MODERN HUMANITIES RESEARCH ASSOCIATION
TEXTS AND DISSERTATIONS
VOLUME 73

A CULTURE OF MIMICRY

MODERN HUMANITIES RESEARCH ASSOCIATION
TEXTS AND DISSERTATIONS

Established in 1970, the series promotes important work by younger scholars by making the most accomplished doctoral research available to a wider readership. Titles are selected and edited by a Board of distinguished experts from across the modern Humanities.

Editorial Board
English: Professor Catherine Maxwell, Queen Mary, University of London
French: Professor William Brooks, University of Bath
Germanic: Professor Ritchie Robertson, University of Oxford
Hispanic: Professor Derek Flitter, University of Exeter
Italian: Professor Brian Richardson, University of Leeds
Portuguese: Professor Thomas Earle, University of Oxford
Slavonic: Professor David Gillespie, University of Bath

Managing Editor: Dr Graham Nelson

A Culture of Mimicry

Laurence Sterne, His Readers and the Art of Bodysnatching

by
Warren L. Oakley

Modern Humanities Research Association
2010

Published by

The Modern Humanities Research Association,
Salisbury House
Station Road
Cambridge CB1 2LA
United Kingdom

ISBN 978-1-83954-585-6 (HB)
ISBN 978-1-83954-586-3 (PB)

© Modern Humanities Research Association, 2010
Transferred to digital printing, 2024

First published 2010

The author has asserted his right under the Copyright, Designs and Patents Act 1988 to be identified as the author of this work. Parts of this work may be reproduced as permitted under legal provisions for fair dealing (or fair use) for the purposes of research, private study, criticism, or review, or when a relevant collective licensing agreement is in place. All other reproduction requires the written permission of the copyright holder who may be contacted at rights@mhra.org.uk.

Copy-Editor: Dr Amanda Wrigley

CONTENTS

Acknowledgements   vii
List of Illustrations   viii
1   Articulating Sterne   1
2   Garrick and Literary Mimicry   29
3   The Redeployment of Uncle Toby   53
4   Erotic Yorick, the Man of Feeling   77
5   William Combe, Esq., Sterne's 'Dear Boy'   107
    Coda   127
    Bibliography   131
    Index   145

ACKNOWLEDGEMENTS

In a letter to a '*dear Lady*' from 1765, Sterne describes the journey of a mutual friend to one particular location in Yorkshire and exclaims 'to Leeds—to Leeds?' as if anticipating her disbelief that anyone would want to travel there. However, the enjoyable and supportive environment of the University of Leeds made this book possible. Without the help of many people at Leeds, I would have conceded defeat a long time ago. I find myself in William Combe's situation, and I hope that the following people will graciously accept my attempt to publicize an association with them in print.

Most importantly, I am indebted to Dr. Robert Jones, whose knowledge and keen critical eye helped to shape and sharpen the ideas in the original thesis. Without his kind assistance over many years, my arguments would have resembled Sterne's illogical narrative lines. I would also like to thank a number of other people for their help: Professor David Fairer, for his friendship and for always having an open door whenever I had a frequent question or problem; Dr. Shaun Regan, for thoughtfully reading my work and helping to take ideas in new directions, as well as spotting my numerous split infinitives and wayward semi-colons; Dr. Jenny Skipp, for casting an expert eye over the subject of Georgian erotica; Professor Peter de Voogd, for generously sharing the invaluable text of the Florida *Letters* before publication and for taking the time to offer advice on epistolary matters; Florence Parkinson, for her gallant support at a difficult time; and Professor John Batchelor for his encouragement of, and belief in, a project on Sterne and the idea of bodysnatching. Any mistakes or errors are, of course, my own.

I have also benefited from the generosity of the Art Institute of Chicago, the Ashmolean Museum, the Brotherton Library of the University of Leeds, the Wellcome Library, and the Yale Center for British Art, which has enabled me to include a number of images. In addition, *The Shandean* has allowed me to reproduce material from an earlier version of Chapter Five. Lastly, I would like to thank my parents, Jack and Aida, the best match since Walter and his wife. This book is dedicated, with love, to them in appreciation of their indefatigable help, understanding, and advice.

LIST OF ILLUSTRATIONS

Cover: Jacques Gamelin, *Nouveau recueil d'ostéologie et de myologie* (1779), volume one, table five. © Wellcome Library, London.

1.1. Johan Zoffany, *David Garrick*, oil on canvas. © Ashmolean Museum, University of Oxford.

1.2. Frontispiece to *Letters of the Late Rev. Mr. Laurence Sterne, to His Most Intimate Friends [...] Written by Himself. And Published by His Daughter, Mrs. Medalle* (1775). Reproduced with the permission of the Brotherton Collection, Leeds University Library.

2.1. Facsimile of *Romeo and Juliet by Shakespear; with Alterations and an Additional Scene by D. Garrick. As it is Performed at the Theatre-Royal in Drury Lane* (1766), p. 69. Reproduced with the permission of the Brotherton Collection, Leeds University Library.

2.2. Simon François Ravenet, *Mr. Garrick and Miss Bellamy in the Characters of Romeo and Juliet* (1753), engraving after Benjamin Wilson. Yale Center for British Art, Paul Mellon Collection, B1977.14.14564.

4.1. Thomas Rowlandson, *A Man of Feeling* (1811), colour print. Art Institute, Chicago: Gift of Joseph R. Shapiro.

5.1. 'Yorick in Clover', the frontispiece to *Sterne's Witticisms; or, Yorick's Convivial Jester* (1782). © British Library Board.

CHAPTER 1

Articulating Sterne

Bodysnatching

As in Hamlet's remembrance of Yorick while he holds the jester's skull, the dead continue to exist in the phantasies of the living. Their identities, reputations, and bodies become controlled and refashioned by the imagination of other people, as illustrated by the posthumous fate of Laurence Sterne. Even his gravestone exists as a testimony to the invention of two admirers who attempted to recreate the famous novelist in the late eighteenth century. This generous gift from two anonymous 'masons' was partly inscribed with a eulogy in verse seeking to reappraise Sterne's literary reputation, through defending this satirical and sentimental writer with 'a sound head, warm heart, and breast humane' against the accusations of 'prudes', an allusion to his notoriety for prurient and bawdy wit. After this homage, the two masons 'W. & S.' carved an audacious piece of self-publicity:

> This Monumental Stone was erected to the memory of the deceased by two BROTHER MASONS, for although He did not live to be a Member of their SOCIETY, yet all his incomparable Performances evidently prove him to have acted by Rule and Square: they rejoice in this opportunity of perpetuating his high and irrepressible Character to after Ages.[1]

This inscription could act as a motto for *A Culture of Mimicry*. Like other attempts to write for and as the departed novelist, this expression of admiration was a guarded attempt, under partial anonymity, to claim Sterne's friendship and imagine the author as belonging to a fraternity and a lifestyle in this public celebration of a secretive brotherhood.[2] In such writing, remembrance becomes an act of identification as Sterne is chosen for oneself and adopted as part of the imaginative community of his admirer. Consequently, as the eye scans the engraving upon this stone, the capitalized words 'STERNE', 'BROTHER MASONS', and 'SOCIETY' are linked in a visual association. Their desire to 'perpetuate' this portrayal of the man and his fiction was both set in stone and quickly erased. Accounts in late eighteenth-century periodicals describe mourners who could not resist scribbling upon Sterne's gravestone in acts of creative vandalism.[3] In one account, a tearful Clarinda adds a eulogy entitled 'To the Memory of Genius' in impermanent pencil. For Clarinda and other visitors, Sterne's headstone existed as a palimpsest where the author's literary image could be continually recreated and refashioned by the fancy of his devotees.

Away from his gravestone, more authors sought to claim ownership of Sterne's posthumous identity through rewriting his personal history and creating alternative, gruesome biographies. In lurid rumours circulated by Georgian publications, and later perpetuated by a variety of other texts from provincial Victorian newspapers to modern biographies, Sterne's corpse was not left undisturbed after being interred on 22 March 1768. These rumours often changed after each writer had employed his invention, yet two details about the afterlife of Sterne remain constant: the bodysnatching of his corpse, and its dissection at one of the anatomy schools. Even when the truth of this scandalous tale was denied in eighteenth-century literary reprints and impersonations of his work, these publications still raised the possibility of this harrowing end.

The desire of *The Public Advertiser*, 24 March 1769, to play upon his authorial pseudonym initially gave momentum to the grotesque anecdote as the newspaper waggishly encouraged the reader to draw parallels between this idea of Sterne's dismemberment and the display of the jester's skull with 'Alas, poor Yorick' also acting as a suitable epitaph for the novelist's horrible fate. One implication of Sterne's original intertextual reference, that the consumptive author would eventually become a collection of bones, was exploited in the *Advertiser*'s imaginative development of his narrative preoccupation with physiology, illness, and mortality. This inspection of Sterne's corpse would have been a strangely fitting conclusion for an author obsessed with 'extraordinary self-study' concentrating upon the heart, lungs, and nerves.[4] During one bout of consumption shortly before his death, Sterne even anticipated the reports of anatomization through his self-portrayal as 'cadaverous goods'.[5] After the *Advertiser* had suggested this fate, new details emerged and old ones disappeared as the idea was repeatedly resurrected in print and Sterne reappeared upon the anatomist's table. If these tales are collated, we find that Sterne was dissected by Dr. John Parsons at Oxford or Professor Charles Collignon at Cambridge; he was recognized by one of the anatomist's friends, acting as his assistant, or by several spectators who observed 'the marked features of the great humourist'; the identity of the corpse was indicated by the remarkable prominence of two or three teeth reminiscent of Sterne's singular physiognomy, or by the number of teeth in each jaw in the Georgian precursor to the modern use of dental records; the body was immediately returned for clandestine reburial after its identification, or fully dissected and left at a London hospital where his articulated skeleton was displayed and belatedly acknowledged by a curious gentleman.[6] These inconsistencies, while weakening the idea that Sterne was a victim of bodysnatching, nonetheless highlight the enduring fascination of this grisly tale in the popular eighteenth and nineteenth-century imagination as well as the interest in rumours about the undignified end of celebrity. Away from the printed page, the story was widely talked about in the 1780s society frequented by the well-connected Edmond Malone, who claimed in a manuscript that 'a gentleman who was present at the dissection told me he recognized Sterne's face the moment he saw the body' in an attempt to lend credence to the scandal.[7] As evidence of the popularity and believability of this tale, the third edition of *Yorick's Sentimental Journey Continued* (1774) attempted to quell rumours concerning the exhumation of Sterne's body.

While it is impossible to know whether Yorick's bones 'remained undisturbed in the grave where they were first laid' or not, circumstances give credibility to the scandalous reports.[8] The burial site of St. George's, an open, isolated space containing paupers' graves, would have been an 'easy target' for opportunistic grave-robbers.[9] As Ruth Richardson recognized, 'the poor state of urban burial grounds had long worked to the bodysnatchers' benefit' and the neglected location of St. George's had a 'high incidence of disturbance'.[10] In one early edition of his *Works*, it was reported that Sterne was buried with 'no bell tolling' which may suggest a secretive ceremony motivated by the graveyard's 'sinister reputation' and an awareness of the vulnerability of the body.[11] In addition, as Georg Christoph Lichtenberg noted in 1775, Sterne's resting place was hardly a gunshot away from Tyburn Hill, one of the main sources of corpses for surgeons in London.[12] With demand from the dissection rooms outstripping the supply from executions, an adult corpse could sell for around two guineas and, for these amoral and clandestine traders, Sterne's body would have been a valuable commodity commanding a premium. The cadavers of figures who were remembered for being 'intellectual', 'eccentric', or simply infamous, had added value for Georgian anatomists.[13] The famous author, who was celebrated for his eccentric literary style depicting heightened nervous sensibility, was potentially an attractive subject for anatomists interested in the body's sensorium and network of nerves.

True or not, the act of bodysnatching provides interesting parallels with the sizeable artistic appropriation of his literary heritage after 1768. As in the embezzlement of Yorick's sermons after his death in *The Life and Opinions of Tristram Shandy, Gentleman* (volume two, published in 1759), the posthumous appropriation of Sterne's novels can also be understood as an attempt to 'plunder him after he was laid in his grave'.[14] Sterne's literary bones were not left undisturbed as his fictional alter egos haunted a variety of locations including London bookshops, Covent Garden theatre, bacchanalian clubs, as well as the lecture theatres of anatomy schools in Oxford and Cambridge. On the shelves of booksellers, his fictional and epistolary personae reappeared in a variety of reworkings as his storytelling was reconceived to produce a diverse collection of genres, from affordable erotica to morally educational anthologies. His characters, including Tristram and Yorick, were resurrected to create burlesque publications and performances with the potential to influence contemporary perceptions of Sterne's personality. In these ways, Sterne's body became a contested site of ownership and interpretation.

The attempt to draw an analogy between the infamous act of bodysnatching and the process of literary impersonation does not presuppose a common moral viewpoint upon these activities during the century; moreover, bodysnatching was not universally condemned, but rather seen as a necessary, if immoral, means to an important end by sections of the medical community. In 1831, the Royal College of Surgeons belatedly admitted that this practice was an inescapable part of 'the acquisition of knowledge'.[15] Despite the uncharitable and disparaging association of such imaginative invention with this necessary evil, Sterne nevertheless provided both forms of employment with commercial opportunities. His fresh corpse was a potential commodity to be bought and sold within an activity that exploited a legal loophole whereby 'a dead body did not constitute real property, and therefore could neither be owned nor stolen'.[16] Similarly, the Georgian book trade approached Sterne's body of work as common property which could be republished, rewritten, and anthologized for financial gain. The customers of Thomas Becket's shop could even purchase a 'bronzed' bust of Sterne for one libra, seven shillings; this bookseller profited from selling Sterne's epistles while also commercially exploiting his physical body, albeit through the medium of sculpture.[17]

Sterne's dissection and articulation provide a physical embodiment of, and a way of understanding, the creative processes of writers, editors, and anthologists who wielded a literary scalpel. If the text is approached as a body, it illuminates their negotiation of his writing on a structural level. Both forms of activity were aware that the subject, either the cadaver or his fiction, was composed of distinct parts and easily divisible sections. The anthologist's recognition of the fragmentary nature of this fiction finds a parallel with the surgeon's awareness of the divisibility of the body into organs and bones once the corporeal links and joints have been cut. The Latin term 'articulosus', a precursor of the English adjective 'articulate', unites the perspective of the anatomist and the anthologist: it describes a body which is full of joints as well as a discourse full of minute divisions and subdivisions. The conversational style of Sterne's narrative, full of divisions and structured around the ubiquitous dash to signify pauses and to connect statements, encouraged the division of his text into passages in the same way that the corporeal joints uniting bones prompted incisions from the anatomist. The nature of Sterne's novels, made up of discrete, easily detachable sentimental set-pieces and comic digressions, provided suitable material for cut-and-paste publishers who compiled self-contained vignettes for popular literary miscellanies and anthologies of beauties.[18] In particular, *A Sentimental Journey through France and Italy* (1768), 'shaped by isolable episodes of delicate stimulation', inspired such anthologization.[19] This narrative style advanced other forms of literary appropriation through providing a structural model that pragmatically reduced the demands upon aspiring literary novices. For such writers, the production of short fragments side-stepped the onerous task of creating a book-length tale as passages and phrases could be easily joined together through the employment of dashes, the literary equivalent of the brass wire used to connect skeletal fragments during articulation.[20]

These literary articulators were not 'hacks', an unhelpful and derogatory term which has been used by René Bosch and Mark Blackwell to label the community who financially exploited Sterne.[21] The compilers of fragments carefully dissected his work to produce desirable segments for the creation of novel texts for new, specific audiences. To achieve this, they did not indiscriminately and carelessly hack and hew; instead they precisely excised stylistically and thematically consistent extracts from Sterne's miscellaneous and morally motley texts. By bringing together the anatomist and the editor in an association, I aim to confer an air of respectability and dignity upon the latter. This way of viewing the text, as a body dissected and displayed, encourages an appreciation of their professional skill, a strategy taken from the surgeons themselves when exhibitions of anatomy were often more concerned with the raising of public esteem and the establishment of medicine as a respectable discipline than with the communication of knowledge. As one surgical colleague said of John Hunter, a high-profile proponent of anatomy who would eventually become 'surgeon extraordinary to King George III' in 1776: 'He alone made us gentlemen'.[22] This struggle for status, and the title of gentleman, also reflects the motivation of William Combe who excised and incorporated snippets of Sterne's writing within the *Original Letters of the Late Reverend Mr. Laurence Sterne* (1788), partly for self-promotion.[23]

Following such surgical selectivity, the anthologist who compiled the initial editions of *The Beauties of Sterne* (1782) extracted the passages of high sentimentality to satisfy 'the heart of sensibility' while discarding inflammatory sections that may have excited other anatomical parts.[24] While the process of medical dissection separated the connections between such organs as the heart, spinal marrow, and genitalia, Sternean writers sought to disentangle the physiological symptoms from these biological sites. Authors of erotica, who exploited Sterne's travelogue, attempted to disconnect the delicate vibrations of Yorick's heartstrings and nervous system from the sexual excitement of his genitalia in a parting of the sentimental from the sexual. *Yorick's Sentimental Journey Continued*, which exhibits Yorick's sexuality at the expense of his heightened sensibility, aimed to satisfy the connoisseurs of erotic material in its concentration upon the stimulation of the phallus. In contrast, the *Original Letters* focused primarily upon Sterne's sentimentality and polite sociability to provide instruction for an aspirational audience. Such selectivity trimmed and streamlined the author's personae for new purposes and audiences, an interpretation that contrasts with David A. Brewer's concept of 'imaginative expansion' in *The Afterlife of Character* to describe the eighteenth-century redeployment of other figures, including Sir Roger de Coverly and Falstaff, in imitative publications.[25]

Significantly, the anatomist would dissect to rebuild and exhibit the body in a new skeletal form for the spectator's pleasure and instruction. Michael Lyser's *The Art of Dissecting the Human Body* (1740) explains the importance of articulated skeletons to the 'young Osteologist' and anatomical professor: when the bony fragments are wired together, they can be continuously redivided and reunited in infinite investigations.[26] In literary acts of division and reconstruction, anthologists and the playwright Leonard MacNally reduced the novelistic whole into constituent narrative parts before rebuilding and reconnecting these elements to voice Sterne's tales in alternative commodities and new forms of entertainment, thereby exploring perspectives upon his cultural value.[27] Both the imaginary anatomist positioned over Sterne's body, and the author who exploited Sterne's body of work, can be understood as articulators in different senses of the word, through their connection of bones or extracts to form joints, and to express Sterne anew. In the visual pun of the cover image, Jacques Gamelin's *Nouveau recueil d'ostéologie et de myologie* (1779) represents these two different meanings of articulation: to read aloud, to express, to give voice to, as well as to connect skeletal parts in scientific investigation.[28] Gamelin's artistic connection of bones to display the human frame in a specific position corresponds to the writer's connection of words and literary fragments to represent Sternean bodies in action.

The physical manipulation of the human frame into different shapes concerns both practices. The skeletal product of dissection was often exhibited in specific positions to demonstrate the physical properties of the body, a practice illustrated by eighteenth-century anatomical primers for artists such as Gamelin's *Nouveau recueil d'ostéologie et de myologie*. Collignon, one figure implicated in the dissection of Sterne, asserted that practical anatomy identified not only 'the Situation' of parts, such as specific bones, but also their 'Action and Use'.[29] Whereas the 'auto-icon' of Jeremy Bentham was based upon his skeleton which had been mounted on a chair and exhibited in a sitting posture, we can only imagine in what position Sterne's articulated skeleton visited the writer who contributed to *The Derby Mercury* in 1874.[30] As seen in Chapters Three and Four, below, Sterne's personae were communicated through the physical expressiveness of the body, its posture, movement, and engagement in action. Sternean erotica focused upon the movement of the literary phallus, while actors mimicked the physical gait of *Tristram Shandy*'s characters upon the stage. The performances of MacNally's 1783 stage adaptation gained an air of notoriety through the casting of Richard Wilson as Uncle Toby, a comic who was infamous for shocking audiences through the exposure of unsightly flesh. Like the fanciful narrative of Yorick's dissection, this entertainment at Covent Garden theatre encouraged the public to imagine one of Sterne's characters as a fleshy, impolite, and distressing spectacle.

In the late eighteenth century, both types of theatre showcased the physicality of the human form and displayed the body as a spectacle, with the potential to create unease.[31] Sites such as Covent Garden, Drury Lane, and the Haymarket exhibited the expressive body through the mimic's manipulation of physiognomy, posture, and movement in a gestural art expertly practised by these specialist performers. During Sterne's visits to London in the 1760s, this theatrical art was a hugely popular form of entertainment and primarily associated with the fashionable spectacles provided by Samuel Foote at the Haymarket, and the patent winter theatres. Of course, while such stage mimicry concerned the representation of the living body and the creation of recognizable contemporary personalities, anatomical lectures involved the presentation of death and the final destruction of personal identity as embodied by the corporeal. Yet, in stories of Sterne's anatomization, his identity survived the process with the emphasis upon the perception of the novelist's famous physiognomy by spectators. The widely disseminated anecdote, like the reworkings, adaptations, and continuations of his literary heritage, perpetuated the fame of Yorick after Sterne's death. The activities of mimics, both theatrical and literary, and the narrators of Sterne's dismemberment shared one purpose within the far-reaching culture of Georgian celebrity, namely the development of the popularity and social prominence of individuals.

One often cited description of Sterne's death by the footman John MacDonald provides a textual connection between the world of theatre and this Georgian fascination with the novelist's end. After being a witness to Sterne's final moments, MacDonald described this episode in his memoirs:

> I went into the room, and he was just a dying. I waited ten minutes; but in five he said, '*Now it is come*'. He put up his hand, as if to stop a blow, and died in a minute.[32]

Kenneth Monkman perceived that these final words were reminiscent of Hamlet's speech in act five: 'If it be now, 'tis not to come; if it be not to come, it will be now; if it be not now, yet it will come — the readiness is all'.[33] Combined with this intertextual echo spoken by Sterne, a theatrical character who MacDonald claims sometimes assumed the name 'Tristram Shandy' and 'sometimes Yorick', was a posture evoking physical action made famous by David Garrick upon the stage. As part of his performative language, Garrick often employed a trademark pose, with one arm extended, hand raised, and fingers outstretched in a defensive physical gesture to express fear and surprise. He employed numerous subtle variations upon this posture in Shakespearean roles, as illustrated by William Hogarth's famous portrait of Garrick as Richard III in 1745 and Benjamin Wilson's depiction of Garrick as Romeo in the monument scene, an image reproduced in Chapter Two below. Clearly, MacDonald's memoirs presented the body of Garrick's friend as a theatrical signal, a dramatic sign the significance of which could be fully decoded with knowledge of acting technique. The writers and actors who created new Sternean narratives also recognized the theatricality of Sterne's literary body and approached invention as a performative act, as the mimicry of his personae and narrative style. To fully understand this process of literary appropriation, before a consideration of its effects upon the portrayal of Sterne, we need to withdraw from the anatomist's table and consider the Georgian stage with its alternative concept.

Mimicry

After leaving aside the anthologists and editors, 'mimicry' becomes central to an analysis of the techniques used by the Sternean writers chosen in this study. These literary mimics wrenched fictional characters from Sterne's authorial ownership and transplanted them into new forms of entertainment. As Brewer has noted, eighteenth-century imitative writers adopted well-known literary characters to indicate the 'fundamental independence and detachability' of these figures and 'their capacity to migrate both into new texts and into the lives of readers themselves'.[34] However, Shandean identities were not completely independent; mimics adopted personae which were, in the memory of London and Parisian society, inseparable from the author's social identity after his intense identification with the personalities who inhabited the world of *Tristram Shandy*. During attempts to 'Shandy it away', and perform these fictional alter egos, Sterne presented his identity as synonymous with such personae, albeit within self-consciously performative acts for the entertainment of spectators.[35] Through these acts of mimicry, to embody and perform novelistic characters in personal correspondence and social gatherings, the author aimed to secure ownership of his creations while giving the impression that 'there was no appreciable difference between Sterne and his narrators'.[36] Whatever 'detachability' his characters may have possessed in the exploitative attentions of other literary mimics was 'accompanied — and probably offset — by a sense that "Sterne" had himself achieved a sort of placeless omnipresence that could not be nearly as readily disregarded'.[37] Paradoxically, Sterne's method of claiming proprietorship over *Tristram Shandy*, giving characters life and fame beyond the confines of the published commodity, may have encouraged competition from the Shandean mimics both during his life and after his death. After all, the link between authorship and ownership is 'destabilised whenever a character in a book becomes more famous than its creator. It then risks being kidnapped by other writers'.[38]

The importance of 'mimicry' for understanding this appropriation is further reinforced by an investigation of the other possible terms to indicate literary similarity in the eighteenth century; unlike this relatively stable and discrete concept, related terms pose a variety of critical problems. The attention of modern theorists upon associated concepts, such as 'imitation', 'plagiarism', 'forgery', and 'counterfeiting', has created a 'stockpile of incompatible definitions' and a disorganised mass of classifications threatening to erode the distinctiveness of these ideas and produce a collection of indistinguishable synonyms.[39] In addition, the semantics of these connected terms changed and fluctuated, to a lesser or greater extent, as the century progressed, resulting in 'confusing and contradictory' critical concepts without clear distinctions.[40] In the most noteworthy example of semantic change, 'imitation' altered drastically. At the beginning of the century, it signified a praiseworthy, noble literary pursuit which was institutionalized as *imitatio*, 'a creative application of the textual know-how taught under the rubric of "rhetoric"' involving 'identifying and systematising the complete repertoire of stylistic devices used by acknowledged masters of the art of writing'. Literary imitation, as epitomized by Alexander Pope's *Imitations of Horace* (1733–38), encompassed both reverence for the chosen model and also the ambition to emulate, or even surpass, such literary achievements.[41] Later in the century, poetry which a generation earlier would have been celebrated for the 'skilful imitation of time-honoured models', became 'denounced as plagiaristic'. 'Imitation' slowly began to mean the slavish reproduction of an original artistic conception, in a century that increasingly valued inspiration leading to 'creative originality' as typified by Edward Young's 1759 discourse, *Conjectures on Original Composition*.[42]

The semantics of 'mimicry' are comparatively stable in the period as a result of its primary application to a form of specialized theatrical performance. Related through etymology to 'mime', this technique ideally involved the reproduction of the 'external characteristics' of an individual with 'minute accuracy'. Like Sterne's novelistic preoccupation with the signifiers of the body and the translation of 'looks and limbs', the mimic concentrated upon the body language of his subject, including 'manner, gesture' and 'mode of action', to amplify physical characteristics for the entertainment of an audience.[43] Samuel Johnson, in the *Dictionary* of 1755, derided this form of spectacle as low comedy, performed by 'ludicrous buffoons' who 'ridicule' through 'burlesque imitation'.[44] His explanation forms a semantic connection between mimicry and burlesque: both terms can signify the ridicule of an individual through the creation of caricatures with a reductive number of individual traits, as typified by Foote's performances. Despite this, Johnson's use of burlesque as synonymous with mimicry is too simplistic. The latter was judged upon the accuracy of the portrayal and whether there existed a close external resemblance between the mimic and his victim; in contrast, burlesque could signify an absurd, unbelievable performance through a mismatch of actor and role, as in the Covent Garden production of *Tristram Shandy*. Whereas mimicry involved precise impersonation to create ridiculous subjects, burlesque indicated the ridiculousness of the attempt. In this semantic tradition, 'mimic' as an adjective once implied deceptive intention and effect, as if the player could be mistaken for the subject in a successful act of identity theft. The application of this theatrical process to literary production encourages a recognition of how Sternean imposters and their printers used strategies to persuade buyers of the authenticity of their publications, whether erotic continuations of Yorick's journey or collections of Sterne's letters. In response to such ploys, one periodical review denounced *Yorick's Sentimental Journey Continued* as a piece of 'finesse' and portrayed it as dangerous because it was potentially believable.[45] Mimicry signifies these attempts at resemblance, the creation of Sterneana with Sternean facets.

Despite such similarities between Sterne and his mimics, all of the publications and entertainments considered in this study involve a simplification of either Sterne's personae or fictional characters within the specialization of his heteroclite writing for new purposes and genres. As mentioned earlier, the practice of anatomization provides a way of understanding the reduction of the Sternean traveller into an erotic hero, even to the extreme of becoming simply a phallus in action as in *La Souriciere: The Mouse Trap* (1794), but such characterization also provides clear parallels with mimicry upon the Georgian stage. The portrayal of recognizable figures by Foote, for example, was essentially an act of simplification through the selection of a limited number of the victim's salient features. As his impersonations focused upon the singularity, as opposed to the complexity, of an individual target, Foote's performative exaggeration of the conspicuous and arresting features of an individual would trigger the audience's recognition. Johnson's disparagement of Foote in 1772 emphasized this tendency:

> he cannot take off any person unless he is very strongly marked [...] He is like a painter, who can draw the portrait of a man who has a wen upon his face, and who, therefore, is easily known. If a man hops upon one leg, Foote can hop upon one leg.[46]

Using such a concentrated focus, erotic authors created a caricature of Yorick that pronounced and heightened the risqué, titillating facet of sexuality at the expense of the moral complexity of Sterne's original figure. Authors who identified with the sexual suggestiveness of *A Sentimental Journey* obsessively magnified this one specific facet of his persona, an action with implications for the perception of Sterne's morality at the end of the century.

Johnson's definition was disdainful of the mimic's ability to ridicule and create socially injurious impersonations. With Foote's ability, a man could become the laughing stock of London. Johnson's aversion may have been motivated by his dislike of Foote's potential power to transform him into such a spectacle; when asked 'did not [Foote] think of exhibiting you, Sir?', Johnson replied, 'Sir, fear restrained him; he knew I would have broken his bones'.[47] In one unfortunate incident recorded by the playwright Richard Cumberland, Foote's satirical portrayal of a companion, who was secretly listening and hidden from view, was represented as the ultimate impolite offence against masculine friendship, especially when performed at the intimate setting of the dinner table. Cumberland felt that such 'an affront' was 'as gross as could well be put upon a man'; furthermore, 'no wit [can] furnish an evasion, no explanation [can] suffice for an excuse'.[48] Foote's mimicry could have been viewed as highly impolite because of his disregard of two of the central precepts of eighteenth-century politeness, as identified by Philip Carter: 'the display of generosity' to others and 'the need for gentlemen to control their conversation so as to show respect'.[49] Showing a distinct lack of generosity and self-control, Foote's ability to offend was further heightened through his transformation of a private personality into a public spectacle for the entertainment of others. Throughout his career, Foote was a threatening figure because of his flair for changing men who valued privacy into ridiculous spectacles upon the alternative setting of the stage. This invasion of privacy is relevant to the understanding of these literary impersonations of Sterne, impersonations which publicized clandestine facets of his personality and lifestyle. Two Sternean writers, John Hall-Stevenson and Combe, also questioned the propriety of placing their names upon such impolite publications that indiscreetly revealed hidden, and potentially scandalous, aspects of their friend's character.

Mimetic texts like Hall-Stevenson's *Crazy Tales* (1762) and Combe's *Original Letters* did not simply relocate versions of Sterne's personality into the public sphere of print; they also transferred his personae into new situations. While literary mimics transplanted Sterne's alter egos into new locations and scenarios, Foote and other mimics at the Haymarket presented their impersonations in novel, imaginary settings. These performances formed sketches as part of a revue such as *The Diversions of the Morning*, first performed in 1747.[50] As James Boswell remarked in a conversation with Johnson, 'it is amazing how a mimick can not only give you the gestures and voice of a person whom he represents; but even what a person would say on any particular subject'.[51] Similarly, 'Timothy Touchit' in *La Souriciere* impersonated Yorick's narrative voice to imagine how Sterne's character would experience and relate alternative, sexually charged situations; Combe in the *Original Letters* conceived how Sterne would sentimentally react to news of his friend's suffering and misfortune.

After Sterne's willingness to conflate his personal character with his fictional and epistolary personae, Hall-Stevenson's association of Shandean characters with the raucous, drunken enjoyment of erotica in *Crazy Tales* — like Combe's portrayal of a violent, impulsive, and unstable epistolary personality in *Sterne's Letters to His Friends on Various Occasions* (1775) — would have implications for the perception of the man. As one mimic claimed, before attempting to influence the reader's perception of Sterne, 'we cannot easily [...] separate the author from his book'.[52] These books had the potential to confirm eighteenth-century preconceptions about him, yet it is important to view them as creative acts of storytelling that manipulate Sterne's personae, not as uncomplicated biographical evidence to support presumptions about his private life. *Crazy Tales* can illuminate Sterne's social life at Skelton Castle, but this world of the Demoniacs also involved witty narrative performances and opportunities to indulge in waggish alter egos. In a letter from May or June 1761, which includes his only mention of the Demoniacs club by name, Sterne asked Hall-Stevenson to 'write me a letter, if you are able, as foolish as this' in the portrayal of writing as partly an expression of friendship and partly an exercise in wit.[53] Hall-Stevenson's *Crazy Tales* and Combe's *Original Letters* involve manipulative storytelling about themselves and Sterne in a creative partnership, not the recording of historical evidence. I have tried to avoid using creative inventions to identify the real Sterne, unlike Monkman's ingenious attempt to find Sterne's skull using comparative measurements from the 1766 bust by Joseph Nollekens.[54] Even sculpture and life drawing, whose merit is partly judged upon visual accuracy, exist as forms of fabrication. After perusing the National Portrait Exhibition in 1867, which included Sir Joshua Reynolds's likeness of Sterne, one Victorian gentleman waggishly complained, 'There is a fine portrait of *Mr. Yorick* — a STERNE reality; but, after the most careful examination, I have failed to discover any representation of *Mrs. Wadman*'.[55] While astutely suggesting that Reynolds's impish portrayal of Sterne may be as much of an invention as any image of the widow would be, he also implies that Sterne's alter ego, '*Mr. Yorick*', was itself an act of creative self-fashioning; it was an achievement comparable to his creation of other characters.

Nonetheless, novel perspectives upon Sterne's social personality were provided by his former acquaintances, perspectives which gain a certain authority and validity through their intimate knowledge of *Tristram Shandy*'s creator. Hall-Stevenson conspicuously celebrated his friendship with Sterne in *Crazy Tales* and, after being identified as 'Eugenius' (Sterne's faithful counsellor), he was subsequently associated with the authorship of *Yorick's Sentimental Journey Continued*. Combe, another acquaintance, covertly identified himself and publicized a relationship with the sociable and sentimental Sterne in the *Original Letters*. The employment of mimicry as a concept provides a perspective upon these texts encouraging the tracing of friendships, that Sterne cultivated during the 1760s, and the subsequent influence of these connections upon the portrayal of his posthumous character. That such fellowship gave rise to impersonations in print is comparable to the reliance of theatrical mimics upon the close observation of friends and professional associates.[56] At the Haymarket, Foote notoriously impersonated other actors and, as his career as a playwright developed, he would create roles for himself which would enable him to mimic well-known London figures, often other performers.[57] In the professional community of the stage, Foote would mimic Henry Woodward and Garrick among others, while Woodward and Tate Wilkinson would mimic Foote. When David Williams attempted to shame Garrick in one pamphlet attack, he stated that the actor's 'powers of mimickry' inevitably led to the victimization of other players, becoming a 'species of robbery' on 'reputation'. Mimicry possessed a satirical edge, to the extent that Williams could blame Garrick for the death of one much maligned and mimicked performer, Dennis Delane.[58] In contrast, mimicry could also exist as a form of flattery if used in the act of self-portrayal as illustrated by Sterne's employment of Garrick's performance technique to create an epistolary voice, as discussed in the next chapter.

Theatrical mimicry, as entertainment that could have been perceived as illicit and illegitimate, is key to understanding the context, in terms of the production as well as the consumption, of a number of Sternean texts in the late eighteenth century. Foote's Haymarket began life as a disreputable and subversive alternative to the two licensed London theatres in the 1740s before it was officially issued with a patent from the Crown in July 1766.[59] The extent to which the theatregoing public of the 1740s and '50s would have approached Foote's mimicry as an illegal form of entertainment, geographically and legally outside of the confines of legitimate theatre, is a contentious issue.[60] However, during the use of the Haymarket without an official patent, he was not required to submit plays to the Examiner, Lord Chamberlain, for the censorship of obscene, libellous, or seditious material.[61] His alarming mimicry of contemporary figures, with the potential to make even Johnson nervous, flourished in such an ambiguous legal position. In this shared environment of entertainment with a very questionable claim to respectability, Sternean mimicry, with its often scandalous implications for the novelist's character, gained momentum from the lack of effective legal supervision and enforcement. While Foote's spectacles eluded the authority of the patent enforced by the 1737 Stage Licensing Act, literary mimics would challenge a different form of prerogative, namely Sterne's authorial authority, albeit a posthumous one after 1768. Both forms of activity existed as statements of creative freedom in the act of seizing the personal property and the commercial rights of others. When the embryonic law on copyright struggled to construct working legal definitions, Sternean mimicry prospered while frequently employing one or more of the following strategies: anonymity, pseudonymity, and inaccurate or fictitious places of publication.[62] As illustrations, we have an erotic version of *Tristram Shandy* 'with a curious Set of Cuts' printed by 'P. Van Slaukenberg' in 'Amsterdam' in 1785, and the risqué *Miss C--Y's Cabinet of Curiosities; or, The Green-Room Broke Open. By Tristram Shandy, Gent.*, printed by 'William Whirligig' at 'Utopia' in 1765.

The commercial activities of Foote and the Sternean mimics belong to a wider culture of unauthorized Georgian entertainment which was characterized by the potential to create moral disquiet. For Jane Moody, theatrical amusements that operated outside of the Licensing Act fuelled contemporary fears concerning the potential for 'moral pollution' and the 'promotion of plebeian immorality'.[63] As a literary embodiment of the boundary between legality and illegality, the acceptable and the immoral, *Yorick's Sentimental Journey Continued* was perceived as both illegitimate as a continuation of the first two volumes and, in the minds of some contemporary moralists, dangerous through the exploitation and amplification of the licentiousness of Sterne's original publication. The infamy surrounding this erotic text and others considered in Chapter Four, below, potentially fuelled the moral condemnation of Sterne as expressed in the polite periodical press, critical monographs which reviewed his work, and compilations of Sternean extracts. Two educational anthologists who appropriated sentimental passages from Sterne, George Nicholson and Vicesimus Knox, portrayed the author as a moral danger: he was 'the grand promoter of adultery, and every species of illicit commerce' through works which 'abound with indelicacy'.[64] In the context of this condemnation of Sterne's narrative content, Hall-Stevenson offers an alternative perspective. This mimic and literary maverick did not simply challenge the moral denouncement of Sterne; his celebration of erotic storytelling in *Crazy Tales* also defied the disapproval of sexual content in print. Furthermore, contributions to *The Public Advertiser* associated with him in 1778 confronted the charge of obscenity, perceiving that such charges were open to scrutiny and objection. Despite such bravado, the contentious material of Sternean erotica was often addressed to specific social situations and gatherings that discreetly contained its accessibility and consumption, away from the eyes of moralistic objectors.

While concentrating upon publications that were often controversial in some way and now little-known, *A Culture of Mimicry* is not simply an analysis of neglected texts or a re-evaluation and critical rehabilitation of works often hastily dismissed as 'rancid' or 'vile' or deserving of 'a great debt of *ingratitude*'.[65] This study also explores the eighteenth-century cultural contexts of these reworkings of Sterne, including a variety of environments from the genteelly polite to the outrageously impolite, from the drawing rooms of the aspirational lower middle class to provincial bacchanalian clubs; these publications also evoke an assortment of geographical locations, from the gallery seats at Covent Garden to the Low Countries upon the Grand Tour. Indeed, to understand Sternean mimicry fully, it is necessary to appreciate the locations and social contexts where such amusements were produced and enjoyed. A number of these texts attempt to influence the act of reading, providing clear indications of the readerships and situations prescribed for their consumption. In this respect, a consideration of both the content and format of a book can present conflicting evidence concerning its possible enjoyment. For instance, the grand first edition folio of *Crazy Tales*, designed for proud, conspicuous display by an aristocratic connoisseur, contains print evoking and celebrating the secretive pleasures of the select club. Through an exploration of texts, this study investigates where, how, and why audiences and readers were encouraged to consume Sternean entertainment, as well as considering the influence of the cultural atmosphere upon their experience.

Biography and Autobiography

To give but one example from many, Cumberland's play *The West Indian* (1771) evoked *Tristram Shandy* to suggest how an audience could enjoy Sterne. Cumberland was another of Sterne's former friends who explored the author's fame and influenced his posthumous literary reputation. On its debut, *The West Indian* aroused the audience's memory of the novelist and proposed two contrasting ways of appreciating *Tristram Shandy* for the benefit of the Drury Lane spectators.[66] In the first meeting between an honourable yet testy old soldier, Captain Dudley, and a dishonourable and unprincipled bookseller, Cumberland's play reflected upon Sterne's literary value:

> DUDLEY: Mr. Fulmer, I have borrow'd a book from your shop; 'tis the sixth volume of my deceased friend Tristram: he is a flattering writer to us poor soldiers; and the divine story of Le Fevre, which makes part of this book, in my opinion of it, does honour not to its author only, but to human nature.
> FULMER: He is an author I keep in the way of trade, but one I never relish'd; he is much too loose and profligate for my taste.

> DUDLEY: That's being too severe: I hold him to be a moralist in the noblest sense; he plays indeed with the fancy, and sometimes perhaps too wantonly; but while he thus designedly masks his main attack, he comes at once upon the heart; refines, amends it, softens it; beats down each selfish barrier from about it, and opens every sluice of pity and benevolence.[67]

This exchange provides a clear paradigm for the act of reading Sterne whereby readers were faced with a stark interpretative choice terminating in two extremes of public opinion. At their most acute, these opposing critical viewpoints either portrayed the author as a sentimental philanthropist, able to stimulate noble, exquisite emotions, or as an immoral erotomaniac, obsessed by the body's sexuality. Dudley's view of Sterne as a 'moralist', refining the reader's heart through the encouragement of 'pity and benevolence', contrasts greatly with Fulmer's view of the author as offering 'loose and profligate' pleasures. As an extension of their comments, Sterne's admirers associated him with such celebrated sentimentalists as Jean-Jacques Rousseau and Johann Wolfgang von Goethe, while his public detractors traced the author's origins to the satirical and scatological tradition of François Rabelais and Jonathan Swift.[68] One mimic, who evoked Yorick's narrative style while recounting *A Sentimental Tour* through Wales and England in 1798, realized that these two perspectives were difficult to separate in the appreciation of his fiction; the praise of Sterne's sensibility prefaces an awareness of the main contemporary objection to him:

> thou masterly portrayer of exquisite feelings. If, however, for thy *Innuendos* I praise thee not, I am not singular [...] Knowing so well the human heart, why didst thou hazard the raising of loose ideas[?][69]

Sterne anticipated this question with another in 'THE CONQUEST' of *A Sentimental Journey*:

> If nature has so wove her web of kindness, that some threads of love and desire are entangled with the piece—must the whole web be rent in drawing them out?[70]

The temptation offered by 'the fair *fille de chambre*' enables him to express the difficulty of disengaging the pleasurable feelings of sensibility from the urges of sexual desire, the duty to protect and nurture from the need to gratify the body. In their dissection of the Sternean text and anatomy, writers attempted to disentangle and separate these different threads to target specific audiences. When faced with Sterne's suggestive 'web' of antagonistic impulses, they had to decide whether the 'CONQUEST' referred to the overthrow of the female or the vanquishment of one's desires. With varying degrees of success, they placed an emphasis upon one of these contrasting interpretations, often without removing all trace of the alternative as illustrated by Combe's *Original Letters*. These letters, lauding a sentimental lifestyle, failed to expunge completely language revealing desire in two brief sections from two hundred and sixteen pages. *Crazy Tales* epitomises the difficulty of separating sex and sensibility: a fervid concentration upon sexual proclivities and activity throughout enables the text to radiate the warmth of masculine friendship, showing a clear sensitivity to the refined feelings that create bonds between men.

In *The West Indian*, Cumberland's view of Sterne is clear. Despite Fulmer's disparaging comments, Dudley's assessment of *Tristram Shandy*'s literary value is supported by Cumberland's evocation of the sentimentality of the novel, with the dramatist's portrayal of the soldier, as a personification of honour and compassion, echoing the sentimental idealism of Sterne. After the depiction of Captain Dudley as 'a person' of an 'obliging compassionate turn' and 'scrupulous honour', Major O'Flaherty can reply to the accusation of dishonesty with the irrefutable riposte of 'look at me friend, I am a soldier, this is not the livery of a knave'.[71] In Cumberland's world, this livery is a guarantee of the moral integrity of the wearer. In a further reverberation of Sterne's narrative, Dudley's financial distress, combined with his reluctant reliance upon charity, potentially sustained the audience's memory of the Le Fevre story, the celebrated sentimental passage mentioned by the old soldier. The dramatist's continuation of the novelist's attempt to be a friendly, 'flattering writer to us poor soldiers' could be interpreted as evidence of his heartfelt support for Sterne's intentions.[72]

In another respect, Dudley and Fulmer's discussion of Sterne represents one fundamental aspect of the novelist's representation in the late eighteenth century. When placed in the context of the play as a whole, their judgements do not simply reflect the polarity of moral opinion upon him; their evaluations also reflect the stage characters' own personality and moral outlook. These comments are self-referential and exist as introductory signposts to their moral integrity at the start of the play. The literary taste of the amoral and financially profligate Fulmer accentuates a facet of Sterne's fiction disregarded by Dudley, a figure who attempts to take the contested title of 'man of honour'. Immediately after their debate, Fulmer hints that Dudley's financial embarrassment could be relieved by the prostitution of his daughter's beauty which provokes the Captain's irate response of 'this you call knowledge of the world? Despicable knowledge'.[73] Just as Fulmer's worldly knowledge influences his heightened perception of Sterne's licentiousness, the virtue of another character, 'Belcour' or 'good heart', mistakenly assumes the integrity of Mrs. Fulmer in Cumberland's duplicitous world. Belcour's inability to appreciate 'the cunning contrivances of the intriguing town' creates the main romantic misunderstanding of this farce.[74] Clearly, characters' judgements of others are merely projections of their own moral standards, a situation observed by Sterne when considering the reception of his fiction. Despite his famous declaration that the reader 'should ever bring one half of the entertainment along with him', he was forced to accept that the subjective perspective of the reader woefully guided the understanding of a publication like *Tristram Shandy* where 'the handle is taken which suits' individual 'passions', 'ignorance', or 'sensibility'.[75]

It is possible to approach the late eighteenth-century reception of Sterne's work, including the interpretation of his character from the evidence provided by his publications, as a reflection of the diverse intellectual and moral preoccupations of contemporary consumers. Within such an approach, the viewpoint of the reader exists as the point of Sterne. As Peter Briggs has recognized in a discussion of reactions during the author's lifetime:

> The significance of his performance was further hedged by the various vantage-points of his audience. To some observers he seemed a hero of social sympathy, personal sensibility, and good humour, while to others he was a scandal, running into the ground his various professions as minister, author, husband, and gentleman.[76]

While Cumberland's dichotomy is a useful starting point for conceiving of the posthumous perception of Sterne, it is too simplistic to cover all of these 'various vantage-points', providing only a partial detail of the diverse portrait of the author. Literary mimicry provides interpretations of Sterne as varied and individual as the mimic's personality. These impersonations create many different Sternes, not simply one; we have a miscellaneous assortment of unlike doubles. Each mimetic reworking and adaptation includes a unique and distinct appraisal of either the social dangers, pleasurable vices, or personal values called forth by Sterne's publication; this is achieved through a magnification of specific aspects of his personae which acts as a critical commentary upon the original text. In a period when his fiction was interpreted as evidence of personal morality, or a lack of it, judgements upon his personality were also conveyed by imaginative mimicry.

The far-reaching influence of Sterneana to shape responses to his work is illustrated by the popularity of Combe's epistles which were widely republished and publicized in the late eighteenth century. Before the *Original Letters* were collected for publication, much of this correspondence was widely distributed by *The Daily Universal Register* and *The Times* at irregular intervals between January 1787 and January 1788. After their appearance in London in one volume, these letters were subsequently translated and circulated in Paris.[77] Even in anthologies of Sterne's 'genuine' work, extracts and clippings from Combe's earlier letters *on Various Occasions* appeared, as demonstrated by the expanded seventh London edition of the hugely successful *Beauties of Sterne* (1783) and, later, *The Works of Laurence Sterne* (1790).[78] Consequently, the prediction of a one shilling pamphlet in 1768 was clearly ill-judged:

> should they publish the *Posthumous* Works, and attempt to foist in anything spurious, in order to swell the Bulk, and enhance the Price, the Public would certainly smoke 'em; for he is so much himself that he cannot be imitated.[79]

This author's pseudonym, 'One of Uncle Toby's Illegitimate Children', while implying an improbable parentage, also relates to Combe and Hall-Stevenson's creative efforts as writers who valued anonymity while engaged in the clandestine, illegitimate reproduction of Sterne's personae. Combe's collections of letters, that merged personal epistolary contributions from both Sterne and himself to create novel correspondence, could be considered as the unowned and unauthorized 'bastard' offspring of their combined literary effort.[80] As an alternative to Combe's letters *on Various Occasions*, the first authoritative collection of Sterne's correspondence, from his daughter Lydia Medalle, appeared three months later, a compilation which invited comparisons with the earlier edition.[81] The preface to Medalle's publication vouched for the genuineness of the letters and emphasized the close family link between the author and the editor. In spite of this, literary historians have noticed her editorial incompetence and her willingness, like

Combe, to rewrite epistles.[82] Her publication is a reminder that posthumous Sternean texts, even volumes marketed as endorsed by familial closeness, exist as creative acts attempting to reclaim and rewrite Sterne's identity, being read for a short time before being replaced and rewritten in a process akin to scribbling upon the palimpsest of his headstone.

To write like Sterne was also an act of autobiography. It is possible to perceive the personality of the writer beneath the personae of Sterne's characters, encouraging us to read the author himself, not simply the text that inspired him. These mimics adopted roles to express and promote the self including a variety of ambitions, anxieties, and 'hobby horses', a form of literary appreciation to reinforce Sterne's belief that the consumer's experience of *Tristram Shandy* was 'like reading *himself*, not the *book*'.[83] Unlike Bosch's dismissive and disparaging study of Sternean publications by 'writing down-and-outers' whose identities and personal motives are unknown, this book attempts to reveal the individuals only partly obscured by acts of mimicry, focusing upon the motivations of these writers, directors, and performers.[84] A visual statement of my approach is provided by Johan Zoffany's unmasking of Garrick in a portrait from the early 1760s (see Fig. 1.1). As an acknowledgement of the actor's friendship and patronage, combining to release the artist from his apprenticeship with Benjamin Wilson in 1762, Zoffany created a picture that disregarded the Georgian tradition of depicting an actor performing a famous role in wig and costume. Instead, Zoffany placed Garrick in a position of retirement from the stage, as seen by the privileged gaze of a friend. He provides a more private, sombre image of Garrick in informal dress, bareheaded and closely shaved to suggest his nakedness in the artistic attempt to depict the man beneath the many roles. As if to emphasize this revelation, the artist places the discarded masks of comedy and tragedy in the foreground. While the impish mask of comedy, worn in the public glare of the theatre, directs his communicative glance at the viewer, the private man in profile disregards his audience.

Following this lead, I attempt to reveal the human stories beneath the literary façades of Shandean performance while also considering the use of comic disguises to engage an admiring audience. In the spirit of Zoffany's portrait, Sterneana such as that created by Hall-Stevenson and Combe can also be read as testimonies to friendship. Both writers provide intimate portraits of themselves and Sterne in private surroundings, portraits which exist as textual wish-fulfilment, as artfully constructed as Zoffany's image. In contrast, Bosch believes that 'usually, nothing is known about the writers' of these 'anonymous texts, whose authors often pose as hack writers, thereby cynically affirming neoclassical assumptions about this trade'; alternatively, I focus upon the emotional investment in Sterne made by his identifiable contemporaries.[85] With the case study of the 1783 Covent Garden production of *Tristram Shandy*, for example, a knowledge of the personnel involved is key to understanding its impact and influence upon the perception of Sterne and his novel.

The assertion that mimics adopted Sterne's style to express individual concerns, in my appreciation of authors and theatre personnel who transported Sterne in new directions and into new contexts, complicates Blackwell's portrayal of

Fig. 1.1. Johan Zoffany, *David Garrick*, oil on canvas.
© Ashmolean Museum, University of Oxford.

Sternean writers as 'hacks', 'who, like hackney horses and hackney coaches, made the same dull round again and again'.[86] Their mimicry can be related to one eighteenth-century understanding of creativity as the making of connections and correspondences between ideas, often unexpectedly between incongruous ones. Indeed, Edmund Burke's claim, that 'by making resemblances we produce *new images*, we unite, we create, we enlarge our stock', provides one perspective on the mimics who identified similarities between Sterne's narrative preoccupations and their own personal interests while seeking to unite with the novelist socially.[87]

When appropriating Sterne, these chosen mimics highlighted compatible, like-minded facets of his personality and recreated his posthumous identity in their own image. The letters published by Medalle provide a visual representation of this authorial phenomenon found in the perpetuation and commercialization of Sterne's celebrity (see Fig. 1.2). The frontispiece represents her identification with Sterne as well as her desire to refashion his epistolary identity. Sterne's bust, itself a creative presentation of his physiognomy and persona, visually corresponds with Medalle's facial features as the daughter clutches the memorial to her father's fame in a gesture of empathy and familial affection. Of course, it is not impossible that the daughter's features actually reflected those of her father; still, the employment of Sterne's image in this engraving emphasizes the visual similarity between the two, a factor accentuated by the presentation of both faces in profile. Here, the representation of Sterne's countenance to mirror Medalle's physiognomy is symbolic of her editorial re-creation of his epistolary voice to address her daughterly concerns. Her editing involved the changing of names and dates and the rewriting of letters to Sterne's infatuation, Eliza Draper, 'to make them appear to be early love-letters to Mrs. Sterne'.[88] In this fantasy of familial closeness, these editorial changes attempted to rescue her mother Elizabeth from the stigma of abandonment and her father from the charges of inconstancy and adultery. This reworking of his public persona for social and not simply financial gain provides a clear parallel with Combe's presentation of Sterne in the *Original Letters*, as discussed in Chapter Five.

While tracing these identifications, it is also necessary to concede that these mimics would have been vulnerable to the charge of authorial vanity as a result of partial self-promotion, despite disguising their identities behind an interpretation of Sterne's novelistic voice. Combe's conspicuous self-portrayal as a gentlemanly correspondent in the *Original Letters*, for instance, failed to follow the 1774 advice from Philip Dormer Stanhope, the fourth Earl of Chesterfield, on polite modesty which concluded 'above all things, and upon all occasions, avoid speaking of yourself, if it be possible. Such is the natural pride and vanity of our hearts, that it perpetually breaks out'.[89] In the light of Chesterfield's guidance, the partial anonymity practised by Combe and Hall-Stevenson can be interpreted as both concealment and disclosure, the act of cautiously and partially revealing authorial identity to a select number of knowing acquaintances. The anonymity of Sternean publications is a noteworthy and distinguishing feature, if not an unusual one, in the eighteenth-century marketplace as a whole. Robert Griffin estimates that 'nearly seventy percent of all novels published in the last thirty years of the eighteenth century were published anonymously' while 'nearly forty percent

Fig. 1.2. Frontispiece to *Letters of the Late Rev. Mr. Laurence Sterne, to His Most Intimate Friends [...] Written by Himself. And Published by His Daughter, Mrs. Medalle* (1775). Reproduced with the permission of the Brotherton Collection, Leeds University Library.

remain unattributed'.⁹⁰ Sternean masquerades provided a safe distance from complete ownership, allowing writers to engage, anonymously or furtively, with controversial preoccupations threatening personal discomfort or danger if detected by unsympathetic contemporaries. Behind the façade of Sterne's literary reputation, Hall-Stevenson trifled with moral outrage and Combe flirted with personal embarrassment. As the act of publication was potentially dangerous on a personal level for both men, a measure of anonymity enabled them to guard their privacy and gentlemanly title. Even the exception of MacNally, who openly published his name on the title page, disguised his creative involvement to the extent that some theatrical reviewers applauded him as an unobtrusive editor. Despite the appearance of an inconspicuous editorial presence, MacNally politicized Sterne's novel and courted political controversy through the selection of extracts and the signposting of Toby's theatrical ancestry.

Overview

One commentator's declaration in 1779 that Sterne had 'captivated numberless copyists' was no exaggeration.⁹¹ Bosch's impressive and considerable bibliography of 'Imitations, Commentaries, Parodies, Forgeries' includes titles published separately in England between 1768 and 1800.⁹² Even for this one period and place of publication, his list could be expanded with the following: Combe's *on Various Occasions*; two additional continuations of Sterne's *Journey* from 1788 and 1793; a number of Maria spin-offs, both narrative and musical from the end of the century, as identified by Carol Watts; as well as the numerous Sternean it-narratives considered by Blackwell.⁹³ In terms of scope, it has only been possible for this study to consider a relatively small cross-section of English Sterneana while placing this selection in its contemporary context through employing approaches from several academic disciplines including theatre history, book history, and literary criticism. As a result, *A Culture of Mimicry* covers the Georgian adaptation of *Tristram Shandy* for the stage; seven titles of anthologies, focusing either partially or wholly upon Sterne; six examples of Sternean erotica; three collections of Sterne's letters; and numerous other publications, including four sentimental journeys in the style of Sterne, to add to the rich contextual background. I have chosen to investigate a number of case studies in depth, from relatively well-known publications in Sterne studies to the disregarded and unappreciated, such as MacNally's transformation of *Tristram Shandy* into a playscript, and the erotic poem 'COUNTER EPISTLES from BRIGHT-HELMSTONE, NUMBER I' (1778) which, for the first time, has been discussed in modern literary study and related to Hall-Stevenson.⁹⁴

These texts have been chosen for one or more of the following reasons: the striking interpretation of the author's fiction and literary personality, the commercial longevity or popularity of the text in the century, and the possibility of identifying the creators and tracing their relationship to Sterne. While not comprehensive, this assortment provides a diverse and representative sample of his portrayal. We have the theatrical Sterne, the patriotic Sterne, the sentimental and philanthropic Sterne, and the erotic Sterne, in a variety of combinations. These publications and entertainments approach the novelist from a number of discrete angles and offer definite, if not definitive, perspectives on the value of Sterne for his anatomists and impersonators. My approach also persues the personal stories expressed by bodysnatching and mimicry while avoiding the potential for superficiality and generalization in trying to group together an immense, diverse, and multifarious accumulation of material to create the semblance of critical order. A focus upon different titles from this vast source would have inevitably offered different emphases on the interpretation of Sterne's fiction and personality. Like the anthology's re-creation of Sterne and his novels through the inclusion and exclusion of narrative strands, my selections provide interpretations that will have to compete with the huge population of other Sternes constructed by editors, anthologists, critics, and biographers since the novelist's death. After all, Sterne really did captivate numberless writers.

When the prospect is widened even further to encompass the eighteenth- and early nineteenth-century world as a whole, these chosen publications from England can be seen to form only one part of a wider literary trend stretching geographically beyond London and its provinces.[95] Sterne's influence spread across the Continent to the extent that editions, translations, and reworkings of *A Sentimental Journey* originated from a wide range of European cities including Amsterdam, Paris, and Vienna. These appropriations can also be contextualized as one authorial subdivision of a larger 'robust market in spurious sequels' exploiting the fiction of high-profile novelists such as Daniel Defoe and Samuel Richardson, a trade in unauthorized reworkings which, according to Christopher Flint, 'characterizes the novel's economics' in the period.[96] In one respect, the piracy of popular literature can be simply explained as a consequence of the market forces of supply and demand in the Georgian book trade. One historian of publishing, Alvin Kernan, has illustrated the commercial profitability of publications in the London marketplace through reference to James Lackington's highly successful 'Temple of the Muses', the remainder bookstore that 'first put bookselling on a large-scale basis with a turnover of about 100,000 volumes in 1791'.[97] Creative reworkings of Sterne's fiction offered profitable new titles for a voracious reading public, satisfying the need for novelty while capitalizing upon their previous enjoyment of his well-known and celebrated back-catalogue. Aside from this profitability, distinctive facets of his literary style could also explain the specific appeal of Sterne for mimics and printers engaged in this trade.

Even though Johnson famously claimed 'nothing odd will do long, *Tristram Shandy* did not last', it was exactly the stylistic and typographical oddity of Sterne's narratives that contributed to their commercial longevity throughout the Georgian period and after. More recently, Thomas Keymer has positively spun Johnson's view of *Tristram Shandy* as 'odd' to maintain that Sterne was 'a novelist among novelists, an innovator among writers of fiction'.[98] While representing his narrative as 'a novel exercise in the novel form', including 'structural, rhetorical, and typographical peculiarities', Keymer does not simply portray Sterne's popularity as a consequence of his innovative eccentricity; his fiction is also of the moment through the parody of the typical representational conventions of the 1750s novel.[99] In an analysis of Sterne's visual appeal, James Cruise has defined *Tristram Shandy* as a 'manufactured story' employing the art of printing and the humorous potential of misprints, as in Sterne's blank page suggesting 'a drunken compositor' or his marbled page hinting at 'a misguided binder who forgets that marbled pages serve a decorative function'.[100] This pictorial playfulness, although not uncommon in the work of other eighteenth-century novelists, was a defining visual feature of his celebrated first novel, a novel 'characterised by the highly unusual nature of its many non-verbal features' including 'an intricate system of hyphens and dashes'.[101] The outlandish typography of *Tristram Shandy*, which at times flirts with the championing of style over narrative substance, did not only encourage writers to explore 'the possibilities opened up by the marks he had made on paper, the actual text'.[102] Printers, who understood the financial demand for Sternean entertainment, were also eager to reappropriate the techniques of print that had been previously manipulated by Sterne.[103] The novelist's laborious attempt, at the bindery, to sign and authenticate every first edition copy of *Tristram Shandy*, volume five, acknowledged that the marks of printed matter could be easily reproduced and hoped that a signature in ink was less vulnerable.[104]

Before exploring the appropriation of his fiction, the following chapter considers Sterne as a literary mimic in an appreciation of the relationship between his writing and the Drury Lane stage. This chapter argues that Sterne's creation of a number of mid-century epistles involved the impersonation of Garrick's performance style, and reflected the staging of plays in his conception of epistolary settings. After this discussion of the art of mime, Chapter Three investigates the literary dissection of Sterne's narratives to create anthologies and a script for performance. MacNally's editorial articulation of Sterne, involving the selection of excerpts and their connection anew, led to the performance of *Tristram Shandy*'s characters at Covent Garden theatre, an entertainment that employed the art of burlesque to comment upon the contemporary beautification of Sterne. The journey from Covent Garden leads to the murky world of the bacchanalian club and the enjoyment of Sternean erotica with its dissection of Yorick's body and physiology to emphasize his carnality, both in terms of his material existence and his gratification of sexual appetite. Chapter Four not only investigates the transformation of Sterne's literary character through the disengagement of the genitalia from the feeling body, but also attempts to understand how, where, and why erotic material was consumed from the 1760s onwards. In contrast to the lascivious and impolite Sternes created by this genre, one writer attempted to redeem the memory of his friend. This final chapter attempts to understand Combe's production of the *Original Letters* using an alternative to bodysnatching and mimicry in the taxonomy of literary appropriation. The legal concept of forgery, as it was applied in eighteenth-century criminal discourse, offers an appropriate term for the comprehension of Combe's personal aims in 1788. To achieve his aspirational goal upon the printed page and gain credit from his former friendship, Combe first had to remake Sterne in his own ideal image, an endeavour which connected all of the writers who creatively exploited him in this study. But, to observe chronology and avoid Walter Shandy's placing of 'the cart before the horse', we need to consider first how Sterne developed his literary personae through engaging with mimicry.[105]

Notes to Chapter 1

1. Taken from Monkman and Day, p. 54. This article describes the footstone subsequently financed by Frederick Carroll in 1893 which also included a certain amount of self-publicity with the inscription of details about the benefactor (pp. 58–59).
2. Monkman and Day, p. 78 note that 'the initials of the two masons are recorded in early transcriptions of the stone, but are no longer visible'. The inscription has commonly been interpreted as a reference to the brotherhood of Freemasons: see, for example, Cash, *Laurence Sterne: The Later Years*, p. 332; and Ross, p. 420.
3. *European Magazine and London Review*, 2 (November 1782), pp. 325–28. Monkman and Day, pp. 55–56 quote an example from *The Gentleman's Magazine*, 56 (1769).
4. Van Sant, p. 99. A number of twentieth-century commentators have shared Sterne's hobby-horse and discussed the influence of medical literature upon the author's depiction of bodily experience: for example, Lawlor; Hawley; and Porter.
5. Sterne, *The Letters*, Part 2, p. 584.
6. See, for example, *The Public Advertiser*, 24 March 1769; *The Works of Laurence Stern* (1769), v: p. clxiii, and later eighteenth-century editions of this title; and *Yorick's Sentimental Journey Continued*, 3rd edn, pp. xxii–xxiii. For the appearance of stories about Sterne's dissection in the Victorian period, see *Willis's Current Notes* (1854), p. 31; *The Western Mail*, 14 April 1874, p. 6; *The Derby Mercury*, 22 April 1874, p. 7; and *The Pall Mall Gazette*, 3 February 1891, p. 6. Cash in *Laurence Sterne: The Later Years*, p. 332, surmises that 'once Collignon knew whose body was on his table, he did the best thing he could: he sent it back to be reburied at Paddington' without reference to any sources for this claim; Ross, p. 420 similarly claims that the body 'was later taken back to London for clandestine reburial' without evidence.
7. The 1787 manuscript is reproduced in Prior, pp. 373–74. Ross, p. 419 comments that the story was 'disseminated widely' in one of Sterne's parishes, Sutton-on-the-Forest.
8. *Yorick's Sentimental Journey Continued*, 3rd edn, p. xxiii.
9. Cash, *Laurence Sterne: The Later Years*, p. 330; and Richardson, p. 60.
10. Richardson, p. 79.
11. Monkman and Day, pp. 48–49.
12. Lichtenberg, *London-Tagebuch*, p. 70: 'er liegt kaum einen Büchsen Schuß von der Stelle begraben, wo die Missethäter hingerichtet werden (Tyburn)'.
13. Richardson's figure for this commercial transaction relates to the 1790s (pp. 57, 64).
14. Sterne, *The Life and Opinions of Tristram Shandy*, 1978 edn, p. 167.
15. On the attitudes of the medical profession, see Richardson, pp. 164–65.
16. Legal discussion from Richardson, p. 58.
17. The advertisement for this 'bronzed' depiction of Sterne can be found at the end of volume one of *Letters of the Late Rev. Mr. Laurence Sterne, to His Most Intimate Friends*.
18. Benedict, *Framing Feeling*, p. 133.
19. Quotation from Van Sant, p. 99.
20. On the challenge of creating a Sternean narrative, see Mayo, p. 339.
21. Bosch, pp. 13–14; Blackwell, p. 193.
22. Information on Hunter from Sappol, pp. 49, 51. This view of the purpose of eighteenth-century displays of dissection and anatomy can be found in Gatrell, *The Hanging Tree*, p. 256; and Egmond, p. 118.
23. Published by the Logographic Press, London.
24. *The Beauties of Sterne [...] Selected for the Heart of Sensibility*, 1st edn.
25. Brewer, p. 2.
26. Lyser, p. 248.
27. MacNally, *Tristram Shandy: A Sentimental, Shandean Bagatelle*.
28. Gamelin, volume one, table five. Of course, the semantic connections between anatomy and discourse can be traced to Latin, one of the languages chosen for the descriptive text accompanying the plates.
29. *The Miscellaneous Works of Charles Collignon*, p. 87.

30. Information on Bentham from Marshall, p. 19.
31. For Richardson, p. 48, 'the element of theatricality implicit in the naming of operating theatres signifies their potential to provide the locus for an action to be performed, a spectacle displayed'.
32. MacDonald, p. 147.
33. Monkman and Day, p. 47. Quotation from Shakespeare, *Hamlet*, 2007 edn, p. 246.
34. Brewer, p. 78.
35. Sterne's claim to 'Shandy it away' can be found in Sterne, *The Letters, Part 1*, p. 242.
36. Brewer, p. 178. Donoghue, Mullan, and — more recently — Brewer discuss Sterne's attempt to maintain authorial control and ownership of his publications.
37. Brewer, p. 180.
38. Ruthven, pp. 112–13.
39. Quotation from Ruthven, p. 35. For example, a comparison of Paul Baines's definition of 'forgery' with Nick Groom's description of 'plagiarism' displays clear overlap in the mutual focus upon the theft of personal, individual identity. For these two writers, both terms involve tangible impersonation, in the financial sense for Baines and the literary sense for Groom. See Baines, pp. 14–15; and Groom, 'Forgery, Plagiarism, Imitation, Pegleggery', p. 74. Additionally, Groom in *The Forger's Shadow: How Forgery Changed the Course of Literature*, p. 45 claims that 'counterfeit also means a more tangible impersonation or impostor — unto the womb, counterfeit children being those fathered in adultery'.
40. Groom, *The Forger's Shadow*, p. 16. The lack of clear distinctions between these associated concepts, and the difficulty of applying individual ones to specific texts, is implied by Bosch's bibliography of Sternean publications under the title of 'Imitations, Commentaries, Parodies, Forgeries', p. 281.
41. Ruthven, p. 123.
42. Kewes, p. 15.
43. Definitions of 'mimic', 'mimicry', and 'burlesque' from the *OED*. Also see Sterne, *A Sentimental Journey*, 2002 edn, p. 77.
44. See the entries for 'mimick' and 'mimickry' in Johnson, *A Dictionary of the English Language*, II.
45. *The Critical Review*, 27 (May 1769), p. 390.
46. Boswell, I: p. 357.
47. Ibid., I: p. 321. Both men were associates of Foote.
48. *Memoirs of Richard Cumberland*, 1806 edn, p. 251 and 2002 edn, pp. 192–93. The editor of the 2002 edition, Richard J. Dircks, is unable to identify Foote's victim, 'Sir Robert Fletcher', with certainty.
49. Carter, pp. 21, 64.
50. From 1747 to 1749, Foote staged a variety of satirical revues at the Haymarket comprising collections of impersonations. *The Diversions of the Morning*, which was first performed on 22 April 1747, was never published.
51. Boswell, I: p. 357. Correspondingly, Brewer, p. 20 claims that eighteenth-century readers engaged in 'endless speculation about what a character might "probably" or "possibly" do in his life off-page'.
52. *Joineriana; or, The Book of Scraps*, II: p. 151.
53. Sterne, *The Letters, Part 1*, p. 197.
54. *The Times*, 5 June 1969, p. 1, details the unearthing of bones at St. George's burial ground and Kenneth Monkman's subsequent attempt to identify Sterne's skull, from among 11,500 others, using Nollekens's bust. Interestingly, a parallel can be made between this enterprise and the creation of Bentham's 'auto-icon'. In the attempt to display a realistic representation of Bentham, a wax head was created for his skeletal body using several artistic sources, including a bust and a portrait.
55. *Punch; or, The London Charivari*, 1 June 1867, p. 2. Details of the exhibition were widely publicized in London newspapers: see, for example, *The Times*, 29 January 1867, p. 4; and *The Pall Mall Gazette*, 26 April 1867, p. 13.
56. In Garrick's letter to Lady Spencer dated 22 October 1777, he passed judgement upon his late fellow performer, Foote: he had 'no feeling, sacrific'd friends and foes to a joke, & so has dy'd

very little regretted even by his nearest acquaintance'. For details of this letter and relationships of mimicry in the theatre, see Foote's entry in Highfill et al., v: pp. 329–30.
57. Tankard, p. 86.
58. Williams, *A Letter to David Garrick*, pp. 10–11.
59. See Foote's entry in Highfill et al., v: pp. 329–30.
60. The interpretation of Foote's 1747 debut in Highfill et al., v: p. 330 as 'a major landslide in the steady eroding away of the Licensing Act, one that led to the "minor theatre" phenomenon' of the late eighteenth century has been reviewed by Moody, pp. 16–17 who claims that the Haymarket occupied a 'unique institutional position, on the border between the two patent theatres and the unlicensed playhouses'.
61. Foote and Murphy, p. 8.
62. It is not my intention to recount the development of copyright law in the eighteenth century which has been described in detail by a number of historians: for example, Rose; Feather; and Englert.
63. Moody, pp. 14–17.
64. Nicholson, p. xxii. Knox's comments appear in Howes, *Sterne: The Critical Heritage*, p. 254. For an example of the condemnation of the first two volumes of *Tristram Shandy* for obscenity, see *Universal Magazine of Knowledge and Pleasure*, 26 (April 1760), pp. 189–90. Howes's *Yorick and the Critics* extensively documents the moral condemnation of Sterne during this period.
65. Condemnation of Hall-Stevenson's *Crazy Tales* can be found in Bosch, p. 113; and Cash, 'Sterne, Hall-Stevenson, Libertinism, and *A Sentimental Journey*', pp. 291, 318. The final quotation, on William Combe's forgery of Sterne's letters, is from Sterne, *The Letters, Part 1*, p. xlviii.
66. *The West Indian* premièred on 19 January 1771. McIntyre, p. 449 acknowledges the huge popularity of Cumberland's farce in the eighteenth century: 'the play ran for twenty-nine nights in that first season, and was regularly revived over the next thirty years. It also sold 12,000 copies'.
67. Cumberland, *The West Indian*, pp. 17–18.
68. See Howes, *Yorick and the Critics*, p. 71.
69. Thompson, p. 198.
70. Sterne, *A Sentimental Journey*, p. 124.
71. Cumberland, *The West Indian*, pp. 25, 46, and 78.
72. Ibid., p. 18.
73. Ibid., p. 20.
74. Ibid., p. 82.
75. Sterne, *Tristram Shandy*, p. 682; and the letter 'To Dr. John Eustace' dated 9 February 1768 in Sterne, *The Letters, Part 2*, p. 645.
76. Briggs, p. 100.
77. For further details, see Hamilton, *Doctor Syntax*, p. 314.
78. Compare *Various Occasions* with *The Beauties of Sterne*, 7th edn, pp. 164–67, 176–77, 251; and *The Works of Laurence Sterne. Complete in Eight Volumes*, 1790 edn, vi: pp. 249–52, 257–64.
79. 'One of Uncle Toby's Illegitimate Children', p. 6.
80. See *Various Occasions* (1775) and *Original Letters* (1788).
81. For the dates of publication, see Curtis, p. 1084.
82. For example, see Cash, *Laurence Sterne: The Later Years*, pp. 351–52.
83. Sterne, *The Letters, Part 2*, p. 646.
84. Bosch, pp. 13, 19, and 35.
85. Ibid., p. 13.
86. Blackwell, p. 193. This view of Sternean texts as slavishly uncreative and unoriginal was earlier voiced by Bandry, p. 49: 'Sterne never filches from his imitators as they do from him, his possible borrowings always being incorporated within a new idea, a new context'.
87. Burke, *A Philosophical Enquiry*, 2nd edn, pp. 18–19.
88. de Voogd, 'The Letters of Laurence Sterne', pp. 181–82.
89. *Letters Written by the Late Right Honourable Philip Dormer Stanhope*, I: p. 354.
90. Griffin, p. 890.
91. Parsons, p. 72.

92. Bosch, pp. 281–93. For an alternative list, see the appendix to Mary-Céline Newbould's *Adaptations of Laurence Sterne's Fiction: Sterneana, 1760–1840* (Ashgate, 2013).
93. *Continuation of Yorick's Sentimental Journey* (London: printed for the author, at the Literary-Press, 1788); *A Sentimental Journey: Intended as a Sequel to Mr. Sterne's through Italy, Switzerland, and France. By Mr. Shandy* (Southampton: T. Baker and S. Crowder, 1793). Watts, p. 245, lists *Maria; or, The Generous Rustic* (London: T. Cadell, 1784), *Maria; or, The Vicarage. A Novel in Two Volumes* (London: Hookham and Carpenter, 1796), and *Sterne's Maria: A Pathetic Story with an Account of Her Death at the Castle of Valesine* (London: R. Rusted, 1800), among others. For a discussion of Sternean it-narratives, see Blackwell, pp. 194–204.
94. Since being mentioned in Howes's *Yorick and the Critics*, p. 64, MacNally's play has been briefly discussed by Hartley in 'Laurence Sterne and the Eighteenth-Century Stage', pp. 149–51, and Newbould, 'Shandying it Away'. While misreading the play as an unsuccessful attempt to dramatize Sterne's novel, Newbould, p. 164 subsequently claims that MacNally's afterpiece 'demonstrates a dissatisfying inability to adapt Sterne's fictional material into the new format of the play' without considering the play in performance at Covent Garden.
95. See Day, and also Asfour.
96. Flint, p. 352.
97. Kernan, p. 220.
98. Keymer, p. 20.
99. Ibid., pp. 1, 156.
100. Cruise, pp. 176–77.
101. Keymer, pp. 63–72, locates the possible origins of Sterne's typographical devices in lesser known eighteenth-century novels including John Kidgell's *The Card* (1755) and the anonymous *The Life and Memoirs of Mr. Ephraim Tristram Bates* (1756). Also see de Voogd, '*Tristram Shandy* as Aesthetic Object', pp. 109, 114.
102. Bandry, p. 39.
103. For one example of a short pamphlet that exploits the typographical elements of Sterne's narrative, see 'One of Uncle Toby's Illegitimate Children'.
104. Cash, *Laurence Sterne: The Later Years*, p. 113.
105. Sterne, *Tristram Shandy*, p. 672.

CHAPTER 2

GARRICK AND LITERARY MIMICRY

Before Sterne haunted the lecture theatres of anatomy schools, he loitered in the stalls and boxes of theatres at London and York. Unsurprisingly, contemporaries of Sterne frequently portray a figure who loves the stage. Charles Churchill in his verse tribute to Garrick, *The Rosciad* (1761), even considers Sterne as a potential judge of performers featured in the poem's fictional competition to find the Georgian successor to Quintus Roscius, the greatest of Roman comic actors:

> Who should be judge in such a tryal:----Who?
>
> For J-HNS-N some; but J-HNS-N, it was fear'd,
> Would be too grave; and ST-NE too loose appear'd:[1]

Churchill's suggestion of 'grave' Johnson and 'loose' Sterne does not simply exploit the contrary personalities of these celebrities for comic effect. His inclusion of 'ST-NE' also exists as a complimentary gesture towards Sterne's knowledge of theatrical entertainment and the on-stage abilities of actors in 1760s London. Theatregoing provided opportunities to see and be seen, and this mention of the celebrated author played upon Sterne's renown for frequent and conspicuous appearances at Drury Lane theatre, a patronage linked in the public consciousness with his much-publicized friendship with its actor-manager, Garrick. Sterne's love of Garrick's art developed when the actor gave the writer a free pass to his box at the theatre for the entire season of 1760–61, a compliment rare enough to be remarked as far away as Paris.[2]

For Sterne, the development of this acquaintance would have far-reaching creative consequences as the hugely famous mimic became an artistic influence upon the writer. Sterne manipulated an epistolary style to engage with Garrick's celebrated acting technique and the theatrical spectacles of Drury Lane, an engagement that culminated in the creation of *Continuation of the Bramine's Journal* shortly before the author's death.[3] Whereas Sterne's fascination with the theatre and theatricality has been recognized at length, there has been no investigation into Garrick's connection to the author's correspondence style.[4] Sterne's authorship of the familiar letter can be seen to mimic the actor's 'busy physicality', a performance style that transformed character into a collection of emotional flashpoints.[5] He used his experiences as a spectator to develop the epistolary identities of Tristram and Yorick, mimicking Garrick's expressive technique involving the representation of emotional experience as a collection of choreographed physical actions, to promote intimacy within communication. Throughout the examples chosen in this chapter, Garrick's presence permeates Sterne's self-expression in forms of entertainment existing outside of the theatre's walls.

The importance of reading the *Journal* in relation to Georgian theatre is encouraged by the frequency of references to dramaturgy as Sterne's performative self-fashioning is placed in locations that are explicitly represented as theatrical, with Shandy Hall becoming a stage for the presentation of the author's sensibility. Sterne complains of the absence of Eliza Draper (1744–1778) by stating:

> there wants only the *Dramatis Personae* for the performance—the play is wrote —the Scenes are painted—& the Curtain ready to be drawn up.—the whole Piece waits for thee, my Eliza—[6]

Throughout, Sterne's presentation of his heightened desire as a form of performance includes a preoccupation with narrative *mise en scène*; his preparations for her wished-for return are expressed as 'work[ing] hard to fit out & decorate a little Theatre for us to act on'.[7] As we shall see, while echoing the mid-century staging conventions of Drury Lane, the *Journal* subtly evokes the theatrical and architectural frames surrounding Garrick's on-stage performances, lending dramatic impact to Sterne's literary spectacles.

Years before the composition of the *Journal*, Hall-Stevenson's lyric celebration of Sterne's new-found literary fame focused upon his friend's experience of theatrical environments. In the first of *Two Lyric Epistles* (1760), he represents theatres as physical spaces providing particular constraints and pleasures; he asks Sterne 'Pray tell me plain, / Whether the theatre in Drury-Lane, / Or that of York, is most commodious'.[8] On one semantic level, 'commodious' indicates the potential of architecture to affect the spectator's enjoyment, in terms of providing suitable or uncomfortable accommodation. Hall-Stevenson's choice of word, with the additional meaning of 'profitable, of use' in eighteenth-century usage, also implies that time spent in indulgent theatregoing can become financially profitable and creatively useful. In the *Journal*, Sterne would combine both meanings of this word: he would exploit his knowledge of stagecraft, theatrical architecture, and the spatial accommodation of audiences, to enclose his literary performances and create emotive narrative locations. Sterne would relocate the contemporary developments in staging at Drury Lane to the theatricality of the *Journal*.

Sterne's desire that the actor should become his artistic mentor was expressed in a letter dated 6 April 1765 which pleaded for Garrick's return from the Grand Tour and derided the performances of his protégé, William Powell (1735–1769). Despite Powell's 'brilliant success' in his first season at Drury Lane, 'performing no less than eighteen capital parts', Sterne sought to flatter Garrick:[9]

> Powel!—Lord God!—give me some one with less smoak & more fire—There are, who like the Pharisees, still think they shall be heard for *much* speaking— come—come away my dear Garrick, <—> & teach us another Lesson—[10]

Even though Sterne's sentiment is primarily designed to compliment, his comparison of acting styles displays shrewd discernment in its anticipation of a related judgement from the experienced former actor turned theatrical commentator, Thomas Davies, in his biography *Memoirs of the Life of David Garrick* (1780). While Sterne criticizes Powell through unfavourably contrasting his excessive reliance upon speech with Garrick's manipulation of the body for the expression of passion, Davies would later describe Powell's overuse of an ineffective and unsophisticated voice: 'among his worst failings we may reckon an inclination sometimes to rant and bluster, and sometimes a propensity to whine and blubber'.[11]

This passage of correspondence is revealing in a number of ways: we gain a glimpse of Sterne's knowledgeable appreciation of mid-century performances; his jocular willingness to be Garrick's pupil; and, most importantly, his use of theatrical references to promote a relationship between the physical marks of punctuation upon the manuscript page and the techniques of conveying emotion in the theatre. In the informal context of this letter, the dash does more than simply divide writing into units of sense. He employs the dash to suggest the delivery of speech in ways that evoke Garrick's performances as well as the use of this typographical mark in translations of those performances upon the printed page. As befitting an avowal of Garrick's tutelage, Sterne's playful rant against Powell conveys a sense of vocal fervour through the use of the dash to separate and accentuate exclamations. Aside from this usage, this chapter primarily comprehends this device as a way of engineering suggestive visual gaps, offering the reader an opportunity both to appreciate pauses and to visualize physical attitudes as an accompaniment to the prose, thereby recalling Garrick's tendency to pause and then strike an affecting pose on stage. For someone like Sterne's addressee, familiar with this style of performance and its representation upon the page, the section '—come—come away my dear Garrick' would provide two such caesuras, inviting him to imagine action to fill the spaces as Sterne attempted to coax and coerce his friend to return home.

There is not the intention to propose that Sterne created a new written style at this moment in 1765 on discovering the communicative potential of the dash. His multifarious use of this mark can be seen in letters, sermons, and novelistic volumes written before and after the duration of his intimacy with Garrick. In numerous critical considerations of Sterne's manipulation of the art of printing in *Tristram Shandy*, attention has been lavished upon his imaginative employment of this feature of typography for a variety of effects.[12] For Janine Barchas and J. Paul Hunter, dashes in his novel exist as prompts, encouraging the reader to translate print into the fluctuations of a narrative voice; they exist as 'visual markers of spoken speech' promoting 'a sense of conversational immediacy' and providing 'a score that the voice can perform by giving the eye a visual diagram of structural transitions'.[13] In this respect, they attempt to place Sterne within a novelistic tradition where typography becomes evidence not of his inventiveness, but of his appropriation of the print techniques from earlier books. He is represented, using charitable terms, as either a 'popularizer' or a 'publicist' of know-how from the 1740s and 50s, traced by Barchas to Sarah Fielding's first novel, *The Adventures of David Simple* (1744).[14]

Focusing upon letters unpublished during Sterne's lifetime removes the complexities posed by the manipulation of print from a discussion of the dash as a method of structuring ideas upon the manuscript page, albeit in ways that potentially evoke the use of this device in other, published texts. This focus partly stems from a desire to approach the dash as a structural principle uncomplicated by the variety of options offered by Georgian print technology, concerning size, length, and position in relation to other print devices and the layout of the page, with the potential for decisions to change with every new edition. This approach discards the printer's obfuscatory art to concentrate upon the forming of connections and relationships between words and sentences with the significance of the dash dependent upon syntactical position and number. After all, even a cursory glance at *Tristram Shandy* reveals Sterne's willingness to exploit the novelties of print to complicate and frustrate the meaning of visual signs, 'by refining typography to the point at which it no longer serves its fundamental communicative purposes'.[15]

However, a consideration of Sterne's letters in the context of his novels can, to a degree, be illuminating. Developing Elizabeth Wanning Harries's observation that Sterne employs fragmentary moments of aposiopesis in *Tristram Shandy* to suggest that words are inadequate and separate characters 'while gestures and glances unite them', this chapter reveals Sterne's recognition of this inadequacy during the opportunities he provides for his addressee to imagine non-verbal forms of communication, thereby compensating for the writer's physical absence.[16] In these letters, the linear marks that prompt the imagination are moving in more than one sense: directing the eye's motion across the page, they give Sterne opportunities to be affecting. As a recognition of the many meanings of the verb 'dash' current in the 1760s, Sterne's strokes of the pen, designed to give the illusion of spontaneous, unpremeditated writing, also served to arouse images of impetuous, madcap action in ways that emotionally stimulated. After the phrase was coined in 1715, Sterne 'cut a dash' in an epistolary sense.

Despite the usefulness of placing Sterne's epistles in the context of his career as a novelist, this investigation provides a different interpretative angle that looks up from the printed page, and the limitations of literary tradition, to another form of influential entertainment. There is, however, a risk of simplification when any account 'imagines a model of textual influence in which the transmission of ideas is seamless, transparent, and free of fiction'. For Markman Ellis, this is especially the case when the purpose and audience for the model and its derivative are different, as in my assertion of the influence of public performance upon a more intimate form of communication.[17] Nevertheless, I support Reiko Oya's methodology in her analysis of texts and commodities inspired by Georgian theatre, namely that we cannot discuss works 'without addressing the company they kept' especially when both parties were conscious and appreciative of each other's activities.[18] My claim of influence illuminates Sterne's writing, irrespective of other independent cultural forces that may have helped to shape it; acknowledging the differences between the two forms of communication reinforces the importance of 'mimicry' as a critical concept. Especially when bearing in mind the pejorative Johnsonian sense of the word in the *Dictionary* of 1755, successful mimicry involves the creation of similarity, between two forms of expression, that can never be exact. Mimicry, as it was practised within Georgian theatre, designated a creative act, one which manipulated recognizable forms of body language for new comic purposes, for an audience whose composition changed every night.

As Garrick entertained theatregoers as a comic mimic, it is fitting that the technique of mimicry provides a number of analogies with Sterne's literary appropriation of the actor's performance style. Sterne's refashioning of his friend's performances represented identity through an exaggeration of manner and gesture. Furthermore, Johnson's disparaging definition highlighted the ambivalent relationship between mimic and subject shared by Sterne's impersonation of Garrick's techniques. The lexicographer derided this form of entertainment as low comedy, performed by 'ludicrous buffoons' who 'ridicule' through 'burlesque imitation'. Sterne's mimicry involved the amplification and burlesque of the actor's physical posturing, a trait also shared by satirical and critical accounts of him in the period. Sterne adapted facets of the burlesque portrayal of Garrick to promote epistolary identities for himself, often involving self-deprecation for comic effect. Like the stage performers, his mimicry of Garrick was only one element of a larger creative process, in this case involving the imaginative situations of his letters. Before Sterne engaged with Garrick, it was first necessary to observe his subject.

'My dear Garrick, teach us another Lesson'

In accounts of the Georgian stage, Garrick has been represented as a protean performer, famous for the creation of roles involving the quickfire transition through a collection of expressive physical attitudes. Davies, who had performed with Garrick's troupe at Drury Lane, celebrated his ability to 'make a sudden transition from violent rage, and even madness, to the extremes of levity and humour', and 'go through the whole circle of theatric evolution with the most surprising velocity'.[19] More recently, Garrick's 'total physicality' has been characterized, according to Kalman Burnim, by the incessant movement from one emotional moment to another as 'his look, his voice, his attitude changed with every sentiment'.[20] Jean Benedetti has described Garrick's method of dividing a character's emotional development into distinct stages involving 'the breaking up of speeches with pauses, followed by sudden starts and shiftings in tone'.[21] Similarly, Tiffany Stern noted that 'Garrick presented "starts" followed by pauses during which an attitude was held [...] Parts were thus divided into a series of "moments"'; like 'Garrick's party-trick of performing each passion in turn, they were detachable'.[22]

Eighteenth-century spectators unimpressed by Garrick represented this characteristic presentation of emotion, these autonomous moments shaped and amplified by the physical body, as violent and spasmodic fits of grotesque, extravagant mime. For such theatregoers, Garrick's collection of physical attitudes did not simply lack cohesion as he performed a role in fits and starts; his manipulation of the body also lacked restraint. In one of the many satirical pamphlet attacks upon Garrick during his career, *An Enquiry into the Real Merit of a Certain Popular Performer* (1760), Thaddeus Fitzpatrick satirically asked the reader to allow 'the manager of Drury Lane [to] fidgit, and bounce and start, and dislocate the members of himself'.[23] Other mid-century criticisms also portrayed a performer who relied upon the illusion of a fitful loss of bodily self-control to communicate extreme emotion, as in Theophilus Cibber's disparagement of Garrick's 'Over-fondness for extravagant Attitudes, frequent affected Starts, convulsive Twitchings' and 'Jerkings of the Body'.[24] The first edition of Tobias Smollett's *The Adventures of Peregrine Pickle*

(1751) acidly criticized this tendency that was the antithesis of the easy, polished composure of the polite gentleman:

> He [...] perverts the genteel deportment of a gentleman, into the idle buffoonery of a miserable tobacconist; his whole art is no other than a succession of frantic vociferation, such as I have heard in the cells of Bedlam [...] convulsive startings, and a ductility of features, suited to the most extravagant transitions.[25]

Here, Smollett recalls the actor's performance of the 'miserable tobacconist' Abel Drugger from Ben Jonson's *The Alchemist*, a role which was synonymous with Garrick's abilities as a comic actor in the period.[26] His performance is presented as a collection of 'convulsive' starts coupled with exaggerated emotional expression suggesting 'frantic', frenzied madness. Garrick's theatrical perversions are evidence of a loss of self-control more suitable in a 'cell of Bedlam', a situation compounded by the actor's new and disconcerting interpretation of Drugger's character. According to Benedetti, the actor's inventive portrayal of Drugger as violent and aggressive, 'wild and stripped off like the famous boxer Broughton', was considered 'a lapse in taste and judgement' by a number of theatrical critics.[27]

Away from these contemporary attacks, Garrick's acting style can be appreciated by looking at his versions of the plays which were performed at Drury Lane and subsequently published. His approach to speech was popularized through the typography of one frequently reprinted edition of *Romeo and Juliet*, '*With some Alterations, and an Additional Scene: As it is Performed at the Theatre-Royal in Drury-Lane*' as described by the 1748 title page. Garrick's reworking of the text, in his altered version of the monument scene, suggestively predates Sterne's employment of the dash in informal mid-century epistles. This scene employed the dash visually both to connect a collection of disjointed exclamations and to represent the pauses in the delivery of speech, indicating the silent spaces created by the actor for the striking of an affecting physical attitude. Typography indicates the location of each dramatic caesura, but is silent about the nature of the action filling the expressive pause made famous by Garrick, prompting the imagination of the reader. In this interpolation (see Fig. 2.1), the actor's communication of emotional intensity is represented by the frequency of the dash, a precursor of Sterne's portrayal of flurried, passionate action using the same visual technique.

While proposing Garrick's influence upon Sterne's epistolary style, the inherent nature of the familiar letter problematizes its use as evidence of authorial development. Even if an editor could resolve all of the ambiguities surrounding the dates of a significant number of Sterne's letters, his informal epistles would still demand appreciation as individual texts with reference to specific factors at the moment of authorship, including the circumstances of composition, authorial purpose, and the level of intimacy between writer and reader. The desire to contrast an author's miscellaneous body of correspondence before and after one event, such as the beginning of a new friendship or association, would unavoidably lead to either the simplistic treatment of this material, or the accumulation of numerous anomalous letters that failed to sustain such a distinction. Instead of a broad survey of Sterne's whole collection of correspondence divided in this manner, this chapter alternatively spotlights the *Journal* (1767) and a small selection of letters from a

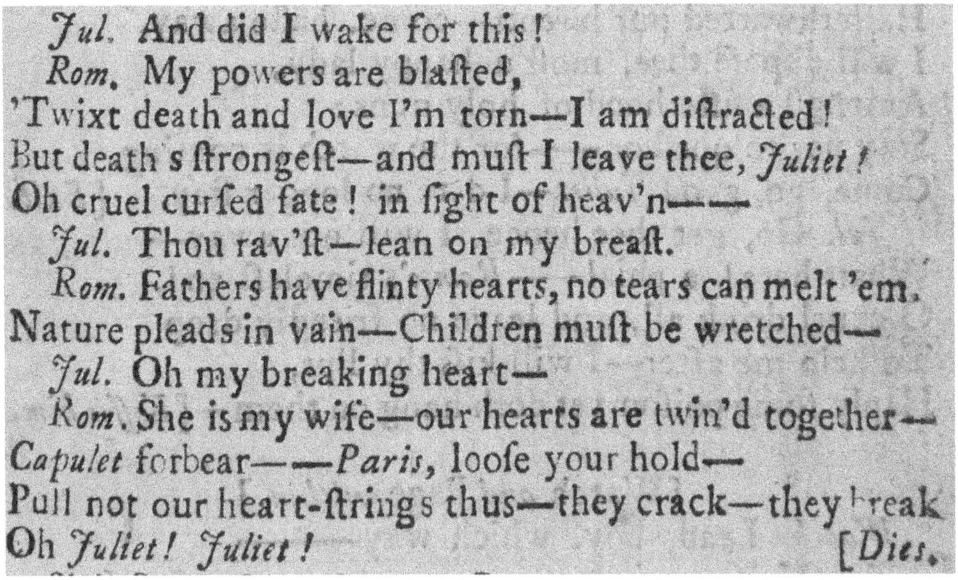

> *Jul.* And did I wake for this!
> *Rom.* My powers are blasted,
> 'Twixt death and love I'm torn—I am distracted!
> But death's strongest—and must I leave thee, *Juliet!*
> Oh cruel cursed fate! in sight of heav'n——
> *Jul.* Thou rav'st—lean on my breast.
> *Rom.* Fathers have flinty hearts, no tears can melt 'em.
> Nature pleads in vain—Children must be wretched—
> *Jul.* Oh my breaking heart—
> *Rom.* She is my wife—our hearts are twin'd together—
> *Capulet* forbear——*Paris*, loose your hold—
> Pull not our heart-strings thus—they crack—they break
> Oh *Juliet! Juliet!* [*Dies.*

FIG. 2.1. Facsimile of *Romeo and Juliet by Shakespear; with Alterations and an Additional Scene by D. Garrick. As it is Performed at the Theatre-Royal in Drury Lane* (1766), p. 69. Reproduced with the permission of the Brotherton Collection, Leeds University Library.

relatively short chronological period (May 1764 to April 1765, although the date ascribed to one letter, without an extant manuscript, is questionable).[28] While acknowledging their individuality, these texts are chosen for their similarity, in terms of stylistic facets employed for comparable aims. In admiration of the actor's ability to encourage intense empathy within his audience, Sterne mimics Garrick's theatrical expression in these letters to grasp unreserved intimacy when faced with the obstacle of a potentially unapproachable or distant reader, whether emotionally, physically, or geographically. This general principle can be illustrated by Sterne's attempt to address and overcome specific inhibitions to emotional closeness: Garrick's annoyance at Sterne's failure to repay a financial debt, the geographical distance from Hall-Stevenson's friendship caused by Sterne's prolonged absence upon the Continent, the indifference of one beautiful and frustratingly unattainable lady, and the departure of Eliza for India.

Sterne's Pantomimic Epistles

Smollett's account of Garrick's 'buffoonery', involving such 'extravagant transitions', could aptly describe Sterne's physical self-presentation within these epistles. Criticisms of Garrick are transformed into comedy as Sterne approaches the written word as performative and attempts self-ridicule, transforming identity into a collection of farcical performances upon the page. He translates perceptions of Garrick's style to develop an epistolary voice that exploits the comic potential of the portrayal of identity as an erratic and fitful collection of disjointed actions and attitudes. On 19 May 1764, Sterne relied upon this theatrical potential to sustain masculine camaraderie with Hall-Stevenson across the distance of the Channel. In this attempt to compensate for the loss of sociable conversation with his 'dear Cosin', Sterne adopted the histrionic persona of the despairing lover and described an intense infatuation in Paris:

> I have been for eight weeks smitten with the tenderest Passion [...] how deliciously I canter'd away with it the first month, two up, two down <fm my hotel to hers>, always upon my haunches, <fr> along the streets [...] the last three weeks we were every hour upon the doleful Ditty of parting—& thou mayest concieve dear Cosin, how it alter'd my gaite and air—for I went & came like any loaden'd Cart; & did nothing but mix tears, & *Jouer des Sentiments* with her from sun-rising even to the setting of the same.[29]

Sterne comically reconstructs his past emotional experience as a collection of extravagant and artfully choreographed movements. In this mimicry of Garrick's on-stage technique, self-portrayal is achieved through a number of playful tableaux and disjointed theatrical moments as emotion is displayed within a series of physical poses which intensify the comic tone of the letter. His farcical image of cantering away provides the epistolary equivalent of a portrayal of pantomime from one theatrical survey, *The Theatrical Campaign for MDCCLXVI and MDCCLXVII*. While this account uses hyperbole to criticize and satirize, with descriptions of actors 'skipping about the stage for an hour or two' and 'constantly running' around 'with imaginary red-hot pokers', Sterne instead recognizes the comic potential of frantic, pantomimic action as magnified by the imagination.[30] As with Garrick's performance style, Sterne's passion is exaggerated and displayed upon the expressive surface of the physical body through the amplification of movement and gesture. Within his self-presentation, emotion has the potential to trigger a comic transformation of the author's mercurial 'gaite and air' with passion represented by speed of movement as Sterne travels through the streets. Like Smollett's description of Drugger, this response to passion involves erratic and fitful forms of action. The image of Sterne manically cantering up and down indicates the resignation of control over the body's movements during bouts of intense desire, an impression reinforced by his obsessive rehearsal 'every hour' of the doleful act of parting.

Such personal correspondence, aiming for jocular intimacy, exists as an exercise in dramatic self-presentation; consequently, letter writing creates a theatrical script which asks to be understood as performance. In another act of role-play in one of his billet-doux, Sterne as 'Tristram Shandy' attempted to seduce 'Lady P.':

> I am kept at a distance—and despair of getting one inch nearer you, with all the steps and windings I can think of to recommend myself to you—Would not any man in his senses run diametrically from you—and as far as his legs would carry him [...]—It is but an hour ago, that I kneeled down and swore I never would come near you—[...] I dine at Mr. C—r's in Wigmore-street, in this neighbourhood, where I shall stay till seven, in hopes you purpose to put me to this proof. If I hear nothing by that time I shall conclude you are better disposed of—and shall take a sorry hack, and sorrily jogg on to the play—Curse on the word.[31]

Again, Sterne's self-fashioning becomes a literary burlesque of Garrick's performances, a frantic collection of physical poses with Sterne's use of the dash to represent the theatrical 'clap-trap' pause followed by a change of attitude. Following the actor's visual style of performance, the emotional temperature of Sterne's persona is expressed through the quality of the movement he rhetorically evokes: for example, the comical expression of fear through running away, and the tearful self-pity represented by the sorry 'jogg'. Moreover, the potential for emotional gratification is conceived as the possibility of achieving progress towards Lady P. within a journey that is frustrated while Sterne is 'kept at a distance'. Emotion here is a physical force capable of manipulating the body into performing paroxysms of action, as typified by Smollett's reading of Garrick's performance.[32] As in this critical commentary, Sterne's loss of self-control subjects the body to a physical, buffeting force.

The novelistic character of Tristram Shandy, like Yorick, became a favourite alter ego for Sterne while involved in mid-century epistolary risk-taking. If the long-standing editorial identification of 'Lady P.' is accepted, his risk-taking becomes audacious, considering that Lady Anne Warkworth (b. 1746) was both married and only nineteen at the date commonly ascribed to this act of seduction by Sterne, then fifty-two years old.[33] Often, when engaging with a risqué or emotionally harmful enterprise, such as the attempt to seduce with the potential for rejection, Sterne approached these identities as comforting disguises. Tristram and Yorick were impish personae which allowed the author to disown responsibility for disreputable actions. Thus, in the 1765 letter to Garrick quoted earlier, Sterne adopted the character 'Shandy' to disavow responsibility for a debt of twenty pounds. After failing to repay this money borrowed over two years earlier, Sterne attempted to withdraw from a confrontation which would eventually signal the end of intimacy between the two men. Using interesting conjecture largely based upon this one surviving letter, Arthur H. Cash attempted to reconstruct the dispute: Garrick became 'worried about the money owed him' after hearing that Sterne was seriously ill and 'wrote several times to Sterne in London. The letters miscarried, said Sterne. When one finally reached him, Sterne was so offended by the tone that he scribbled an angry reply. Garrick shot back that Sterne was scalping him. Then Sterne tried to retreat', with this second note:[34]

> I scalp You!—my dear Garrick! my dear friend!—foul befall the man who hurts a hair of y^r head!—and so full was I of that very Sentiment,—that my Letter had not been sent to the Office ten minutes, before <I> My heart smote me; & I sent to recall it—but fail'd. You are sadly to blame, Shandy! for this; quoth I, $^V\&^V$ leaning with my head on my hand [...]—thou knowest, Shandy, that he loves thee—why wilt thou hazard him a moment's pain?[35]

This playful impersonation of Garrick calculatingly adds an element of flattery to a letter designed to placate, as Sterne's self-fashioning is again achieved through literary tableaux which recall Garrick's technique of producing 'a series of defining emotional statements' upon the stage.[36]

Like Garrick's Drugger, Sterne's epistolary voice here aimed to provoke laughter through relinquishing emotional self-control. Within Georgian guides to politeness, such self-control was synonymous with acceptable behaviour; it was championed as an indispensable trait for polite gentlemen who were concerned with achieving sociable accommodation and complaisance. According to *The Polite Companion* (1760), for example, 'A Man must be Master of himself, his Words, his Gestures and Passions, that nothing may escape him, to give others a just Occasion to complain of his Demeanour'.[37] As illustrated by Carter's detailed discussion, self-discipline was deemed essential for a polished social complaisance which suppressed comments 'that shocked, embarrassed or intruded into others' privacy'.[38] Smollett's description of Garrick's inability to be 'Master of himself' in *The Alchemist* depicted the actor as the stage embodiment of impoliteness. Garrick's depiction of intense emotion upon the stage could be applauded; but within the polite world away from the theatre, displays of passion could provoke unease. Possibly, Sterne closely mimicked Garrick's performance style to ensure that his emotionally extravagant letters would be accepted as harmless entertainment akin to the diversions offered by an actor. Sterne aimed to entertain, not offend, his readers.

Advice from the former actor-manager Thomas Sheridan on the repression of emotion in everyday affairs provides a useful commentary on Sterne's epistolary conversation and indicates how his letters could have been negatively received. Sheridan, the best known elocutionist in the century, condemned passionate expression and the dangerous influence of theatre upon private meetings in *A Course of Lectures on Elocution* (1762). In particular, Sheridan highlighted the danger of allowing extravagance and excess to colour and distort the art of conversation:

supposing a man [...] acquired a manner of delivery in private life, and in his
usual discourse, very disagreeable and disgusting; supposing he should have a
habit of distorting his features, of using aukward and extravagant gestures, and
uttering strange and discordant tones; is he not in such a case, to endeavour to
get the better of these, whenever he speaks [...?] His business is, to set about a
reformation of all such faults, first, in private life.[39]

Sterne's appropriation of Garrick's emotional histrionics within such an intimate form of communication would have been 'disagreeable and disgusting' when judged by Sheridan's polite etiquette. Sterne's self-portrayal (as an actor upon a stage) in the *Journal* implicitly conceded that displays of intense emotion were more acceptable in some locations than others.

When polite commentators advocated the suppression of passionate communication in the private areas of refined society, Garrick was creating a semi-enclosed, secretive stage for the expression of extremes. As the century progressed, performances were increasingly framed with secluded and withdrawn settings which, on one level, satisfied the eighteenth-century spectator's 'need to maintain his sense of privacy' and achieve a safe distance from 'ever more persistent appeals to his feelings'.[40] His stage management attempted to stifle the interaction between performer and audience through the embryonic development of the fourth wall of the proscenium arch, the spatial barrier between the performance space and the auditorium. This strategy encouraged the audience's viewing of the stage 'as a harmonious and completed vision', 'a world not participated in by its immediate audience — a "window on the world" for an essentially passive spectator'.[41] The endeavour to separate actor and spectator, and therefore heighten the illusion of reality on the stage, ultimately cast the theatregoer as a voyeur of distant, confidential displays of emotion. Sterne's mimicry of Garrick eventually reflected these developments in staging as the author relocated his epistolary performances to theatrical yet discreetly private locations within the *Journal*. To fully appreciate the influence of Garrick's spectacles upon Sterne, we need briefly to tour Drury Lane.

Secretive Spectacles

Critical voices on the theatre of mid-eighteenth-century London have presented a communal, interactive space shared by audience and performers alike. For instance, Mark Auburn has claimed that 'the lights of the great chandeliers in the auditorium were not dimmed, so audience and actor were illuminated throughout the presentation' and 'the interaction was constant', a development of Allardyce Nicoll's proposal that the Garrick stage possessed the 'characteristic atmosphere' of a 'close association of actors and spectators'.[42] In contrast to such views, other writers have stressed that the stifling of interaction between audience and performer characterized the English experience in the mid-century period and after. The new season at Drury Lane under Garrick's management in 1747 included one major change: gentlemen were banned from taking their seats on the stage or wandering backstage during the performance.[43] Such innovation spatially distanced the audience from the stage and prevented their observation of the actors when 'physically separate from their scenic context'.[44] This banishment of the audience has been portrayed as Garrick's desire 'to remove an anomolous visual element' even though it sacrificed intimacy.[45] His act of enlarging the audience capacity of Drury Lane in 1747 and 1762 would have again diminished the intimacy of this environment for a significant section of the crowd. It has been estimated that the capacity would have been approximately 1268 after the alterations of 1747 and about 2206 after 1762, a very significant increase.[46]

The descriptions from one German tourist, Georg Christoph Lichtenberg, can be used to oppose the scene of a brightly lit, rowdy, and noisy setting, characterized by the vociferous interaction between audience and actors. Lichtenberg depicted an alternative image of this physical space while emphasizing its importance as an influence upon his experiences at Drury Lane in the 1770s. His accounts, 'remarkable for all the detail they contain and unsurpassed in their vividness', have become an important part of anthologies of theatrical criticism. One anthologist, Stanley Wells, has provided a reason for this surge in popularity: these 'marvellous letters written (for publication)' have 'rarely been bettered for accuracy of observation' and they offer 'a sense of what it felt like to be there'.[47] Lichtenberg's descriptive prose dated 1 October 1775 recounts the moment that Hamlet, played by Garrick, confronted the ghost of his father:

> The theatre is darkened, and the whole audience of some thousands are as quiet, and their faces as motionless, as though they were painted on the walls of the theatre; even from the farthest end of the playhouse one could hear a pin drop [...] His [Garrick's] whole demeanour is so expressive of terror that it made my flesh creep even before he began to speak. The almost terror-struck silence of the audience, which preceded this appearance and filled one with a sense of insecurity, probably did much to enhance this effect.[48]

The space of the theatre, packed with a submissive audience, heightens the emotional experience for Lichtenberg; the 'terror-struck' silence of this passive crowd enhances the disconcerting effect of this tense dramatic moment. The image of a motionless audience in a shadowy auditorium presents their gaze as secretive and surreptitious while their emotional response to the spectacle is amplified by the silence and the lack of physical and vocal interaction. Lichtenberg is surrounded by theatregoers who react by stealthily watching and waiting to the extent that 'from the farthest end of the playhouse one could hear a pin drop'.

Lichtenberg's transfixed spectator in a hushed, dark space also implies the audience's distance from the performance and each other, limiting all forms of interaction except the emotional connection controlled by the performer. Lichtenberg vividly presents his enjoyment of isolation, and separation from the society surrounding him, while occupying a bubble of experience 'without your even once being aware of yourself, or of London, Drury Lane and Garrick. This happens only in the general clapping which follows this scene'.[49] John O'Brien suggests that a turning point in the relationship between actor and spectator occurred in 1765 when Garrick 'replaced the chandeliers over the stage and auditorium with a more sophisticated lighting system' which made it possible 'to dim the illumination in the audience and to throw more concentrated light onto the playing area'.[50] This lighting system, which combined stage footlights with auditorium black-outs, did not simply intensify the audience's awareness of the spectacle through discouraging conversations, arguments, and flirtations between theatregoers;[51] such lighting also visually separated the worlds of the audience and the stage, as strikingly represented by Lichtenberg's account.

During Garrick's revolutionary management, the theatrical space was reconceived in other ways. Lichtenberg's comment that the audience were akin to portraits 'painted on the walls of the theatre' describes the spectators' reactions through applying an image relating to staging during this period. This image, where theatregoers merge into the theatrical scenery, connects to Garrick's adoption of the aesthetic of landscape and his transformation of the actor into one facet of an all-encompassing visual spectacle. In his theatre, the actor's dramatic pose, as if painted on the backcloth, formed only one visual aspect of the dramatic vista as a whole. Consequently, performances became picturesque displays, 'views worthy and reminiscent of a painted picture', with players transformed into landscape figures by the use of increasingly detailed settings.[52] The manager's reform of *mise en scène*, involving lighting, scene painting and set design, presented 'dramatic movements within settings, framed like pictures'.[53] Such on-stage displays emphasized the spatial insignificance of the individual performer who existed as one component of a larger, sweeping visual scene. In one early illustration of this from 1749, Aaron Hill requested that his play *Meropé* should be staged with 'significantly busied groupes of interested people' painted on the wings and shutter 'to extend the prospect with scarce a sensible distinction, from the *real* life' of the actor.[54] Similarly, when watching the ghost scene from *Hamlet*, Lichtenberg noticed Garrick's exploitation of this technique involving the merging of actor and vista:

> The Ghost looked very good; the colour of his armour was practically indistinguishable from the colour of the scene, and he was already standing there quite quiet and motionless, before I, who probably like every other spectator had my eyes riveted on Hamlet, noticed him.[55]

Garrick's awareness of the player as a mere figure within a larger spectacle allowed the dramatic concealment and revealment of character. The colour of the ghost's armour enabled his startling entrance and exit through the illusion of 'disembodiment' with the ghost 'seeming to melt away into the castle walls'.[56] While improving the presentation of time and place upon the stage, such stagecraft again compromised the social interaction between performer and audience as the actor merged into the backcloth; and, when faced with such pictorial representations of landscape, the spectator self-consciously exists outside of the scene in a position of 'separation and observation'.[57] This desire to maintain the theatrical illusion, through distancing the audience visually, complemented Garrick's style of delivery as he attempted to discount the audience's presence during the performance of Shakespearean soliloquies, a strategy applauded by Lichtenberg who felt that 'it should be almost a sin to look at the audience' at such moments.[58]

Benjamin Wilson's artistic portrayal of Garrick's monument scene from *Romeo and Juliet* at Fig. 2.2 provides one representation of a dramatic tableau within a detailed, picturesque frame. Burnim's approach to Wilson's painting as a 'photograph' may exaggerate the accuracy of the depiction; this image nonetheless

FIG. 2.2. Simon François Ravenet, *Mr. Garrick and Miss Bellamy in the Characters of Romeo and Juliet* (1753), engraving after Benjamin Wilson. Yale Center for British Art, Paul Mellon Collection, B1977.14.14564.

provides an indication of Garrick's possible staging of Shakespeare's play.[59] With the widespread use of the dash to hold together Romeo's numerous, disjointed exclamations in Garrick's version of this scene, one can only imagine which dash in the exchange between the two lovers provided the opportunity for him to produce the pose immortalized by Wilson's image. The merging of performer with scenery would have been heightened by Garrick's transformation of emotion into a collection of static tableaux. The intimate setting suited Garrick's overall design for Shakespeare's *Romeo and Juliet*. As Nancy Copeland has discovered, Garrick's editorial cuts 'emphasize the primacy of the love story and, by diminishing the public aspect of the action, present that love story as an essentially private event', a position restated by Vanessa Cunningham.[60] The atmosphere of privacy in Garrick's domestic drama is reinforced by this theatrical equivalent of a peephole. Wilson's image nicely encapsulates the experience of mid-eighteenth-century theatregoers who joined the watchful Sterne, an audience with a clandestine and surreptitious gaze.

Sterne's *Journal*, 'a little Theatre for us to act on'

The staging of theatrical spectacles, as part of a secretive space, provides an instructive context for a consideration of Sterne's construction of the narrative *mise en scène* in the *Journal* as well as his contradictory self-portrayal as a performer soliciting an empathetic crowd while desiring seclusion. His desire to be seen and applauded for heightened, sentimental displays of emotion is tempered by an awareness that unrestrained behaviour should be inaccessible and unseen by others. His 'little Theatre' is a space for clandestine exchanges of passion; his theatre will 'not [be] before a crouded house [...] it shall be as secluded as the elysian fields'.[61] The act of appealing emotionally to a readership while desiring to preserve privacy is represented, by Patricia Meyer Spacks, as an authorial strategy typical of eighteenth-century sentimental publications where 'the efflorescence of writing about sensibility emphasises the urgency of audience, the appeal to a public in even the most apparently private experience'.[62] This self-consciousness of sentimental fiction, in its engagement of readers, is partly accounted for by Christopher Nagle's proposition that the 'Sensibility model' is concerned with 'establishing relationality' and 'the possibility of bringing people in an increasingly alienated society together in real and imagined intimacy'.[63] As this 'relationality' in the *Journal* is conceived theatrically, inviting potential spectators to connect emotionally with the author, it does not solely bear comparison with the contemporaneous *Journey*, where Yorick 'if he does not have an immediate audience, he must imagine one — the audience for whom he writes, revealing himself on the stage of his own fantasies'.[64] The communication of emotion in the *Journal*, both stimulating and denying sentient readers, is also comparable to Lichtenberg's experience as a theatregoer. Like his experience of being emotionally courted while spatially isolated by the darkness of Drury Lane, the *Journal* stimulates empathy while attempting to sequester the reader, reflecting the partial seclusion desired within Sterne's contradictory urge for both communal sympathy and personal retirement.

Sterne's self-fashioning can be partly understood as a reaction to the circumstances of his relationship with Eliza; the *Journal* was, after all, a very personal and potentially dangerous document, a literary response to his distress caused by the wife of another man, Daniel Draper of the East India Company. As both the author and the addressee were trapped in marriages to other people, it was a text with potentially scandalous consequences if seen by unsympathetic readers. Befitting Sterne's inconsistent self-portrayal in the *Journal*, his relationship with Eliza had also involved the social display of intense feelings for her. Before her departure, he had proclaimed his affection for Eliza publicly, showing her picture and letters to acquaintances all over London and employing these sentimental possessions as props for the performance of emotion among friends.[65] As in John Hamilton Mortimer's frequently reproduced painting, *A Caricature Group* (c. 1766), the locket containing Eliza's miniature proved a valuable prop for Sterne's public self-congratulation in the safety of boisterous gatherings of male friends.[66]

To approach the *Journal* as a private and personal manuscript, bearing little relationship to Sterne's authorial strategies in material for publication, would be to overlook his consciousness of a readership, albeit a restricted one, as well as his attempt to relate manifestations of feeling to both literary and theatrical entertainment. Despite his frequent protestations that the *Journal* is primarily written for one privileged reader only, a text which 'must be put into Eliza's hands by Yorick only' as if fearful of the scandalous revelations that could be publicized by an interloper outside of their bond of intimacy, Sterne also hints at a potential readership greater than this one addressee. By mentioning acquaintances who share his confidence — such as Anne James (d. 1798), Lady Margaret Georgiana Spencer (1737–1814), Peter Lascelles (d. 1775), John Talbot Dillon (1734–1806), and Hall-Stevenson — Sterne places this seemingly private record in the context of sentimental pleasures enjoyed within a sociable network of friends.[67] While making his repetitive expression of the fear of exposure seem like rhetorical posturing for affect, to communicate the titillating potential of engaging furtively in a dangerous liaison, this context also raises the potential for the circulation of extracts within a sentimental coterie readership. Mark S. Madoff's belief that the *Journal* 'serves to teach an undefined audience of other initiates into sensibility about the savouring of intimacies' rightly attempts to expand the potential readership beyond the solitary gaze of an absent figure.[68] But, Sterne's promotion of sociability does not involve his self-portrayal as the sole author and master of sensibility instructing 'an undefined audience'. Entries are often portrayed as a form of communal composition involving transcriptions of conversations with named, sympathetic friends who, as in the case of Anne James, both provoke and respond emotionally. When sentimental interactions take a literary form, Sterne admits the possibility of transcribing and incorporating these texts, such as the letter about Eliza sent to Dillon or Hall-Stevenson's 'affecting little poem' about the imminent arrival of Sterne's wife, with the unfinished *Journal* promising to be, but never becoming, a patchwork of sentimental exchanges with the whole arranged by Sterne.[69]

In this document, staunchly defended as private and secretive where the fantasy of reunion is dependent upon the retreat from society, Sterne also relates the *Journal* to various forms of publication with wider, unrestricted, and personally unknown readerships. While showing no firm textual evidence of an intention to publish, the

Journal flirts with the possibility of revelations in print, to popularize his personal connection to Eliza and testify to his celebrity. Referring to the apostrophe to Eliza in the *Journey*, he claims:

> I have brought y^r name *Eliza!* and Picture into my work—where they will remain—when You & I are at rest for ever—Some Annotator or explainer of my works in this place will take occasion, to speak of the Friendship wch Subsisted so long & faithfully betwixt Yorick & the Lady he speaks of—[70]

During this exposé of the imagination, their intimacy is only fully revealed by the future creation of a posthumous biography, as if to restate the privacy offered by the unpublished *Journal* as well as its unsuitability for public consumption. Whereas the *Journal* was not presented for public scrutiny in the same way as the *Journey*, it nonetheless enjoys exploring the textual conditions, both real and imaginary, where personal associations are made publicly known. On one occasion, Sterne copied a revelatory notice from *The Public Advertiser* for 20 July 1767:

> "We hear from Yorkshire, That Skelton Castle is the present Rendevouz, of the most brilliant Wits of the Age—the admired Author of Tristram—Mr Garrick &c. being there, & Mr Coleman & many other men of Wit & Learning being every day expected"—when I get there, wch will be to morrow night, My Eliza will hear from her Yorick—her Yorick—who loves her more than ever.[71]

This act of copying embellishes and transforms the original by turning the journalistic hint of 'Mr G.' into 'Mr Garrick' and the addition of Mr Coleman's name.[72] Sterne's use of George Colman the elder (1732–1794) would have been an obvious choice. In the previous year of 1766, both Garrick and Colman collaborated in the writing of *The Clandestine Marriage*; Colman also acted as artistic manager at Drury Lane during Garrick's absence on the Grand Tour from 1763 to 1765.[73] Sterne's alterations may merely signify a name-dropping fantasy to impress Eliza, but the novelist's theatrical connections would not have made their attendance at such a gathering an impossibility.[74]

Shakespearean drama, championed by Garrick throughout his management, contributes significantly to Sterne's self-fashioning. Upon Sterne's Coxwold stage haunted by the ghost of Cordelia, he evokes the '*Dramatis Personae*' of Shakespearean tradition to role-play and conceive, in different ways, his sentimental connection with the younger Eliza, then twenty-three years old.[75] In the *Journal*, he is involved in different kinds of borrowing to create the mercurial 'I': his transcription and rephrasing of extracts from scripts is combined with the manipulation of prose structure to exaggerate Garrick's style of delivery during emotive moments. In the appropriation of one extract, from the famous scene between Hamlet and the ghost popularized by his friend, Sterne employs the dash in ways reminiscent of the use of typography to represent Garrick's performance in the altered version of *Hamlet* from 1763. A comparison of one moment in Garrick's text with its phrasing in earlier mid-century versions of *Hamlet* reveals the actor's insertion of two dashes at passionate flashpoints. These dashes are included in Hamlet's reply to the ghost's command of 'remember me':

> O hold, My Heart——
> And you, my Sinews, grow not instant old:
> [...] remember thee——
> Yea, From the Table of my Memory
> I'll wipe away all trivial fond Records.[76]

This employment of punctuation, as a sign of breathless agitation with the opportunity for emotive gesture, is developed by Sterne's flurry of dashes in the *Journal*, to claim that the intensity of Hamlet's emotion will pale in comparison with Eliza's lament at the loss of Sterne:

> "remember thee! Pale Ghost—remember thee—whilst Memory holds a seat in this distracted World—Remember thee,"—Yes, from the Table of her Memory, shall just Eliza wipe away all trivial men—[77]

In this moment of apostrophe, Sterne's transcription of Hamlet's lines provides him with both words to imagine Eliza's vow of commitment, and a literary analogy to indicate the depth of affection he desires from her. By attributing Hamlet's voice to Eliza, Sterne's writerly perspective becomes identified, by association, with the ghost demanding remembrance.

Through quotation and allusion, Sterne situates his emotions within specific moments in diverse Shakespearean relationships including those between the ghost and Hamlet, Falstaff and Hal, and Othello and Desdemona; his invocation of 'Cordelia's spirit' also encourages the recollection of the bond between Lear and his daughter.[78] All of these distinct pairs perhaps shared a common dimension for Sterne as they all, in individual ways, involve emotional demands made by an older generation upon a younger, and question the longevity of personal loyalty and affection. Within the context of Sterne's circumstances, his echo of Falstaff's forlorn pose, while 'as melancholly & sad as a Cat', evokes the knight's doomed relationship to the Prince in *1 Henry IV*. Sterne provides an analogy with his own plight through the inclusion of this textual echo of a play that concludes with the experience of rejection and loss. His reworking of Desdemona's explanation of her attraction to Othello, to create the phrase '*Ill love thee for the dangers thou hast past*', possibly fulfils another purpose: Sterne's application of Desdemona's sentiment to his own situation encourages a recognition that the affections of a man for a younger woman can be based upon motivations other than sexual desire.[79]

While these '*Dramatis Personae*' from the repertoire of Drury Lane are important, functioning to portray and interrogate a relationship, the influence of Garrick's theatre extends far beyond a consideration of such textual appropriation. Sterne, in the flow of continuous prose, relates emotion as discrete performative units of expression which mimic Garrick's acting technique:

> when Molly spread the Table Cloath, my heart fainted with in me—one solitary plate—one knife—one fork—one Glass!—O Eliza! twas painfully distressing,—I gave a thousand pensive penetrating Looks at the Arm chair thou so often graced on these quiet, sentimental Repasts—& sighed & laid down my knife & fork,—& took out my handkerchief, clap'd it across my face, & wept like a child—[80]

By employing punctuation, including the dash, there is the conspicuous separation of each physical attitude, giving full weight to each emotional stage in the transition towards the climax of weeping 'like a child', whether it involves laying down his knife and fork or clapping a handkerchief across his face. As with Garrick's combination of the performative and the private, these actions are placed within a sequestered space, Sterne's residence.

The conspicuous employment of homely commodities does not simply communicate to Eliza the comfortable, furnished home prepared for her imaginary return. Items of furniture also exist as concrete signals of his loss within the carefully constructed scene of domesticity, as Sterne 'relates the objects within four walls to mental states'.[81] While writers of sentimental fiction aggrandized 'the investment of those feelings that betokened sensibility in items worn or situated in domestic space', Sterne similarly declares his emotional sensitivity through his projection of his experience of grief onto the commonplace articles of Shandy Hall.[82] As in Sterne's appreciation of Father Lorenzo's 'little horn box' in the *Journey*, one narrative strand of sentimental literature valued commodities for their ability to act as reminders of absence and consequently induce emotion in characters and readers alike.[83] This preoccupation with the communicative power of possessions, instead of their practical uses or financial cost, would eventually spawn the eighteenth-century word 'keepsake', one small lexical legacy according to Deidre Lynch.[84]

Sterne's approach to commodities as memorials to Eliza's absent personality exists as part of a literary tradition, but their application in the *Journal* can also be related to sentimental exchanges in the theatre where props played a vital role in stimulating an audience to indulge in reciprocal emotion. Sterne's working knowledge of a fictional form does not preclude an examination of the theatre as an instructive context in which to understand his use and presentation of these domestic objects so beloved of sentimental fiction. His visual separation of each homely possession, as in '—one solitary plate—one knife—one fork—one Glass!—', provides the literary equivalent of an actor brandishing props as these signifiers of abandonment are flourished and displayed. Emotion is conveyed through his engagement with, and employment of, these possessions, thereby providing another parallel with perceptions of Garrick's acting technique in the period. Despite objects being commonly used by all players on the eighteenth-century stage, observers frequently remarked upon Garrick's manipulation of props to communicate intense emotional states, as in one example of Smollett's criticism. Smollett claimed that Garrick's Hamlet 'expresses no passion but that of indignation against a drinking glass, which he violently dashes in pieces on the floor'.[85]

In contrast to theatrical self-display, the *Journal* presents Sterne's complete self-absorption, as emphasized by his 'thousand pensive penetrating Looks at the Arm chair', that relegates the reader to a position outside of the narrative scene. As at Drury Lane, Sterne employs setting to alienate the spectator's clandestine gaze while simultaneously aiming to provoke empathy:

> was with our faithful friend all the morning; & dined with her & James—What is the Cause, that I can never talk ab\ my Eliza to her, but I am rent in pieces—I burst into tears a dozen different times after dinner, & such affectionate gusts

of passion, That She was ready to leave the room,—& sympathize in private for us—I weep for You both, said she (in a whisper,) for Elizas Anguish is as sharp as yours—her heart as tender—her constancy as great—heaven join Your hands I'm sure together!—James was occupied in reading a pamphlet upon the East India affairs—so I answerd her with a kind look, a heavy sigh, and a stream of tears—[86]

In this description of a visit to the residence of Commodore William James (?1721–1783) and his wife, in April 1767, Sterne establishes an atmosphere of mundane domesticity which is epitomized by James's concentration upon the homely act of reading a pamphlet in spite of the emotional turmoil surrounding him. At a time when East India affairs were suffering a state of financial crisis, the mention of this publication also implies the threat of intrusion by the public world of finance into the domestic space of personal feeling. The intimacy of this scene is underlined by the secretive closeness of Anne's relationship with Sterne, as illustrated by her willingness to 'leave the room,—& sympathize in private'. The telling detail of Anne's 'whisper' reinforces the air of confidentiality surrounding this dialogue concerning Sterne's illicit friendship with Eliza. Akin to a stage whisper, Anne's expression of sympathy exists as a private act, performed secretively, yet with an audience potentially greater than the recipient after Sterne's act of transcription. In this carefully choreographed scene, self-expression again involves the theatricality of discrete emotional stages: 'a kind look, a heavy sigh', and then 'a stream of tears'. Sterne's phrase 'gusts of passion', to portray the violence of his emotion, anticipates one eighteenth-century description of Garrick's acting style, a style based upon 'sudden bursts of passion'.[87]

There is a complex relationship between such performative self-presentation and the denial of the reader's existence. Sterne invites an engagement with the text by providing opportunities to visualize physical attitudes and to accept the call for empathy, while continually forcing the reader to eavesdrop on displays which are placed within unwelcoming narrative spaces of seclusion:

It was thy dear Packets from Iago—I cannot give vent to all the emotions I felt even before I opend them—[...] I instantly shut the door of my Bed-chamber, and orderd myself to be denied—& spent the whole evening, and till dinner the next day, in reading over and over again the most interesting Acc^t [...] I read & wept—and wept and read till I was blind—then grew sick, & went to bed—& in an hour calld again for the Candle—to read it once more—[88]

After courting the reader's gaze, Sterne 'instantly shuts the door' to create a claustrophobic scene of concealment by candlelight forcing the reader to observe events through a keyhole; within the seclusion of the bedchamber, he gives full expression to repetitive, compulsive displays of emotion: 'I read & wept—and wept and read'. Interestingly, this emotional display is triggered by the act of reading an intimate form of correspondence addressed to Sterne, the sole recipient. An act of personal communication, located in the most reserved part of a private residence, is the narrative subject for an intense dramatic appeal for the reader's sympathy.

In February 1767, two months prior to Sterne beginning the *Journal*, Ralph Griffiths in the *Monthly Review* described the newly published volume nine of

Tristram Shandy as the 'pantomime of literature', a reminder that an appreciation of Sterne's theatrical prose can extend beyond the confines of the texts chosen in this chapter.[89] Griffiths's use of the concept of 'pantomime' is incongruous with the emotional torment of the *Journal*; the diary is, after all, an account of the author's emotional suffering. Despite this, eighteenth-century pantomime, which existed 'as a species of metatheatricality' through its mimicry of other forms of Georgian drama, can be usefully compared with Sterne's *Journal*.[90] Like pantomime, Sterne's diary creates a performance that self-consciously gestures towards contemporary theatre in terms of acting technique and staging conventions. Griffiths's comment could easily apply to Sterne's creation of personae in the *Journal* as well as the selection of letters in this chapter, personae which mimic Garrick's physical style of performance in writing. In addition, the *Journal* places the expression of theatrical, yet hermetically private emotion in narrative frames that relate to the stagecraft of Drury Lane. Through his investigation of the emotionally expressive potential of the body, Sterne clearly applied his experiences, both as a theatregoer and as a friend to Garrick, to good effect.

After Sterne's death, his employment of Garrick's style of performance was replaced by the mimicry of Sterne's themes, characters, and literary style for new purposes. Just as Sterne subtly impersonated Garrick's dramatic techniques to create entertaining epistles, the novelist's admirers reworked and performed his fiction to produce novel forms of entertainment. During the 1780s, for example, MacNally's playscript *Tristram Shandy: A Sentimental, Shandean Bagatelle* helped to transform Sterne's prose into a spectacle that combined a number of different perspectives upon this narrative; its appearance before audiences at Covent Garden and provincial theatres is the next event.

Notes to Chapter 2

1. Churchill, p. 3.
2. Cash, *Laurence Sterne: The Later Years*, p. 8.
3. References throughout this chapter are to the 2002 edition of Sterne's *A Sentimental Journey and Continuation of the Bramine's Journal*.
4. Hafter's 1967 article, focusing solely upon the composition of *The Life and Opinions of Tristram Shandy*, is the only discussion of Garrick's creative influence upon Sterne.
5. Sechelski, p. 380.
6. Sterne, *Bramine's Journal*, p. 206.
7. Ibid., p. 214.
8. Hall-Stevenson, *Two Lyric Epistles*, p. 7.
9. *The Letters of David Garrick*, I: p. 388.
10. Sterne, *The Letters*, Part 2, p. 406.
11. Davies, II: p. 93. The editors of Sterne, *The Letters*, Part 2, p. 408 note that 'in March 1765, Sterne could have seen [Powell] play Lear and Othello'.
12. See, for example, Moss; Hunter; Barchas; and Harries.
13. Barchas, p. 160, and Hunter, p. 49.
14. Barchas, p. 164, and Hunter, p. 44.
15. Moss, p. 187.
16. Harries, p. 47.
17. Ellis, *The Politics of Sensibility*, p. 23.
18. Oya, p. 185.
19. Davies, II: p. 79.

20. Burnim, p. 60.
21. Benedetti, p. 59.
22. T. Stern, p. 258.
23. Fitzpatrick, p. 15.
24. *Theophilus Cibber to David Garrick, Esq., with Dissertations on Theatrical Subjects*, p. 56.
25. Smollett, II: pp. 138–39.
26. Garrick would perform the role of Abel Drugger at least eighty times in the course of his career.
27. Benedetti, p. 122.
28. In the absence of the manuscript, it is necessary to question both the date and addressee of one letter chosen from Sterne, *The Letters, Part 2*, pp. 416–17. The editors of the Florida edition accept, with a number of caveats, the long-standing identification of the recipient as Lady Anne Warkworth, with the date of 23 April 1765.
29. Sterne, *The Letters, Part 1*, p. 358.
30. *The Theatrical Campaign, for MDCCLXVI and MDCCLXVII*, pp. 13–14.
31. In the absence of a manuscript, the authority for the authenticity of this letter rests upon its appearance in *Letters of the Late Rev. Mr. Laurence Sterne, to His Most Intimate Friends [...] Written by Himself. And Published by His Daughter, Mrs. Medalle*, III: pp. 128–33; it is included in Sterne, *The Letters, Part 2*, pp. 416–17.
32. In the same letter, Sterne claims 'I feel myself drawn into a vortex, that has turned my brain upside downwards' (ibid., p. 416).
33. Information on the relative ages of Sterne and Lady Warkworth in 1765 is taken from the editorial notes to *The Letters, Part 2*, p. 418.
34. Cash, *Laurence Sterne: The Later Years*, p. 214.
35. Sterne, *The Letters, Part 2*, pp. 405–06.
36. T. Stern, p. 258.
37. *The Polite Companion; or, Wit a-la-Mode*, p. 76.
38. Carter, pp. 64–66.
39. Sheridan, pp. 164–65.
40. Woods, p. 142.
41. Baugh, 'Philippe James de Loutherbourg', p. 110.
42. Auburn, pp. 14–15; Nicoll, p. 91; and T. Stern, pp. 277–78.
43. Holland and Patterson, pp. 260–61.
44. Baugh, *Garrick and Loutherbourg*, p. 43.
45. Baugh, 'Philippe James de Loutherbourg', p. 103.
46. Burnim, p. 65.
47. Quotations from J. P. Stern, p. 29, and Wells, p. 8. For examples of the anthologization of Lichtenberg's account, see again Wells, and also Holland and Patterson, p. 264.
48. Translation from Lichtenberg, *Lichtenberg's Visits to England*, p. 10. The original text in German is in Lichtenberg, *Werke*, p. 322: 'Das Theater ist verdunkelt, und die ganze Versammlung von einigen Tausenden wird so still und alle Gesichter so unbeweglich, als wären sie an die Wände des Schauplatzes gemalt; man könnte am entferntesten Ende des Theaters eine Nadel fallen hören [...] in seiner Miene ist das Entsetzen so ausgedrückt, daß mich, noch ehe er zu sprechen anfing, ein wiederholtes Grausen anwandelte. Die fast fürchterliche Stille der Versammlung, die diesem Auftritt vorherging und machte, daß man sich kaum sicher glaubte, trug vermutlich nicht wenig dazu bei'.
49. Translation from Sutton, p. 9.
50. O'Brien, *Harlequin Britain*, pp. 68, 243.
51. Clery, p. 41.
52. Baugh, 'Philippe James de Loutherbourg', p. 114. Williams, *Keywords*, p. 109 notes that the terms 'dramatic' and 'picturesque' were closely associated in the eighteenth century: '*picturesque*' involved 'costume or action as good to look at as, or having evident qualities in common with, a *picture*'.
53. Nicoll, p. 118.
54. Letter to Garrick reproduced in *The Works of the Late Aaron Hill, Esq.*, II: pp. 375–77.
55. Translation from Sutton, p. 8. The original text in German is in Lichtenberg, *Gesammelte Werke*,

I: p. 1037: 'Der Geist erschien sehr gut, die Farbe seiner Rüstung war nicht sehr von der Farbe der Szene unterschieden, und er stand gewöhnlich schon ganz ruhig hingepflanzt da, ehe ich, der ich meine Augen wie vermutlich jeder Zuschauer auf den Hamlet gerichtet hatte, ihn entdeckte'.
56. Sutton, p. 11.
57. Williams, *The Country and the City*, p. 120.
58. Translation from Sutton, p. 9.
59. See Baugh, *Garrick and Loutherbourg*, p. 64, and Burnim, p. 137.
60. Copeland, p. 6. Cunningham, p. 75 emphasizes that 'Garrick's alteration of *Romeo and Juliet* [...] turns inward, away from the wider social and political world, to concentrate on characters' feelings and interactions at the personal and family level'.
61. Sterne, *Bramine's Journal*, p. 214.
62. Spacks, p. 83.
63. Nagle, pp. 8, 24.
64. Spacks, p. 83.
65. Cash, *Laurence Sterne: The Later Years*, p. 285.
66. Reproduced in Cash, *Laurence Sterne: The Later Years*, Appendix II, unpaginated.
67. Sterne, *Bramine's Journal*, pp. 175, 189, and 210; for biographical information, see the accompanying editorial notes on pp. xxi, 398, 411, and 413.
68. Madoff, p. 48.
69. Sterne, *Bramine's Journal*, pp. 210, 211.
70. Ibid., p. 202. For the apostrophe to Eliza in *A Sentimental Journey*, see p. 58.
71. Ibid., p. 219.
72. Ibid., pp. 417–18.
73. Benedetti, p. 180.
74. See Cash, *Laurence Sterne: The Later Years*, p. 300; and the editorial comments by New and Day in *Bramine's Journal*, pp. 417–18.
75. The spirit of Cordelia is mentioned on pp. 172, 223, and 224 of the *Bramine's Journal*; the significance of this figure is discussed in the editorial notes on pp. 386–87.
76. For example, compare this quotation from Shakespeare, *Hamlet, Prince of Denmark*, 1763 edn, p. 18 with the text published by J. and P. Knapton in 1751. The altered version from 1763, which is prefaced by the Drury Lane cast list including Garrick as Hamlet, is attributed to the actor in the editorial commentary of *The Plays of David Garrick* edited by Pedicord and Bergmann (IV: p. 432).
77. Sterne, *Bramine's Journal*, p. 192.
78. In their editorial notes to Letter 153 ('To the Countess ******/Eliza'), in which Sterne reflects upon the ruins of Byland Abbey close to his Coxwold retreat along with the ghostly 'Cordelia', New and de Voogd interestingly claim that '"Cordelia" would seem to have nothing to do with King Lear's daughter [...] Sterne may have thought it an appropriate "monastic" name, based on *cordeliers* (a French term for Franciscans; Sterne would introduce a Franciscan monk into the early pages of *ASJ*). Alternatively, he perhaps had had access to an unpublished poem by Mark Akenside, "To Cordelia" (1740)' (Sterne, *The Letters*, Part 2, p. 440). However, in the different context of the *Bramine's Journal*, with its conspicuous theatricality and numerous references to both dramaturgy and Shakespeare, the reader is encouraged to associate this Cordelia with the heroine from *King Lear*.
79. Quotations from Sterne, *Bramine's Journal*, pp. 172, 216, and 222; the relationship between these passages and Shakespeare is discussed within the editorial notes on pp. 387, 416, and 421.
80. Ibid., p. 172.
81. Tristram, p. 238.
82. Quotation from Barker-Benfield, p. 209.
83. Sterne, *A Sentimental Journey*, pp. 26–27.
84. Lynch, p. 63 follows the *OED* in dating the word 'keepsake' to 1790.
85. During this critical account, Smollett, I: p. 138 also claims that Garrick 'starts at the image of a dagger which he pretends to see above his head, as if the pavement was a looking glass that represented it by reflection'. For another example of his use of stage props, see Benedetti,

pp. 120–21 who describes Garrick's famous mishandling of the urinal for comic effect in Ben Jonson's *The Alchemist*.
86. Sterne, *Bramine's Journal*, p. 174.
87. Description of Garrick from Williams, *A Letter to David Garrick, Esq.*, p. 30.
88. Sterne, *Bramine's Journal*, p. 222.
89. Cash, *Laurence Sterne: The Later Years*, p. 266.
90. Description of Georgian pantomime from O'Brien, 'Harlequin Britain', p. 497.

CHAPTER 3

THE REDEPLOYMENT OF UNCLE TOBY

In the autumn of 1782, Thomas Harris had many reasons to anticipate the forthcoming theatrical season with great confidence. As Drury Lane still struggled to recover from Garrick's retirement, Harris moved to establish further the dominance of Covent Garden. While retaining the services of Richard Wilson (1744–1796), a notorious low comedian and the favourite of gallery audiences, Harris strengthened his troupe of comics through poaching the seasoned actor and singer Charles Bannister (1741–1804) from the rival theatre after doubling his salary from six to twelve pounds. Months earlier, Bannister had gained fame as Polly in a burlesque version of John Gay's *The Beggar's Opera* at Drury Lane through causing the death of one spectator, Mrs Fitzherbert, after she failed to recover from a bout of hysterical laughter.[1] To further strengthen the theatre's future, Harris had architecturally redesigned Covent Garden to create a completely '*New*' theatre with nothing remaining of the old structure 'but the outside Wall' according to *The Public Advertiser*. After the sumptuous refurbishment and ornamentation of the auditorium to increase the spectators' pleasure, the same newspaper claimed 'we do not remember to have seen the Audience more highly gratified than they appeared' on the opening night, an observation illustrated by their report of 'the most unbounded and continued Applause'.[2] Following Harris's 'magnificent decoration' of the theatre and his assembly of 'a very select company of performers', there were fears for the fortunes of his competitors: 'the new managers of Drury-lane theatre must exert themselves in an extraordinary degree, or their spirited and judicious rival Mr. Harris will get the *whip hand* of them for several seasons to come'.[3]

Harris, the manager of Covent Garden between 1774 and 1820, is barely remembered in histories of eighteenth-century theatre and has been represented in rare critical narratives as an astute businessman who knew 'how to capitalize on every resource'. For Judith Milhous, it was Harris's concentration on financial considerations that led to his successful management of a patent theatre for a longer spell than that of any other eighteenth-century figure, including Garrick.[4] Biographical accounts have suggested that Harris prospered in the 1770s and '80s by offering popular, frivolous entertainment such as pantomime, away from the intellectual pleasures of 'serious drama' at the relatively sophisticated, and financially insecure Drury Lane.[5] This view of Harris as a populist manager, concerned with the dumbing down of entertainment in favour of financial gain, can be contextualized and considered through a focus upon his directorial practices and creative decisions in the staging of one play. In 1783, in his opulent new theatre, he put on a successful production of Leonard MacNally's adaptation of *Tristram Shandy*. MacNally's afterpiece achieved a successful run of seven nights beginning in April

1783, followed by five nights in September during the following season. In the words of *The Morning Herald and Daily Advertiser*, the first night was accepted 'with loud and universal Plaudits from all Parts of the Theatre', and *The Morning Chronicle* similarly reported that 'the piece throughout was received with repeated marks of applause'.[6] MacNally's script became a popular retelling of Sterne's tale as testified by the play's reception in London and its subsequent journey to the theatres of Hull, York, and Bath.[7] Its success even led to a production at Dublin and, subsequently, one in America, at the Church-Street Theatre in Charleston, South Carolina.[8] The warm London reception led to the publication of two editions of the play under the title *Tristram Shandy: A Sentimental, Shandean Bagatelle, in Two Acts*.[9]

Any attempt to understand the presentation of *Tristram Shandy* at Covent Garden needs to follow the various stages of theatrical adaptation, which involves scriptwriting, casting, performance, and reception. Tracing this sequence acknowledges that the eighteenth-century playscript is only a partial and imperfect record of the original theatrical entertainment. The text in performance includes 'a considerable extratextual gain' involving the combination of scripted dialogue with music, spectacle, and play acting. The playscript is the text minus the theatre.[10] These scripts provided springboards for mimics who employed improvisation and off the cuff comments, often of a political nature, about current events and people. Indeed, the skeletal nature of the script, before it has been fleshed out in performance, can lead to surprises when it is compared with contemporary theatre reviews that draw attention to the extratextual. Consequently, this chapter attempts to relate MacNally's play to its interpretation upon Harris's stage within performances that can be faintly perceived through the piecing together of theatrical history.

Both MacNally's script and Harris's production are testaments to the heteroclite nature of Sterne's novel and its complex mixture of the patriotic, the sentimental, the comic, and the salacious; however, in their approach to this combination, each man placed the emphasis differently. Whereas the text by MacNally primarily portrayed *Tristram Shandy* as a sentimental and jingoistic celebration of British military might without sacrificing the suggestive humour of the original novel, Harris's stage production instead seized upon the script's potential as a burlesque and ribald farce at the expense of the scriptwriter's noble sentiments appropriated from Sterne's fiction. Harris refashioned a new form of entertainment, giving a ludicrous treatment of MacNally's script as well as a contrasting judgement on the literary value and social relevance of Sterne's narrative.

As Sterne's fiction was passed from scriptwriter to theatre manager to actor, *Tristram Shandy* became converted into different narratives, a process that provides surprising and competing evaluations of Sterne's novel in the early 1780s. These creative stages provide contradictory information on the late eighteenth-century understanding and representation of Toby, a character who was constructed using a variety of conflicting interpretations by those involved in shaping this dramatic entertainment. The scriptwriter viewed Toby as a potential figurehead for British patriotism, but this role was performed by an actor who pandered to the gallery's relish for low, bawdy comedy and sexual innuendo. In Harris's production, Sterne's personification of sensibility and philanthropy was performed by Wilson, an actor '*lost to decency*' who was infamous for cross-dressing, self-exposure, and outrageous comic tricks upon the stage. His appearance would have transformed MacNally's script and provided a unique and unexpected embodiment of Sterne's character.

MacNally, the Literary Articulator

MacNally's production of a viable script involved his celebratory appropriation of passages, with editorial changes, from Sterne's narrative. Act one brings together a number of incidents from the novel including the following: Trim's description of military life and his eulogy on the soldier (volume six, chapter seven), Trim's affecting oration on death (volume five, chapters seven, nine, and ten), the fate of Le Fever highlighting Toby's generosity and intense fellow feeling (volume six, chapter eight), Dr. Slop's distress after his collision with Obadiah (volume two, chapter nine), and the birth of Tristram with a crushed nose, followed by Walter's lament. While the first act is a medley of extracts, act two primarily focuses upon one narrative strand, the relationship between Toby and Widow Wadman leading to their agreement to marry. This second act includes the widow's amorous attack on Toby, by announcing that 'something has got into this eye' (volume eight, chapters twenty-four and twenty-five), and the misunderstanding concerning the exact location of his wound (volume nine, chapter twenty).[11] The diversity of this collection, representative of Sterne's combination of the sentimental and the comic, is knitted together by two sentiments that reverberate throughout the play: soldiers are embodiments of bravery and integrity, as illustrated by the figure of Toby, and the dangers of a military life demand appreciation in terms of both awareness and gratitude. One celebration of this life appropriates Toby and Trim's memories of battle from volume five, chapter twenty-one:

> TOBY. The French, brother; had the advantage of a wood; and give them a moment's time to retrench themselves, they are a nation will pop, and pop at you for ever—There is no way but to march cooly up to them, receive their fire, and fall upon them—
> TRIM. Pell, mell—
> TOBY. Ding dong—
> TRIM. Horse and foot—
> TOBY. Helter skelter—
> TRIM. Right and left—
> TOBY. Front and flank—
> TRIM. Sword in hand—
> TOBY. Blood and 'ouns—
> BOTH. Huzza!—huzza![12]

Here, MacNally's adoption and development of material from Sterne's narrative culminates in the dramatist's addition of 'Huzza!—huzza!', inviting the audience to shout their approval of a soldier's exploits and such devil-may-care valour.

Ironically, two years before MacNally's *Tristram Shandy* hit the stage, the dramatist criticized acts of literary appropriation as practised by the Grub Street '*cut* and *paste*' author. In *Sentimental Excursions to Windsor and Other Places* (1781), which mimics Sterne's novelistic style, MacNally disparaged the rapid, mercenary and exploitative craft of the editor who 'will *cut* down and *paste* up half a dozen volumes' before the writer 'who can *conceive* and *write* well' can 'invent and arrange a whole page'.¹³ But MacNally publicized Sterne's narrative by carefully selecting and piecing together these Shandean fragments. Unlike the anthologist, MacNally distilled and dramatically reconceived Sterne's sprawling novel. The creativity of MacNally's interpretative act as a scriptwriter partly involved his editorial choice and abridgement of excerpts to construct a narrative structure that suited the time limit and audience expectation of a two-act afterpiece. His theatrical remodelling can be displayed by a comparison of the original novel with a shorter extract from MacNally's script:

> my uncle *Toby* had scarce a heart to retalliate upon a fly.
> —Go,---says he, one day at dinner, to an over-grown one which had buzz'd about his nose, and tormented him cruelly all dinner-time,—and which, after infinite attempts, he had caught at last, as it flew by him;---I'll not hurt thee, says my uncle *Toby*, [...] I'll not hurt a hair of thy head:---Go, says he, lifting up the sash, and opening his hand as he spoke, to let it escape;—go poor Devil, get thee gone, why should I hurt thee?----This world surely is wide enough to hold both thee and me [...] This is to serve for parents and governors instead of a whole volume upon the subject.¹⁴

> SHAN. he hasn't a heart to hurt a fly—Go, says he, one day to an overgrown one, which he had caught as it buzz'd about his nose, and tormented him cruelly, poor devil, I'll not hurt a hair of thy head. Go, said he, lifting up the sash, the world is wide enough for thee and me.—It was a lesson which might serve governors and parents better than a whole volume on the subject of humanity.¹⁵

Sterne's highly sentimental and idealistic description of Uncle Toby's mercy survives with minor lexical alterations. The most significant lexical change involves MacNally's initial substitution of 'hurt' for 'retalliate', a rewording which lessens Sterne's emphasis upon Toby's endurance of provocation within the context of the whole passage. Unlike 'hurt', Sterne's original choice emphasizes the unfailing strength of Toby's mercy as the philanthropist refuses to kill the fly despite the case for justifiable retaliation in response to the annoyance suffered. Also, we have the omission of Sterne's repetition of Toby's merciful refusal to 'hurt', as well as the removal of the original textual underscoring of the captain's lack of irate frustration despite fruitless 'infinite attempts' to catch the fly. MacNally sacrificed the textual prominence of Toby's long-suffering submission in order to condense the narrative description and add brevity to the dramatic dialogue.

MacNally's textual excisions provided performative opportunities, whether taken or not, for actors to use physical actions and thereby supply the omissions from this abridged narrative. This removal of action and gesture from Sterne's description, including 'after infinite attempts he had caught at last' and 'opening his hand as he spoke, to let it escape', allows the mimic opportunities to animate the speech visually using the original narrative as an optional directorial commentary. Through relying upon omissions to encourage dramatic movement and action, MacNally capitalized upon the novelistic style of *Tristram Shandy* where 'the characters' actions, and the mode of description of these actions, turn the novel into a stage', a feature of the text recognized by Alexis Tadié.¹⁶

MacNally's compilation of extracts followed an established publishing tradition which commenced after the novelist's death. Just as popular report claimed that Sterne's remains had been stolen and sold for dissection, Sterne's body of texts came under the editorial knife to create numerous, financially rewarding compilations. Sterne was articulated through the removal and connection of textual fragments in new forms and publications. When these literary articulators chose passages from *A Sentimental Journey* or *Tristram Shandy* to reprint, they often conservatively recycled a widely accepted selection. Within this eighteenth-century 'culture of the excerpt' which developed the commercial potential of the literary anthology, editorial procedure was governed by an 'unwritten taboo on invoking individual taste'.[17] Consequently, a comparison of MacNally's choice of extracts with *The Beauties of Sterne* (1782) is revealing. Nine out of the ten extracts employed in act one also previously appeared in the first edition of *The Beauties* and all later eighteenth-century editions of this anthology.[18] These nine substantial passages appropriated by *The Beauties* and MacNally also reappear, partially or wholly, in one or more later compendiums from a list including *The Narrative Companion and Entertaining Moralist* (London: J. Wenman, 1789), Knox's *The Prose Epitome* (London: C. Dilly, 1791), *Gleanings from the Works of Laurence Sterne* (London: C. Whittingham, 1796), and Nicholson's *Extracts from the Tristram Shandy and the Sentimental Journey of Law. Sterne* (Ludlow: G. Nicholson, 1796). Such chains of articulation, displaying relationships of influence as well as the uniformity of editorial choice, offered a conventional approval of Sterne's literary merits. MacNally's adoption of '*The Story of* LE FEVER' as the centrepiece of act one mirrors the editorial decision to include this fragment in all of the prose anthologies consulted.[19] Such widespread inclusion emphasizes the importance of this narrative section, this speech on 'the strength of the bond of suffering and support acquired throughout the hardships of war', for establishing Sterne's late eighteenth-century reputation as a writer of high sentiment and philanthropy.[20] Through the popularity of these anthologies, the widespread posthumous appreciation of one highly sentimental narrative strand threatened to eclipse the public's awareness of the narrative whole of *Tristram Shandy*.

Editorial consistency also relates to the 'long-standing tension' between 'the economic incentives to recycle earlier editorial principles or even to reuse old plates' and 'the demand for new editions to edge older ones out of the market'. This tension, identified by Leah Price, is supported by the evolution of the Sternean anthology; later compendiums reprinted established extracts, and also attempted to include novel additions. Later Sternean anthologies, both new titles and revised editions, increasingly became unwieldy textual monsters through the continual addition of fragments and the refusal to revise or excise previous celebrated choices. These anthologists also attempted to 'disclaim originality' through reprinting the popular editorial choices of previous anthologies to give second generation selections an air of cultural authority to boost sales. For Price, such declarations of unoriginality kept Knox's successful text, *Elegant Extracts* (1784), in print and subsequently plagiarized by other editors.[21] The avoidance of novel choices is nicely illustrated by the *Gleanings*'s refusal to reduce the accepted, authoritative selection of *The Beauties* while adding copiously to this voluminous authority.

MacNally's significant editorial debt to *The Beauties*'s select act of republishing emphasized the authority of this anthology which reached a seventh edition within a year.²² In an effort to fill Covent Garden, MacNally approved the strategy of *The Beauties* that had distilled *Tristram Shandy* and extracted publicly acclaimed and commercially successful episodes from a miscellaneous text. MacNally's conservative editorial approach to Sterne in act one could be symptomatic of his cautious anticipation of the reactions of an audience including traditionalistic admirers of Sterne who had been nurtured upon such selective *Beauties*. The late Georgian veneration of Sterne was fuelled by compilations confirming an accepted selection as the 'beauties' of this author, a fact acknowledged by MacNally's attempt to 'bring the beauties of poor Yorick's page' onto the stage.²³ Despite this approval of *The Beauties*, the first night review for the *Morning Chronicle* criticized the length of MacNally's afterpiece and advised that the 'pruning pen' should remove passages which, if accurately described, appear to have no correlation to anthologized extracts. Such criticism focused upon 'the kitchen scene between Slop and Susannah, and the discourse on geography between Toby and the Widow'.²⁴ Unlike articulators of the human body, who attempted to create uniform, proportioned skeletons from miscellaneous collections of bones, MacNally was criticized for not following the literary equivalent. They chose skeletal fragments with similar proportions, appearance, and points of connection; his initial selection, a mixture of the bawdy and the sentimental, celebrated the variety of Sterne's original novel instead of striving for uniformity. As a result, he created an inconsistent, misshapen, and ungainly script, according to the reviewers. MacNally appears to have followed the advice and produced a revised text for publication with the removal of the confrontational kitchen scene involving Slop and Susannah. It exists only in the manuscript licensed for performance (Huntington MS LA 621).

In contrast to *The Beauties*'s selection, MacNally created a second act focusing upon Toby's courtship of the Widow Wadman which profited both theatrically and financially from the literary material that the anthologists wanted to discard in their attempt to cleanse and purge Sterne's heritage for an educational use. While he exploited the bawdy and comic promise of Toby's relationship, the widow was completely and conspicuously expunged from Sterne's original text in all of the other compilations from the 1780s and the '90s. Only two anthologies, *The Beauties* and the *Gleanings*, reprint a section of *Tristram Shandy* which originally included the figure of the widow; yet her presence is edited out of this passage. The excerpt entitled 'The Beguine' sanitizes Sterne's text and removes the widow's breathless interest in Toby and Trim's discussion on groin injuries as well as her commentary on the sexual innuendo originally woven by Sterne into Trim's sentimental account about falling in love.²⁵

MacNally's act of embracing novelistic corruption was at odds with the educational impulse of anthologists who advertized the value of Sterne's works for the promotion of virtue, philanthropy, and emotional refinement. The preface to an edition of *The Beauties* presented editorial decisions as a method of censorship. Before *The Beauties* arrived:

the CHASTE lovers of literature were not only deprived themselves of the pleasure and instruction so conspicuous in this magnificent assemblage of Genius, but their rising offspring, whose minds it would polish to the highest perfection were prevented from tasting the enjoyment likewise. The CHASTE part of the world complained so loudly of the obscenity which taints the writings of STERNE.[26]

This textual moral guardian reads like an A to Z of eighteenth-century conceptions of virtue and vice for the would-be sentimental man about town. Each excerpt is arranged alphabetically on the content pages with such individual titles as 'Compassion', 'Charity' and 'Contentment', with too many moralistic headings to list.[27]

The afterpiece's dramatic success in London may only be partly explained by MacNally's celebration of these 'beauties' in act one, and it would be unfair to unreservedly follow *The Monthly Review*'s appraisal of his piece as 'little more than a cento from Sterne'.[28] Throughout the script, MacNally appeals to patriotism in a time of war through the selection of a backbone of excerpts preoccupied with the promotion of military life and the presentation of Toby as a national hero, a figure of martial pride, honour, emotional sensitivity, and sentimental philanthropy. Even before his appearance, MacNally's script celebrated this character through the inclusion of Sterne's famous anecdote about Toby's meek inability to 'hurt a fly', an extract immortalized within numerous eighteenth-century Sternean anthologies. MacNally's appropriation of this extract immediately signalled his intention to present Sterne's martial ideal of benevolence and enlist this character to bolster nationalistic pride within a climate of fragile national morale that contrasted with the mood at the novel's first appearance. The first six volumes of *Tristram Shandy*, published between 1759 and 1761, capitalized upon the notable military successes of the Seven Years War (1756–63) through nostalgically evoking King William's Wars (1689–97). Despite the faint memory of such victories as Namur within the popular imagination, MacNally's 1783 afterpiece entered a more fraught atmosphere of nationalistic self-consciousness. During the same month as *Tristram Shandy*'s second run at Covent Garden, Britain and America signed the definitive treaty formalizing American Independence and the release of the Thirteen Colonies, a time of 'bitter humiliation and of persistent anxieties'.[29]

MacNally's script expresses a more positive political message through his reduction of Sterne's text into sections of blatantly jingoistic dialogue in the attempt to emphasize that the empire was bigger than America, an empire safe in the hands of Sterne's military heroes. MacNally focuses on Toby and Trim's nostalgic remembrance of past victories over France and Spain at a time when Britain had enjoyed successful military campaigns to safeguard colonial interests in Gibraltar, the Bengal, and the West Indies.[30] In a piece of blatant morale boosting propaganda, the two retired soldiers laud Britain as the moral guardian of unstoppable military might. Toby and Trim contrast the complete lack of 'principle in the powers which oppose her', with the 'principle, power' and 'justice' of Britain 'able to drive France and Spain and—and the devil if he should join them, out of the field'. Even before Toby's appearance, MacNally chooses Trim's idealistic opinion of his master as a man who 'fears not death, he fears only what every honest man fears—doing a wrong thing'. In the script, the role of Toby exists as the embodiment and epitome of the British soldier as moral hero governed by conscience. Moreover, Toby's entrance is anticipated by Trim's praise of the soldier's religious and national devotion: both men are willing to fight for their king, country, and honour while also finding time to 'pray as often of his own accord as a parson'.[31]

Positive nationalism is also partly reflected by MacNally's original ending which culminates in the marriage of Toby and the widow and concludes with Walter Shandy's request:

> (*joins their hands*) and since peace is now established, I hope every unmarried man and single woman will follow the example of you and the widow, and encrease the strength of the nation by raising supplies for the next war.[32]

MacNally adopts a common afterpiece ending, involving marriage with the potential for children, to emphasize the importance of procreation for national strength, an essential consideration when such superannuated soldiers as Toby and Trim populate the stage. This ending develops Yorick's belief in volume eight that 'the procreation of children [is] as beneficial to the world [...] as the finding out the longitude', equating childbirth with a skill necessary for the successful management of colonial interests and their protection through naval warfare.[33] Like Yorick, MacNally's conclusion confirmed the popular eighteenth-century political assumption that 'population growth' was synonymous with 'national power' at a time when the people were forced to accept that Britain was 'too underpopulated, with too restricted a standing army to conduct successful, large-scale land warfare on imperial or any other territory over a protracted period'.[34] The nationalistic fervour of this afterpiece, looking forward to the 'next war', sits uneasily within an historical period that forced Britain to accept defeat prior to the Peace of 1783.

The Claims of Ireland

Any interpretation of political bias in the script of *Tristram Shandy* must also consider MacNally's relationship to the conflicting ideologies of British unity and Irish separatism. These ideologies are significant, given that MacNally, at the time of adapting *Tristram Shandy*, was preoccupied with the colonial government of Ireland during intense periods of insurrection. Protestant Dublin's political relationship with England included both an acceptance of protective, economically stable union and a desire for political independence that inescapably encompassed the worrying threat of Catholic ascendancy. As MacNally created *Tristram Shandy*, the retention of parliamentary institutions at Dublin made possible 'a potentially revolutionary brand of Irish nationalism', spurred on by America's combative opposition to English colonialism. Such Irish insurrection included 'a powerful and at times acrimonious response to anything that smacked of imperial imposition'.[35] However, the usefulness of this distinction between unity and separatism has been challenged by historical analysis showing that Irish writers were often torn between these opposing political options.[36] In the light of this, any attempt to understand MacNally's choice of patriotic statements as expressions of his political bias is problematic: political allegiances can be complex areas of personal conflict. The dramatist's contradictory political career is difficult to reconcile with the seemingly straightforward patriotic jingoism of the script.

Born in Dublin in 1752, he initially gave active support to the 'Irish Revolution', including the demand for economic and legislative independence in the wake of American political autonomy. In the year before *Tristram Shandy*'s first run, he published *The Claims of Ireland and the Resolutions of the Volunteers Vindicated*, a pamphlet which gave support to a group that was 'a form of extra-constitutional agitation' working closely with the patriot opposition in the Irish Parliament.[37] Despite the fact that MacNally was to become an original member of the Society of United Irishmen, and would fight a duel with Sir Jonah Barrington to vindicate their honour, he could in the early 1780s be interpreted as being merely opportunistic, riding the waves of political change and championing the inevitable development of legislative independence in Ireland. Such change was signified in 1782 when England and Ireland witnessed the annulment of the Declaratory Act of 1720, which Paul Langford has interpreted as allowing the Irish Parliament to 'demolish the remains of Privy Council supervision of Irish legislation'.[38] MacNally's combination of political inconstancy and ruthless pragmatism is displayed by his actions from 1794 onwards. While apparently supporting revolutionary Irish activity, he betrayed numerous leading agitators to the British government for financial reward. At the trials of the conspiratorial 'defenders' in 1798 and 1803, MacNally accepted briefs for the defence in a government prosecution, then disclosed their contents to the Crown lawyers.

Before *The Claims of Ireland*, he dedicated his *Sentimental Excursions* to the famous actor-dramatist Charles Macklin. In this preface, he expressed a staunch identification with Irishness alongside a call for ethnic equality and the removal of prejudice. This dedication shares a common concern, expressed by eighteenth-century Irish dissenters, that England should appreciate an Irish humanity 'different from the reductionist images insisted upon by English historians and dramatists'.[39] MacNally proclaims:

> DEAR SIR,
> YOU are to consider this Dedication as a grateful return to the warmth of your friendship, a just tribute to the integrity of your heart.—Seven years intimacy have convinced me of both—
> Exclusive of these motives, I have another—
> The author of SIR CALLAGHAN O'BRALLAGHAN, merits respect from every Irishman.—That character has been of national service, by being a means of removing, in a great measure, illiberal prejudices which had too long promoted enmity between sister-kingdoms, but are now happily diminished.[40]

After initially viewing Macklin on a personal level as an intimate friend, MacNally subsequently presents a figure of political importance, a cultural icon whose work deserves 'respect from every Irishman'. Here, Macklin's worth exists solely through his authorship of *Love à-la-Mode*, a play that redefined the theatrical presentation of Irishness and countered English prejudice through the creation of Sir Callaghan O'Brallaghan.[41] MacNally's flattery shrewdly focuses upon the actor's only emphatic success as a writer which was a source of Macklin's great pride as well as financial support during the wane of his acting career. By comparison, the actor's celebrated career upon the stages of London and Dublin, eventually spanning nearly seventy years at his retirement in 1789, is conspicuous by its absence from this eulogy.[42] Even though he emphasized 'friendship' and 'intimacy', the celebration of the play was more important than the celebration of the man. MacNally's concerns are primarily national, not personal, and it is difficult to view this dedication as anything other than a proud call for equality. Such honouring of Macklin could not reflect a self-serving attempt to curry favour with a figure of wealth or up-to-the-minute fame: Macklin, at least eighty years old at the time of the dedication, was a spent cultural force rarely performing on stage while suffering poverty.[43] The actor's goodwill and praise of MacNally's publications would not have greatly affected the public's perception of the author's efforts. Such a choice of dedicatee may be contrasted with Sterne's mercenary flattery of Garrick after the publication of the first two volumes of *Tristram Shandy*; Sterne's solicitation of the celebrated actor at the height of his fame proved a marketing masterstroke.[44]

Michael Ragussis and Paul Goring have discussed the importance of *Love à-la-Mode* for the eighteenth-century presentation of theatrical stereotypes. Goring identifies that Macklin breaks the theatrical mould to produce an Irish character who is 'no stereotypical comic butt', and Ragussis similarly, but more emphatically, claims that the play represents Macklin's conscious attempt 'to fight anti-Irish prejudice, particularly as it had become crystallized in the blundering, fortune-hunting stage Irishman'.[45] Principally, *Love à-la-Mode* concerns the comic rivalry between four suitors (an Englishman, Irishman, Scotsman, and 'Beau Jew') for the hand of a wealthy English heiress; Macklin's farce 'plays the suitors off one another in an intricate struggle not only for Charlotte but also for ethnic significance and supremacy'.[46] In a reversal of stereotypical expectations, the Irishman Sir Callaghan successfully triumphs as a result of his willingness to sacrifice wealth for love upon hearing of Charlotte's supposed penury. He wins this struggle, allowing the achievement of cultural unity, through his adoption by the wealthy merchant family who exist at the margins of the English aristocracy.

Goring's emphasis upon rivalry and antagonism overlooks *Love à-la-Mode*'s scripted celebration of inclusive Britishness. Despite Macklin's farcical use of these stereotypes to imply national disunity, the playscript presents Sir Callaghan as a figure representing laudable military allegiance giving social cohesion and political solidarity to the British nation. Macklin made Irish supremacy palatable for the partisan majority of the London audience through the portrayal of Sir Callaghan as a veteran of the German campaign that was part of the successful Anglo-Prussian alliance within the Seven Years War. When the play was first performed in 1759, this Irish character was a figure who demanded remembrance by the nation 'while Britain or British gratitude have a name'.[47] As in Shakespeare's *Henry V*, such cohesion upon the battlefield potentially helped to strengthen British identity within the confines of the theatre. The popularity of Macklin's afterpiece, which played twenty-one times during its first run, may have been partly dependent upon the clap-trap applause for Sir Callaghan's military exploits serving the whole nation and removing division. Ultimately, the swagger of Irish romantic success was acceptable for a British military servant who represented a successful Anglo-Irish partnership upon the battlefield. As the anonymous and critical pamphlet *A Scotsman's Remarks on the Farce of Love a la Mode* (1760) noted, Sir Callaghan 'is made a Prussian officer, to introduce him under that passport more favourably to the crowd'.[48]

MacNally's admiration of Sir Callaghan guided the scripting of Toby. The parentage of the Shandean stage figure can be partly traced to the hero of *Love à-la-Mode* as Macklin's hugely successful farce influenced what MacNally chose and consequently neglected from Sterne's novel. When this literary connection is acknowledged, the Toby of Covent Garden can be interpreted as an Anglo-Irish hybrid, a new articulation of Sterne's martial Englishman to evoke Macklin's heroic Irishman. The guidance of *Love à-la-Mode* is expressed through MacNally's textual choices which serve to remember Sir Callaghan and the qualities associated with his particular theatrical embodiment of Irishness. Toby became a reincarnation of the spirit of Sir Callaghan clothed by the careful choice of passages from Sterne. The possibility that an audience would perceive parallels between the two theatrical figures is bolstered by *Love à-la-Mode*'s status as a favourite afterpiece throughout the century. Indeed, regular Covent Garden theatregoers had the opportunity to compare both plays within days of *Tristram Shandy*'s first stage appearance, as MacNally's afterpiece opened on Saturday 26 April 1783 with a familiar revival of *Love à-la-Mode* on the following Wednesday evening.

When approaching these two scripts solely as texts upon the page, without considering their production histories, these two idealised martial roles represent a curious combination of obsessive military madness, reckless bravery, passive meekness, and selflessness. In *Love à-la-Mode*, the script constructs Sir Callaghan as the epitome of steadfast, devil-may-care courage upon the battlefield, to the extent that 'Danger [...] is the soldier[']s profession, and death his best reward', but it also presents his pacifism as a matter of personal principle within civil society. Despite his warlike heroism, the social principles of this 'man of honour' lead to Sir Callaghan's confession of his dislike for personal dispute, a quality contrary to the quarrelsomeness of the eighteenth-century stage Irishman: 'there are two things I am always afraid of', he admits, 'the one is of being affronted myself, and the other, of affronting any man'.[49] After the play's performance at Drury Lane in 1760, one commentator portrayed this combination of meek civility and an enthusiasm for war as a contradiction, with the lack of consistency interpreted as a sign of authorial weakness. For this critic, it was surprising to see a soldier, who every morning 'drank gunpowder tea for his breakfast' and 'swallowed pistol balls, *like sugar-plumbs*, by way of helping digestion', suddenly appear 'with all the mild vacancy of looks that denote a good-natured, untravelled young man' and with 'language and demeanor of the gentlest cast'.[50]

While these contrary qualities are integral to Sterne's protagonist, and therefore not peculiar to Macklin's figure in the literary context of the 1760s, it is nonetheless significant that MacNally's script pinpointed and championed the facets of Toby's character that corresponded to the qualities of Sir Callaghan within a form of entertainment associated with the Irish soldier. As with Macklin's model Irishman, the same combination of reckless courage and polite social conscience is given prominence within MacNally's Toby:

> TRIM. There's Captain Shandy fears not death, he fears only what every honest man fears—doing a wrong thing. He's as kind an officer as ever stepp'd before a platoon, and would march up to the muzzle of a cannon, tho' there were a lighted match at the touch-hole. He'll take care of Lefevre's son—I'd serve him to the day of my death for love.[51]

In another example from numerous parallels, MacNally emphasizes Toby's philanthropy through his selection of the Le Fever narrative, in a scene dealing with brotherly compassion and humanitarian aid that highlights the willingness of the old soldier to give a 'shilling' 'for each man's need'.[52] Such Sternean sentiments can be related to Macklin's 'Generous man' whose complete indifference to Charlotte's wealth leads to the success of his romantic suit.[53]

Macklin's playscript also helped to shape MacNally's transformation of a collection of fragmentary extracts into the framework of a two-act afterpiece; through following the structure of Macklin's blueprint, MacNally was able to 'leave out digressions, and connect by plot' as expressed by the prologue.[54] Instead of Sterne's tale of romantic frustration expressed by a digressive narrative, both afterpieces employ the traditional structure of a successful courtship followed by the celebratory denouement of marriage. To achieve this, MacNally's editorial choices remodel Sterne's naïve, overmodest, and unlikely wooer to create a figure who, like Sir Callaghan, is comic because of his romantic contradictions. After Susannah's introductory point that Toby is 'as mild as new milk [...] so modest a gentleman, that you must court him', the text encourages a confident, rakish display of passion from him in act two.[55] In one tête-à-tête between the lovers in the second act, the warmth of Toby's expressions leads the widow to assert 'I see, Captain, you are acquainted with the soft passions of love as well as the horrors of war'.[56] This restyled Toby conspicuously inverted, and thereby potentially recalled, Sir Callaghan's character development. After the Irishman's brave romantic 'declarations [about] attacking, storming, making a coup de *main*, or dying upon the spot', he becomes full of 'respectful bashfulness and timidity', someone who can only approach Charlotte while 'trembling'.[57]

To enable Toby's bold seduction of the widow at the conclusion of *Tristram Shandy*, MacNally selects Sterne's military metaphors, just one of the many languages of sexual attraction from the novel, to create a point of linguistic comparison with Sir Callaghan's martial language of love. Like Sir Callaghan, Toby relies upon this diction to express sexual desire:

> TOBY. And the [eye is] most dangerous, Madam—an eye is for all the world, in this respect, exactly like a cannon, that it is not so much the eye nor the cannon themselves, as it is the carriage of the eye and the carriage of the cannon, by which both the one and the other are enabled to do so much execution—
> WID. Then there are many kinds of eyes—
> TOBY. Yes, widow, and many kinds of cannon.
> WID. The rolling eye—
> TOBY. And the battering cannon.
> WID. The commanding eye—
> TOBY. And the field piece.

> *WID.* The languishing eye—
> *TOBY.* And the howitzer.
> *WID.* The forbidding eye—
> *TOBY.* And the horn petard.[58]

After Toby's first comment (an appropriation of the opening paragraph of volume eight, chapter twenty-five), MacNally develops Sterne's 'comparison' of 'an eye [which] is for all the world exactly like a cannon' to produce this flirtatious cut and thrust exchange. Using this simile as a creative starting point, he invents the rest of the exchange, except for one phrase, 'the rolling eye', which is taken from Sterne's later attempt to define the widow's beauty.[59] Unlike Sterne's Toby, whose military obsession distracts his attention from the widow's amorous intentions, MacNally's Toby employs his knowledge of military terminology to flirt with the widow and actively develop their courtship, a new emphasis upon his character which evokes Sir Callaghan during the Irishman's moments of confidence.[60]

MacNally's development of this Sternean conceit linking courtship with warfare shapes a character whose language is comparable to Macklin's military lover, a man who states 'I was for carrying on my approaches like a soldier, A-la-militaire'.[61] At the conclusion of *Love à-la-Mode*, Sir Callaghan, 'a mere rough hewn soldier', adheres to the 'rules of war':

> *Charl.* And I yield sir to your disposal with unfeigned pleasure.
> Sir *Call.* By the glory of a soldier I had rather be at her foot, than at the head of a regiment—and now she's mine by all the rules of war—I have a right to lay her under contribution, for her kisses are lawful plunder *(kisses her)* O ye are a little tight creature.—'Pon honour her breath is as sweet as the sound of a trumpet.[62]

In the light of MacNally's earlier celebration of Sir Callaghan in *Sentimental Excursions*, the fact that this literary analogy between love and war was widely used in the period hardly weakens the underlying point that this shared language suggests Macklin's influence upon MacNally's editorial choices, resulting in a literary parallel between the two stage characters.

In both plays, successful romantic perseverance leads to a celebration of the importance of unity within the nation. Whereas the Anglo-Irish union that concludes *Love à-la-Mode* parades British ethnic solidarity, the concluding marriage of *Tristram Shandy* is an event of national importance whereby family unity reinforces the health of the political state, 'encreas[ing] the strength of the nation by raising supplies for the next war'. Both scripts present a positive, patriotic image of British nationhood. Through the piecing together of narrative fragments, Sterne's reclusive Englishman from the 1760s novel is newly articulated as a British Sir Callaghan figure of 1780s theatre. Such a development of Toby represents a theatrical gesture towards national unification, where soldiers can possess the same ideal qualities, and defend the empire in equal measure, irrespective of their ethnicity.

However, these two theatrical attempts to encourage political harmony between the 'sister-kingdoms' were received very differently in Ireland. After both plays had achieved success in London, they made the customary journey across the Irish Sea with markedly contrasting fortunes. *Love à-la-Mode* proved successful in Dublin and subsequently travelled to numerous provincial towns including Cork, Ennis, and Limerick; *Tristram Shandy* was 'damned' and 'condemned' on the first night in Dublin.[63] Despite the puff inserted in *The Morning Herald and Daily Advertiser*, which stated that MacNally's bagatelle was playing 'with the greatest success' at the 'Theatre Royal in Dublin', the fact that it never reached the provinces — unlike his other plays *Retaliation* (1782), *Robin Hood* (1784), and *Fashionable Levities* (1785) — gives credibility to different reports that *Tristram Shandy* was never listened to by an angry Dublin audience.[64] When political opponents sat cheek by jowl in the intimate confines of Dublin theatres, 'choosing an Irish play for such an audience was sometimes like choosing the bomb that might do the least damage' according to Christopher Morash.[65] In this explosive environment, it is easier to understand why *Tristram Shandy* failed rather than why the manager of Dublin's Theatre Royal ever thought that it was acceptable theatrical fare for such a volatile audience. This scripted flag-waving of the Union Jack would have been incredibly divisive for Irish audiences who were moved by the badges of nationality in the early 1780s.[66] Although Toby recalled Macklin's theatrical celebration of Irishness, there was a clear difference in political emphasis between the two scripts which accounts for their different reception. Whereas Macklin employed the concept of the British nation to enable a positive embodiment of Irishness in theatres from London to Kilkenny, MacNally evoked the Irish stalwart Sir Callaghan to celebrate the British nation. The latter was a political sentiment likely to find violent opposition from an audience which included supporters of Irish separatism.

Of course, MacNally could not be held fully responsible for the success or failure of *Tristram Shandy* on the London stage after relinquishing artistic control. There is evidence that Harris's actors moved MacNally's script in new directions, and employed improvisation to include satire upon contemporary politics, with the exact content of the afterpiece changing on a nightly basis. By allowing his actors to interpret the script in ingenious ways in order to comment upon the current political climate, Harris made *Tristram Shandy* topical and satirical in a way that avoided the censorship of the Licensing Act, an act that focused upon scripts before their performance. Interestingly, while the printed version of MacNally's afterpiece gives no obvious indications of any satire against political figures, *Parker's General Advertiser* noted that the first night included 'a few well-adapted political remarks, chastly pointed at some great characters' that were 'well received, and seemed to coincide with the opinion entertained by the public of a certain learned Caledonian Lord'.[67] The reviewer's use of 'learned' to imply the legal profession does not help greatly with identification, as Scottish law officers as a whole were often much hated in Georgian England. Henry Dundas (1742–1811), the Lord Advocate of Scotland during the American War, provides a likely target for Harris's satire, especially considering the politician's change of heart in the early 1780s. Initially, Dundas offered passionate support against the rebels in the early stages of the conflict; after the British surrender at Yorktown in 1781, he publicly and boldly abandoned his support and proposed that the profitless war should end. Possibly, Obadiah's search for a horse in act one offered Harris's troupe the opportunity to pass judgement upon Dundas's change of opinion. In Obadiah's conversation with Trim and Susannah, he concedes that 'the Scotch horse is gall'd, and can't bear a saddle upon his back' while observing that another, 'poor Patriot', has been 'sold'.[68] If the script was employed to insinuate that 'gall'd' Dundas was disloyal and unfit for purpose after his withdrawal of support for the British troops, such an extratextual commentary would have complemented MacNally's textual support for British military intervention in his literary call to arms.

Wilson as Toby

In the light of this reading of *Tristram Shandy* as a political afterpiece in a sensitive context, Harris's casting decisions seem strange and curious, implying an attempt to burlesque MacNally's jingoistic adaptation after recognizing the comic potential of one bawdy episode in act two. Startlingly, in the main role of Toby, his production introduced one of the most disreputable and scandalous low comedians of the 1780s London stage. The inclusion of this infamous comedian potentially undermined the scriptwriter's noble sentiments as *Tristram Shandy* was reconceived as theatrical entertainment for the plebeian audience of the gallery. Wilson — known as '*Shuterkin*' in the popular press as an acknowledgement of his likeness to the recently deceased comic actor, Edward (Ned) Shuter (?1728–1776) — would have clearly gratified this section of the theatre. Like his protégé Wilson, Shuter was 'more the player of his acquaintances than of the audience: in general, he was not without his familiars among the gods [galleryites]', noted *The Theatrical Examiner*.[69] An understanding of the actor who was selected to represent Toby evokes a portrayal of Sterne's Captain that worked against the scriptwriter's idealized figure.

The importance of Wilson for the longevity of MacNally's play in the theatre is revealed by the commercial life-span of *Tristram Shandy*. While Wilson was part of the Covent Garden cast, he performed the role fourteen times during the three seasons 1782–83, 1783–84, and 1784–85. He was a casting constant within a variety of different line-ups during these runs and he evidently made the role his own. After his departure from Covent Garden in the summer of 1786, the afterpiece was revived on just one further occasion, with Toby this time played by John Fawcett (?1768–1837), before being completely abandoned by the London stage.[70] Theatrically, Toby became defined by Wilson's presence, even if this actor was not solely cast for reasons connected with his suitability to become the embodiment of Sterne's hero. Harris's decision may have been guided by financial considerations that indirectly affected the presentation of Sterne's narrative. His commercial acumen exploited the actor's current notoriety for sensational acts of bawdy self-exposure and theatrical cross-dressing. In her consideration of casting, Katherine West Scheil has explored the importance of 'practical realities', such as 'how to attract a paying audience' and 'how to harness the talents of actors', in early eighteenth-century productions of Shakespearean comedy.[71] Such sentiments are easily applicable to the theatre world later in the century: the availability of comic actors within the Covent Garden troupe as well as the current public profile of these performers would have influenced Harris's choice, irrespective of the implications for the theatrical construction of Toby.

The *Tristram Shandy* production was not the first time that Wilson had helped transform a celebrated tale, familiar to the London audience, into a burlesque entertainment for comic effect. He had performed Mrs. Peachum in a cross-dressing parody of *The Beggar's Opera*, gender roles having been reversed for the whole cast of this traditional repertoire piece at the Haymarket Theatre. When Harris received MacNally's script months later, this version of Gay's opera guided his production values, as implied by his staging of these two plays together in *Tristram Shandy*'s first season. In his production of Gay's play, Harris employed the Haymarket's idea of reversing gender roles, and cast Mrs Margaret Kennedy (d. 1793) as Macheath, the actress who would also perform the role of Widow Wadman in the following afterpiece.[72] The influential nature of the Haymarket performances upon Harris's plans for *Tristram Shandy* is suggested by the casting not only of Wilson, but also the comic actor John Edwin (1749–1790) in the role of Trim, an actor who had played Lucy in the *Opera*. For an entrepreneur like Harris, the publicity and infamy surrounding Wilson's earlier involvement in the Haymarket production could have influenced his casting decisions while conceiving a burlesque of Sterne's famous novel. Consequently, descriptions of the Haymarket entertainment, and the responses generated by Wilson's performance, combine to provide an insightful commentary upon the manager's motives for employing these comics.

Throughout the month of August 1781, Wilson was continually attacked by a number of critics in *The Morning Herald and Public Advertiser* for his 'stupid absurdity and gross indecency' as Mrs. Peachum.[73] They were responding to one of his performances where the laughter of the gallery encouraged Wilson to expose himself with his 'petticoats drawn up to his knees, exposing the counterparts of two collars of brawn to all those not prevented by disgust from seeing the same'.[74] Mrs. Peachum's attack on her daughter's sexual availability in Gay's script, *'And when she's dressed with Care and Cost, all-tempting, fine and gay, / As men should serve a Cowcumber, she flings herself away'*, would perhaps have provided Wilson with the best opportunity for such self-display.[75] After his performance on 9 August, the second night, writers to *The Morning Herald* made strident attempts to shame him. Wilson's approach to this role as a burlesque comic actor was treated as a revelation of his corrupt personal character: the 'brazen-faced' Wilson, as he was called, was repeatedly portrayed as a figure *'lost to decency'*. These letters do not interpret his behaviour as an attempt to fulfil the audience's expectations or the specific demands of a comic role; they exist as judgements upon the man, not the actor. The scandalous personal attacks, displayed across the pages of a popular London newspaper, surely impacted upon the perception of Wilson's Toby given that an actor's personal identity was often confused with on-stage performances in contemporary accounts of the stage.[76] In the immoral hands of Wilson, Sterne's 'child' with his 'innocency of heart' would have immediately raised the audience's expectation of bawdy obscenity.[77] Following his performance in the *Opera*, Wilson became infamous as an actor who encouraged laughter through obscene displays which were below the belt, flaunting his masculinity through ribald exhibitionism.

In reply to the criticisms of *The Morning Herald*, Wilson presented himself as a blunt, forthright character. His first brief reply, under the transparent and unconvincing pseudonym of 'SOMERSET', described one critic as a 'rascal' and a 'scoundrel'. Both brusque and pugnacious, Wilson's second defence proudly owned the first letter and declared his name and address as '*R. Wilson, No. 7, Suffolk Street, Haymarket*'. Through these two letters, the actor was displayed to the public as a bullish, hot-headed figure eager to defy any detractor in a face to face confrontation, yet uncomfortable and unconfident with the literary challenge of a 'paper war'. The public perception of this performer's personality, through Wilson's self-promotion as fearless and irascible, would have provided a marked contrast with Sterne's Toby whose peaceful and placid nature was famously patient of injuries. Harris's casting creates a moral mismatch of Wilson's bullish, shockingly coarse, and morally dubious character with the modern critical perception of Sterne's figure as the personification of delicate moral and emotional sensibility.

To undermine further the nobility of Sterne's original Captain, Harris matched Wilson's Toby with Thomas Hull (1728–1808) as Walter Shandy. In the spirit of Sterne's original narrative, in which he creates a brotherly relationship that comically contrasts their characters, Harris matched two very different actors to create a classic pairing of comic with straight man. His decision, to combine two socially contrary figures, worked to spotlight their moral antithesis and emphasize Wilson's social imperfections. Hull was regarded as 'a respectable performer' of 'tender sensibility' fitted for the 'graver parts of comedy'; he was a performer whose repertoire consisted of 'impersonating old trusty *Stewards*, and parts that require an apparent honest sincerity of expression, such as flow at once from the heart'. In contrast, Wilson specialized in ludicrous old men and the raising of laughter through obscenity and low, disreputable humour. Beyond the stage, the public's perception of Hull and Wilson could not have contrasted more. Hull is primarily remembered as a hardworking, responsible and dependable actor who 'boast[ed] that he had missed the prompter's call but once in 54 years — and then he was in bed with a violent fever'.[78] After decades of financial prudence while in the acting profession, he became a shareholder at Covent Garden and also a famous philanthropist who organized a 'Theatrical Fund for the relief of distressed Actors and Actresses'. He was a man portrayed by the late eighteenth-century press as one of the most virtuous and respectable actors of his era.[79] As Harris's deputy manager in the early 1780s, Hull was responsible for the day-to-day supervision of the cast including his troublesome on-stage brother. One article in *The London Evening Post*, from 10 January 1782, illuminates the managerial hierarchy through describing the dismissal of Wilson after he left Covent Garden for Portsmouth without Harris's permission despite informing Hull. While Hull was responsible for the mundane, day-to-day organization of the theatre, including instructions to actors concerning their availability, Harris made the far-reaching managerial decisions such as the selection of plays for performance as well as the hiring and firing of actors. As Hull's antithesis, Wilson was a notorious rogue both on and off the stage. His disregard for polite conduct on the stage was matched by his disreputable inability to honour debts; the 'only Low Comedian of importance in the Metropolis' was a dissolute bankrupt who spent a lifetime evading capture.[80] In the 1784 summer season, only months after the second run of *Tristram Shandy*, Wilson's financially precarious life became part of the dramatic entertainment. One of his performances at the Haymarket was interrupted by an audience member who leaped from the King's Box onto the stage in an attempt to arrest him. Wilson's continuous financial embarrassment, through 'too great an indulgence in the follies of the town', led to his imprisonment and eventual death in the King's Bench prison in June 1796.[81]

Through Wilson, the production comically took advantage of the potential distance between this actor's human imperfections and the novelistic idealism of Sterne's martial figure. The success of the Covent Garden production partly rested upon the comic potential of the appearance of this notorious actor as the Sternean figure of ideal humanity and philanthropy. This casting of Wilson encourages a revision of much twentieth-century criticism, which has viewed Sterne's protagonist as the epitome of heightened masculine sensibility, and creates alternative ways of understanding Toby. For commentators such as Robert Erickson and Richard Lanham, Toby exemplifies 'original innocence and pure-spirited generosity' and 'an ideal-type representing the best aspects of collective masculine feeling'.[82] In contrast to such views, contemporary reviews of this stage production never questioned a casting decision that implied a vastly different conception of Toby's character in the decades shortly after Sterne's death. While Wilson's selection may have been an example of casting against type for comic effect, it is also important to appreciate how this decision exploited some of the textual ambiguities surrounding Toby, especially in relation to his sexual virility.

Modern reviewers of Sterne's soldier have become preoccupied with authorial insinuations about the absence or presence of Toby's damaged masculinity after the wound suffered at Namur; this fascination with what exists below Toby's belt has led to the construction of a sexually suspect figure in modern discussions of Sterne's narrative of sexual impotence.[83] Mark Sinfield's attempt to defend Toby's potency has been met with a critical response giving weight to the idea that Toby is just 'not able'.[84] As Judith Hawley realized:

> Sterne continually nudges us into thinking that his characters are impotent: we are encouraged to speculate about their noses, about Toby's wound, Tristram's accident with the sash window and his disaster with Jenny, to say nothing of the failure of the Shandy bull.[85]

Wilson, who was infamous for dressing as a woman on stage, had the potential to accentuate such a view of Toby as emasculated and lacking sexual potency. In another respect, Wilson's on-stage antics strangely qualified him for the Sternean role. On a semantic level, his infamy, created by a willingness to expose himself upon the stage, was appropriate for a character whose name 'Toby' existed as an eighteenth-century slang term for the buttocks.[86]

If the paternal and martial pretensions of Wilson's Toby seemed highly dubious, at a time when 'sex was repeatedly seen as an activity which would restore the country's fearsome fighters', the casting of Kennedy as the widow would have made the successful presentation of alluring womanhood, with the potential for fruitful union, even more unlikely.[87] Harris's choice of Kennedy would have undermined a straightforward patriotic message and presented a grotesque stage depiction of Sterne's heroine, especially after the audience had seen her perform Macheath earlier in the evening. The actual figure of Kennedy contrasted blatantly with the Sternean invitation to create a sexually seductive fantasy: 'Sit down, Sir, paint her to your own mind—as like your mistress as you can—as unlike your wife as your conscience will let you [...] please but your own fancy in it'.[88] Sterne's overriding conceit that 'beauty is in the eye of the beholder' seems apt when applied to Kennedy. This actress, who towered over Hull and possessed a large, clumsy, robust figure and a deep vocal tone, gained equal fame for playing male as well as female roles.[89] While the widow of MacNally's play exists as a figure of sexual fascination for Toby with 'fire!—fire!—shooting from every part' of her eye, this choice of actress moved the courtship towards a ridiculous, implausible spectacle.[90] Harris's casting of Kennedy highlighted the incomplete nature of Sterne's original text and exploited one of the creative gaps of the novel which the author encouraged the reader to fill. Such 'an aesthetic of the unfinished' in the novel leads to 'an aesthetic of participation', a playful participation in the case of Harris.[91] With the narrative description of the widow's physical appearance absent, Harris, as reader and theatre manager, explored the creative opening to reconceive the comic style of Sterne's text. The casting of a man infamous for playing women opposite a woman famous for playing men would have undermined all notions of conventional romance and sexual attraction upon the stage.

When considering this romance, a number of reviewers debated the acceptability of Wilson's performance. Newspaper comments interestingly indicate that Wilson did not fully exploit his penchant for crude humour in this role. One spectator enjoyed Wilson's self-restraint and insisted that the actor 'appears in a new light — he gives Uncle Toby in his native simplicity'; another reviewer, who also anticipated edgy comedy, instead lamented that Wilson's performance was 'sadly indeed below Par!'[92] Both comments did not simply judge his acting in relation to his past performances, and applaud or damn him accordingly; they also suggest that Wilson approached Toby as a burlesque role involving 'the ironic stance' of 'underlying sobriety which leaves its audience in a state of interpretive perplexity'. Just as 'the burlesque teases its audience with a glimpse of a performance which they are destined never to see', Wilson's appearance promised both the explicit ridicule of Sterne's novel as well as obscene action, but disappointed theatregoers who were either relieved or disgruntled at the sight of Toby's sobriety and simplicity.[93] One episode from MacNally's script created an opportunity for Wilson to encourage, and subsequently disappoint, the audience's expectations:

> WID. You are so gallant, so ardent, I wonder a gentleman of your figure could so long have lived comfortably alone, without a bosom to rest your head on, or trust your cares to. But then that dreadful wound—where did you receive it, Captain?
> TOBY. You shall see, Madam, the very spot where I—*(pulls out a plan.)* [...] I suppose you understand the geography of the place.
> WID. A fig for the geography—We were speaking of love and matrimony.

> TOBY. But must postpone the conversation, sweet widow, for here comes my brother.
> WID. What an interruption! *(aside.)* Well, Captain, I shall take a view of your fortifications, as soon as I pay a short visit to poor Mrs. Shandy.[94]

Wilson's recent scandalous reputation offered extra resonance to the line 'You shall see, Madam, the very spot where I—*(pulls out a plan.)*' This potentially wild declaration would have stimulated the thrill of expectation for an audience familiar with the actor's theatrical past, irrespective of their knowledge or ignorance of Sterne's original text. As Wilson groped around, a knowing audience surely appreciated the actor's self-conscious gesture towards his past theatrical misdemeanours before the appearance of the harmless map. Despite such a failure to deliver, Wilson's embodiment of Toby nevertheless became an act of theatrical bodysnatching: we have a performance that bawdily focused the audience's attention upon the physicality of Sterne's figure, including the presence or absence of genitalia, by an actor whose performances were infamous for the display of unsightly flesh.

The casting of Wilson and the creation of a burlesque, with the representation of 'mean Persons in the Accoutrements of Heroes' as defined by Joseph Addison, did not simply have political implications, but also literary ones.[95] This casting not only undermined the heroic, martial, and virile Englishman of MacNally's script, but also the sanitization and reformation of Sterne which gained momentum in the early 1780s through the success of *The Beauties*. Just as popular Victorian burlesques of Shakespearean plays contested 'an *idea* of Shakespeare', Harris's entertainment decades earlier contested an idea of Sterne.[96] His choice of Wilson challenged the selective representation and reinvention of Sterne for the polite tea table, a remaking championed by essayists lauding Sterne's sentimental style and editors tirelessly choosing sentimental extracts from Sterne's body of work. Wilson's introduction flaunted Sterne's earthy humour and acted as a counterweight to MacNally's appropriation of the sentimental in act one.

Commercially, the production of *Tristram Shandy* illustrates Harris's successful ability to give the public what they wanted. His casting decisions show the impresario's expertise in pleasing the common afterpiece audience of the gallery who would have taken advantage of half-price admission. Harris pragmatically and safely aimed his farcical entertainment at Wilson's 'familiars', the 'galleryites', who might have responded less enthusiastically to the patriotic flag-waving of MacNally's script, at a time when audiences in the higher tiers were 'renowned' for their capacity to interpret the politics of plays 'in inventive and unpredictable ways', sometimes leading to expressions of anger; as an illustration of unpredictability, Gillian Russell describes the reactions of one upper gallery audience a decade later who threw missiles at members of the pit audience who participated in a rendition of 'God Save the King'.[97] In the context of the 1780s, involving military defeat in a war far from universally supported, it is possible that a celebration of nationhood based upon a willingness to engage in conflict had the potential to create dissent in the shilling gallery, especially considering that the nation's war policy involved conscription and press-ganging, measures which exploited the society who populated that section of the auditorium.[98] As Marilyn Butler has asserted, war was 'unpopular among many sections of the community, since it was felt to defend or enrich those who already had a stake in America', profiting from 'the poor, who provided the soldiers'.[99] After the gallery spectators had poured out into the Covent Garden streets, they may even have been confronted with the common sight of an injured and wounded military veteran begging in order to survive, a reminder of the stark realities overshadowed by MacNally's eulogy of military men.[100] While avoiding the danger of simplifying the multitude of possible reactions in the gallery to MacNally's celebration of military life, it is worth recognizing that appeals to patriotism did not always meet with approval and applause: one response described the expressions of British triumph in *Love à-la-Mode* as 'begging *clap-trap* [...] springes to catch woodcocks'.[101]

Ultimately, a comparison of MacNally's *Tristram Shandy* with Harris's production emphasizes the difficulty of judging the effect of a performance merely from reading the published script. As MacNally primarily aimed to promote the patriotic facets of Sterne's narrative without neglecting the humour of the relationship between Toby and the widow, Harris alternatively sought to create a burlesque entertainment. The scriptwriter's celebration of martial prowess became a farce played out by Wilson and Kennedy, parodic and grotesque versions of Sterne's hero and his seductive heroine. Michael Seidel's definition of satire can apply to Harris's treatment of MacNally's adaptation. For Seidel, satire involves the transformation of noble figures into 'monstrous' and 'degenerate' forms; satire is both 'descend*ant* and descend*ent*'.[102] Wilson, who specialized in performances and comedy that descended to parts of the anatomy unmentionable in polite society, became the theatrical descendant of Sterne's virtuous ideal. And for some spectators, Harris's *Tristram Shandy* may have been their only experience of Sterne; Wilson's performance was, possibly, their only meeting with Toby.

Notes to Chapter 3

1. See *The Morning Post and Daily Advertiser*, 5 August 1782; and Hogan, pp. 511, 548, 604.
2. *The Public Advertiser*, 24 September 1782.
3. *The Morning Post and Daily Advertiser*, 5 August 1782.
4. See C. Price, p. 108, and Milhous, p. 12. The first biography of Harris by Warren Oakley — *Thomas 'Jupiter' Harris: Spinning Dark Intrigue at Covent Garden Theatre* (MUP, 2018) — considers the labyrinthine and fraudulent financial dealings that supported his theatre.
5. See, for example, Matthew and Harrison, xxv: p. 469 and Highfill et al., vii: p. 138.
6. *The Morning Herald and Daily Advertiser* and *The Morning Chronicle and London Advertiser*, 28 April 1783. The Larpent manuscript of *Tristram Shandy* — the officially licensed playscript — is held at Huntington MS LA 621. However, it is only a record of what was licensed and not a copy verbatim of the potentially ever-changing text in performance.
7. MacNally's *Tristram Shandy* was performed during the 1783–84 season at Hull and York; the Bath production did not occur until the 1800–01 season. For further details, see Fitzsimmons and McDonald, and Hare.
8. Hartley, 'Laurence Sterne', p. 150. Smock Alley, Dublin, 9 February 1784.
9. Both editions of the play were published in 1783; this chapter throughout consults and quotes the second, and final, 1783 edition which was printed for S. Bladon in London. Quotations which have no presence or origin in MS LA 621 are noted.
10. Genette, *Palimpsests*, p. 280.
11. Quotation from MacNally, *Tristram Shandy*, p. 18.

12. Ibid., pp. 23–24.
13. MacNally, *Sentimental Excursions*, p. 67.
14. Sterne, *Tristram Shandy*, pp. 130–31.
15. MacNally, *Tristram Shandy*, p. 2.
16. Tadié, p. 83.
17. L. Price, pp. 5, 69.
18. A number of MacNally's selections from Sterne's *Tristram Shandy* to create act one, 1783 edn: p. 28 (l. 18–22), p. 130 (l. 26–28), p. 131 (l. 3–7, 23–24), p. 265 (l. 21–22), p. 432 (l. 18–21), p. 434 (l. 20) to p. 435 (l. 15), p. 436 (l. 10–16), p. 436 (l. 20) to p. 437 (l. 2), p. 437 (l. 14–17), p. 437 (l. 20–25), p. 438 (l. 3–4). All page and line numbers refer to Sterne, *Tristram Shandy*, 1978 edn.
19. Sterne's 'Story of LE FEVER' comprises volume 6, chapters 6 to 13 of *Tristram Shandy*, pp. 499–520.
20. Quotation from Descargues, p. 64.
21. L. Price, p. 69.
22. Howes, *Yorick and the Critics*, p. 62.
23. See MacNally's prologue to *Tristram Shandy*, p. iii.
24. *The Morning Chronicle and London Advertiser*, 28 April 1783.
25. For the extract reproduced by *The Beauties* and the *Gleanings*, see *Tristram Shandy*: p. 693 (l. 21) to p. 695 (l. 8), p. 696 (l. 11) to p. 698 (l. 24), p. 699 (l. 5–24), p. 700 (l. 8) to p. 702 (l. 16), p. 702 (l. 20) to p. 703 (l. 11), p. 703 (l. 15) to p. 704 (l. 4).
26. *The Beauties of Sterne*, 11th edn, pp. iii–iv.
27. See *The Beauties of Sterne*, 1st edn.
28. *The Monthly Review*, 69 (December 1783), p. 439.
29. Colley, p. 237.
30. Langford, p. 556.
31. MacNally, *Tristram Shandy*, pp. 10, 6, 3; 'able [...] field' not present in MS LA 621.
32. Ibid., p. 28; not present in MS LA 621 although the sentiment exists.
33. Sterne, *Tristram Shandy*, p. 721.
34. See Langford, p. 638, and Colley, p. 208.
35. Langford, p. 325.
36. Powell, p. 414 claims that 'the presence of the Catholic majority, and the issue of dependance on British security, meant that Irish patriotism had both internal and external limits'.
37. Langford, p. 546.
38. Ibid., p. 558.
39. McLoughlin, pp. 36–37.
40. MacNally, *Sentimental Excursions*, p. i.
41. Kinservik, p. 179.
42. For further details, see Appleton, pp. 122–24.
43. Highfill et al., x: p. 20.
44. See Cash, *Laurence Sterne: The Early and Middle Years*, pp. 294–96.
45. Goring, p. 71, and Ragussis, pp. 779–80.
46. Goring, p. 70.
47. Macklin, p. 13.
48. *A Scotsman's Remarks on the Farce of Love a la Mode*, p. 5.
49. For these quotations which illustrate the character of Sir Callaghan, see Macklin, pp. 12, 14, and 16.
50. *A Scotsman's Remarks on the Farce of Love a la Mode*, pp. 9, 14.
51. MacNally, *Tristram Shandy*, p. 6.
52. Ibid., p. 2.
53. Macklin, p. 27.
54. From the prologue of MacNally's *Tristram Shandy*, p. iii.
55. Ibid., p. 16; not present in MS LA 621.
56. Ibid., p. 20; not present in MS LA 621.
57. *A Scotsman's Remarks on the Farce of Love a la Mode*, pp. 14, 33.
58. MacNally, *Tristram Shandy*, p. 19.

59. Compare Sterne's *Tristram Shandy*, pp. 707–08 with MacNally's *Tristram Shandy*, p. 19.
60. In Sterne's narrative, p. 668 the widow's romantic scheme is frustrated by Toby's military obsession: 'it was plain that widow Wadman was in love with my uncle Toby. My uncle Toby's head at that time was full of other matters, so that it was not till the demolition of Dunkirk, when all the other civilities of Europe were settled, that he found leisure to return this. This made an armistice (that is speaking with regard to my uncle Toby—but with respect to Mrs. Wadman, a vacancy)—of almost eleven years'.
61. Macklin, p. 14.
62. Ibid., pp. 5, 28.
63. On the reception of *Tristram Shandy* at Dublin, see Oulton, I: pp. 121–22; and Baker, Reed and Jones, III: p. 352. On the performance of plays by Macklin and MacNally at provincial Irish theatres in the century, see W. S. Clark, pp. 292–93, 320–21.
64. *The Morning Herald and Daily Advertiser*, 20 February 1784. Subsequent dates indicate the first performances of MacNally's plays at Covent Garden.
65. Morash, p. 71.
66. Political context from Morash, p. 71.
67. *Parker's General Advertiser and Morning Intelligencer*, 28 April 1783.
68. MacNally, *Tristram Shandy*, p. 7.
69. Highfill et al., XIII: pp. 380–81.
70. See Hogan. On 9 May 1783, Wilson chose this play for his benefit with receipts of £255 17s. 6d.
71. Scheil, p. 219.
72. For notices of both plays on the same night, see *The Gazetteer and New Daily Advertiser*, 3 May 1783; *The Morning Post and Daily Advertiser*, 13 May 1783; and *The Public Advertiser*, 13 May 1783.
73. The letters to *The Morning Herald and Daily Advertiser* appeared on the following dates: 17, 24, 25, 28, and 31 August 1781.
74. This newspaper extract on Wilson's performance is quoted in Highfill et al., XVI: p. 170.
75. Gay, p. 9.
76. Straub, pp. 12–13 has discussed the intense eighteenth-century curiosity about the private lives of players; she claims that roles were often taken as indications of an actor's personal identity within the public consciousness.
77. Sterne, *Tristram Shandy*, p. 706.
78. For details on Hull's career, see Highfill et al., VIII: pp. 34–36; and *Candid and Impartial Strictures on the Performers Belonging to Drury-Lane, Covent-Garden and the Haymarket Theatres*, p. 56.
79. See Haslewood, II: pp. 233–36.
80. Ibid., II: p. 265.
81. See Gilliland, II: p. 1013; and Highfill et al., XVI: p. 173.
82. On the presentation of Toby as a masculine ideal, see Erickson, p. 239; Mazella, p. 162; and Lanham, pp. 77, 85–86. Peter de Voogd in 'Uncle Toby, Laurence Sterne and the Siege of Limerick', p. 207 suggests that Toby was partly modelled upon Sterne's nostalgic remembrance of his father, Ensign Roger Sterne.
83. Seidel, p. 257 claims that 'the opening of the narrative hints that in the face of time the Shandean line is weakened, if not impotent'.
84. Compare Sinfield, pp. 54–55 with Hawley, p. 89; Erickson, p. 239; and McMaster.
85. Hawley, p. 90.
86. de Voogd, 'Uncle Toby, Laurence Sterne and the Siege of Limerick', p. 207.
87. In the first Covent Garden run of *Tristram Shandy* from 26 April 1783, in a season that ended in June, the widow was played by Margaret Kennedy, not 'Mrs. Morton' as stated in the cast list of the second edition of the play. Quotation on the political context from Harvey, p. 143.
88. Sterne, *Tristram Shandy*, p. 566.
89. For this account of Kennedy, see Highfill et al., VIII: pp. 416–18.
90. MacNally, *Tristram Shandy*, p. 19.
91. Harries, p. 45.
92. *The Public Advertiser*, 29 April 1783; and *Parker's General Advertiser and Morning Intelligencer*, 5 May 1783.
93. Schoch, p. 104.

94. MacNally, *Tristram Shandy*, p. 20.
95. *The Spectator*, II: pp. 467–68.
96. Schoch, p. 56.
97. Russell, p. 16.
98. Gilliland, I: pp. 135–37 described the 'shilling gallery' as the cheapest seating at Covent Garden before the theatre was redesigned by Harris in 1792.
99. Butler, p. 31. Russell, pp. 9–12 also describes English attitudes to the Army and Navy in the 1790s, including the animosity caused by press-ganging.
100. Watts, pp. 67–68 observes that 'the military veteran was a recurrent figure in mid-century culture, and a familiar spectacle in London streets, for the maimed and infirm who did not receive pensions were allowed to beg in public as a reward for their sacrifice to king and country'.
101. *A Scotsman's Remarks on the Farce of Love a la Mode*, p. 16.
102. Seidel, p. 263.

CHAPTER 4

Erotic Yorick, the Man of Feeling

On one particular Tuesday in March 1787, a gentleman perusing the front page of the daily newspaper, *The World and Fashionable Advertiser*, to discover the performances scheduled for that evening at Harris's Covent Garden, may have been distracted by a titillating advertisement from William Holland, purveyor of erotica, flagellation literature, satirical prints, and caricatures. At a time when, according to Julie Peakman, a new sub-genre of erotica emerged, 'which concentrated specifically on flagellation as a sexual predilection', this announcement was intended to place Holland's Drury Lane business at the forefront of this literary trend:[1]

> *Man of Feeling and Miss Walton*
> SUBSCRIBERS to the PRINT of HARLEY and OLD EDWARDS, &c. from the MAN of FEELING, are respectfully informed, it will be ready for delivery the 25th of this Month.
> The Companion will be Miss WALTON's visit to the Cottage of Old Edwards.
> To be published by William Holland, No. 66, Drury-Lane;
> Of whom may be had,
> A Sale of English Beauties in the East-Indies [...] Exhibition of Female Flagellants, in two parts, with 12 superb Prints; Lady Bumtickler's Revels; the Sublime of Flagellation; Tristram Shandy, with illustrative Prints [...] Madame Birchini's Dance, with large additions, and an elegant collection of other literary and print curiosities.[2]

This announcement of images and publications is an arresting collection of strange bedfellows adding force to Karen Harvey's claim that the taste for erotica was not 'a marginal or underside feature of the eighteenth century; it was not fenced off' from the rest of culture.[3] Available from Holland, for the observer's pleasure, are illustrations of two highly sentimental scenes from Henry Mackenzie's highly sentimental novel, *The Man of Feeling* (1771); an erotic picture, 'A Sale of English Beauties' by James Gillray, a Georgian caricaturist well-known to art historians; a selection of specialist erotic literature for those with an interest in flagellation and, finally, *Tristram Shandy* 'with illustrative Prints'.[4] As Georgian newspapers attracted attention by juxtaposing a variety of advertisements in 'a textual space requiring the reader to make sense of and to synthesize diversity', we can only wonder if *The World*'s readers connected Holland's notice to another in the next column, for 'PATENT WHIPS, SPURS, AND BRIDLES, SOLD CHEAP', that potentially offered similar pleasures.[5]

When Sterne's novel was advertised by Holland in such salacious company, a reprint of *Tristram Shandy* with engravings depicting sexual anatomy and activity was circulating in London, possibly from his shop.[6] The exact content of Holland's version of *Tristram Shandy* is not known for certain; still, his advertisement clearly related this text to flagellation erotica and, through this textual association in a single notice, classed these commodities as sharing a common audience and purpose. Holland was not solely responsible for this association between Sterne's fiction and the genre of erotica. Looking back to the early eighteenth century, *A Sentimental Journey* can be related to an earlier erotic literary genre that employed travel and geographical exploration to consider the female body and its sexual anatomy. This tradition, involving such popular titles as *Merryland Displayed* (1741) and *A New Description of Merryland* (1741), provided 'a guide to the female body under the cloak of a geographic survey'.[7] The *Journey* does not employ extended analogies between the body and landscape as commonly found within these erotic publications, providing one of many differences between the two; this narrative nonetheless combines travel with the exploration of female anatomy, to the extent that journeying enables Yorick's study of desirable bodies and their circulatory systems.

Furthermore, when the *Journey* is related to a later erotic genre, it is possible to perceive that Sterne's novella anticipated late eighteenth-century flagellation literature, in terms of the heightened focus upon the pleasurable sensations offered by the surface of the skin. As in the 'scenes of flagellant drama' discussed by Niklaus Largier, the intimate moments between Yorick and women have a primary concern with 'the skin, with its keen sense of touch and feeling, its sensitivity to excitement'.[8] The peak of Yorick's intimacy with the Calais lady and the Parisian grisset involves his tactile awareness of 'the pulsations of the arteries' beneath the skin. Physical closeness involves Yorick's reception of their repetitive throbs which strike his sense of touch, a sensation that would be intensified by the rhythmic beats and strokes of flagellation literature. While episodes of discipline in such erotica would climax with the display of blood, the intensity of Yorick's sensuous experience culminates in the discovery of blood pulsating below the surface of desirable female companions.[9] In another episode of temptation, alone with the *fille de chambre*, he enjoys the 'warm tint' of her skin and imagines the blood rising to her cheeks. Yorick's reciprocal blush, with 'the sensation of it [...] delicious to the nerves', increases his enjoyment of the self-flagellation of denial; he adds that Stoics without sexual passion should be whipped to enable their appreciation of his stirring experience.[10]

Another curious textual connection is suggested by the fetish for gloves in flagellation fantasies as writers followed Sterne's narrative gaze and portrayed the hands, wrists, and forearms of dominant females as sites of arousal. As a sign of fetishism, writers would adorn these body parts with ornaments including jewellery and gloves.[11] In the stories of the *Bon Ton* magazine during the 1790s, the donning of gloves by female disciplinarians became narrative code to introduce an episode of punishment; as a result, this article of clothing was 'used to signify the power' of the female flagellator, 'denote sexual experience in whipping', and indicate 'a shift from the business of everyday life into a sexual performance'.[12] The *Journey* draws attention to this item of clothing in narrative episodes dealing with Yorick's experience of emotion in response to a female companion's power to affect. In the narrative employment of this article of dress, the feeling of the grisset's pulse precedes Yorick's purchase of two ill-fitting pairs from her after a dominant 'attack' upon his senses; his physical intimacy with the lady at Calais is introduced through a precise and detailed description of her 'black pair of silk gloves open only at the thumb and two fore-fingers', openings that allow him to communicate his desire through throbbing fingertips.[13] A relationship of textual influence between the literary flagellators and Sterne's peregrinator is difficult to ascertain and, to an extent, involves the consideration of parallels rather than an appreciation of differences; yet it is interesting that while the subject of birching was mentioned as far back as seventeenth-century erotica, there was a marked increase in the popularity of this erotic genre from the 1770s onwards along with the introduction of gloves as a narrative motif in the 1790s by the connoisseurs of carnal flagellation.[14] Given such dates, the commercial guidance of Holland could have alerted the future writers of flagellation literature to the pleasures offered by Sterne.

Holland's advertisement acknowledged that there was a fine line between the vibrations of the nerves enjoyed by the man of feeling in a state of emotional distress and the smart experienced by the nerve endings of the feeling man who was sexually aroused by, among other things, Madame Birchini's rod. In one print sold by Holland in the following year, Thomas Rowlandson would pun on the title of Mackenzie's popular novel and equate tactile sensibility with the sexual to suggest that 'the true man of feeling felt women's breasts'.[15] Rowlandson revisited this idea in 1811 (see Fig. 4.1) to produce a tinted drawing for Thomas Tegg who had two years earlier printed his illustrations for an edition of *A Sentimental Journey*.[16] The titular hero of *A Man of Feeling*, a grotesque figure dressed in clerical black whose facial profile has similarities to Thomas Patch's 1765–66 caricature of Sterne in oils, leers at and enjoys touching the curves of his younger female companion.[17] The possessions of this devotee of sensibility include a closed book, placed in the bottom right-hand corner, inscribed with the word 'ARRATINO' upon its side, a reference to the sixteenth-century erotic poet, Pietro Aretino, who was associated in the Georgian period with a genre of engravings depicting sexual positions known as *Aretino's Postures*.[18] A conversation between John Cleland and Sterne, as reported by Boswell, reveals this connection between sex and sensibility through the eighteenth-century semantics of 'sensation':

> CLELAND. "Sterne's bawdy too plain. I reproved him, saying, 'It gives no sensations.' Said he: 'You have furnished me a vindication. It can do no harm.' 'But,' [I said,] 'if you had a pupil who wrote c— on a wall, would not you flog him?' He never forgave me."[19]

Cleland initially employs 'sensation' to signify refined mental feeling, the intense emotions aroused by the senses, a usage current in the mid 1750s. After Sterne playfully interprets the word as signifying physical feeling, the thrill of bodily sensation, Cleland's retort immediately connects their new understanding of this term to the sexual anatomy. As both men eventually acknowledge, the senses create the sensitive, physical body with the potential for both emotional and carnal, fleshly pleasures.

Like his response to Cleland, Sterne's mischievous *Journey* would combine

80 EROTIC YORICK, THE MAN OF FEELING

FIG. 4.1. Thomas Rowlandson, *A Man of Feeling* (1811), colour print. Art Institute, Chicago: Gift of Joseph R. Shapiro.

emotional with tactile, physical pleasure, bridging the divide between the sentimental and the sensual. His portrayal of masculine sensibility in the *Journey*, involving the vibrations of the nervous and circulatory systems, clearly offered later literary imposters creative possibilities. After Sterne's narrative focus upon the sentimental traveller who gauges the emotions and benevolence of attractive women through feeling the pulsations running through their wrists and fingertips, writers would explore the erotic opportunities provided by Yorick's travels, while booksellers like Holland would exploit the subsequent commercial ones. These figures rewrote and restyled Sterne's prose to amplify the sexually suggestive to the detriment of the sentimental. In a fundamental difference between Sterne and his followers, these erotic writers would dislocate the reproductive organ from the sensitive nervous system of the Shandean traveller and privilege the former, thereby breaking the textual intercourse between the sentimental and the sexual as explored in *A Sentimental Journey*.

Holland and his Drury Lane business partner, George Peacock, were conspicuous as advertisers who repeatedly announced the sale of erotic material in the daily press, but they were not alone in producing and peddling Sternean erotica.[20] This chapter identifies five examples of this genre from various publishers, and considers three of them in depth: Hall-Stevenson's *Crazy Tales* (1762), *Yorick's Sentimental Journey Continued* (1769), and Timothy Touchit's *La Souriciere: The Mouse-Trap. A Facetious and Sentimental Excursion through Part of Austrian Flanders and France* (1794).[21] When these publications are placed in the context of the number of other titles inspired by Sterne but without erotic content, then we appear to have a minority genre. For example, in England between 1768 and 1800, at least eleven titles appeared which all include reference to either a sentimental journey or the character of Maria upon the title page, display stylistic facets of Sterne's travelogue, and eschew the sexual as the focus of the narrative.[22] The relatively small number of erotic titles gives no indication of their huge popularity, or of their appearance in a variety of different formats. There is evidence of eight different eighteenth-century editions of *Crazy Tales*, and twelve editions of *Yorick's Sentimental Journey Continued*, as a text issued separately or combined with Sterne's original narrative.[23] Clearly, Sternean sex sold well.

Sternean Erotica

'Sternean erotica' refers to texts that form a relationship to, or mimic facets of, Sterne's literary style; this mimicry also involves the simplification of his narrative focus to emphasize the sexual through, for example, describing the sexual anatomy and encouraging the readers' arousal. It includes an obsessive and reductive focus upon genitalia and sexual action, whether it is the representation of Miss C--Y's 'mighty pretty' cabinet 'fringed about with curling Ornaments, and precious Jewels—A Cabinet that the greatest Monarchs would have delighted to have laid their Hands on' in *Miss C--Y's Cabinet of Curiosities [...] By Tristram Shandy, Gent.*, or the illustration of Sterne's *Tristram Shandy* with graphic images in the 1785 edition.[24] In erotic reworkings of *A Sentimental Journey*, when the Sternean traveller is not reduced to the phallus in action as in *La Souriciere*, Yorick's personal encounters are transformed into overtly sexual experiences as presented by *Yorick's Sentimental Journey Continued*. The teasing sexual suggestiveness of Sterne's original narrative is explicated, displayed in detail, made explicit. As one reviewer of *Crazy Tales* noted, while his friend Tristram 'knew how to intimate his ideas imperfectly by asterisms', this poet 'is capable of expressing himself on the most delicate occasion, in plain German'.[25]

I have grouped these titles together as erotic texts through both textual analysis and a consideration of their reception. This approach avoids a sole reliance upon subjective analysis to differentiate between sexual and nonsexual publications in a period when the dividing line can be difficult to discern as the erotic is often fused with other literary genres in one text. *Miss C--Y's Cabinet of Curiosities* places graphic descriptions of sexual anatomy, and the sexual fetishes of 'depraved Appetites', within a miscellany of jests, bawdy stories, songs, and titillating biographical details of the eponymous heroine, most likely the actress Ann Catley (1745–1789); *La Souriciere* combines the erotic with facets of the Georgian tour guide; and 'COUNTER EPISTLES from BRIGHT-HELMSTONE' by '*The Author of* CRAZY TALES' (1778) connects religious satire to erotic content.[26] Even Cleland's *Memoirs of a Woman of Pleasure* (1748–1749), arguably the most infamous of all eighteenth-century erotic publications, is a hybrid narrative that shares traits with 'mainstream' Georgian novels and differs 'only in its explicit and obsessive interest in sexuality; its mingling of romance elements with realistic presentation is commonplace for its time'.[27]

While Sterne's bawdy suggestions invited disapproval, Sternean erotica was seen as morally dangerous upon its first appearance. *La Souriciere* was 'filthy and nauseous, and incapable of being relished by any but the most degenerate palate' and 'calculated to do evil'; *Yorick's Sentimental Journey Continued* was 'obscene', full of 'immorality' and 'deformities'; *Crazy Tales* made one reviewer feel 'ashamed for the Writer' with a 'few' lines all that he could extract from the publication, 'containing one hundred and fourteen pages, without hazarding the resentment' of readers.[28] The use of readers' reactions to classify texts can be related to the identification of modern 'pornography' as 'a matter of opinion'.[29] To create the literary category of erotica using the subjective responses of contemporary consumers understands the erotic, in the words of Frances Ferguson, '*less because of what it is than because of what it does in a particular situation.*'[30] Whether considering the disgust of the studious reviewer at his desk or the drunken enjoyment of members in the bacchanalian club, this chapter attempts to approach the erotic through the responses generated by it in specific situations. These two methods for comprehending erotica, 'what it is' based upon textual analysis and 'what it does' based upon reader response, are not unconnected: they are reconciled by the actual print and presentation of *Crazy Tales* and *La Souriciere*. Both texts can be distinguished by their use of strategies to indicate how erotica can be enjoyed in a climate of potential moral condemnation.

Sterne's influence is expressed in a number of different textual ways, such as the adoption of his literary personae or the celebration of friendship with him. In *La Souriciere*, it is primarily expressed through textual allusions and the structure of its fragmentary prose, full of digressions and anecdotes, whilst also retaining the confidential tone of speech between friends. The anonymous *Yorick's Sentimental Journey Continued*, later identified as by 'Eugenius' upon the title page of the second edition, gave new life to Sterne's persona as it revisited the scenes and characters of Yorick's original journey. When reviewing this last example, periodicals either begrudgingly acknowledged, or denied and therefore implied, its likeness to Sterne's fiction.

The Gentleman's Magazine was caught between attempts to educate its readership through claiming that *Yorick's Sentimental Journey Continued* had no 'resemblance to [Sterne's] works but in their deformities', thereby preventing assumptions concerning the authenticity of the narrative, and the desire to admit that such 'obscene' erotica perfectly befitted the memory of Sterne. He was remembered by some as a prurient womanizer. Such long-lived scandal survived Sterne's death, as illustrated by the comments of one reviewer in 1769: 'For tho' the Rev. Mr Sterne was a great wit, it cannot be said that he was a desirable companion for a woman of delicacy'.[31] Georgian suspicions about Sterne's lack of sexual restraint were subsequently made explicit in the biographical sketches of nineteenth-century newspapers; one boldly stated that in the brief periods when Sterne was not 'continually after his female servants', he went to York where 'he rarely spent a night without a girl or two'.[32] It is possible that the 1769 continuation, which attempted to assume an air of authenticity, especially fuelled the construction of Sterne as an erotomaniac. Here, the writer adopted the literary persona of Yorick to exploit the memory of mistrust and suspicion surrounding his creator and to develop the dark social scandal surrounding Sterne's infamously tangled dealings with women. As one cause of such infamy, Ian Campbell Ross details Sterne's 'flagrant and repeated infidelities' which included scandalous visits to York's prostitutes in the 1740s leading to possible infections with syphilis and gonorrhoea.[33] This emphasis upon the erotic potential of Yorick's travels in the 1769 continuation potentially fuelled the public understanding of Sterne as a 'licentious wit' who attempted 'to inflame by an artful series of lewd adventures'.[34]

Periodical reviewers focused upon the continuation's attempt to recreate Sterne's novelistic style, even after they had drawn the reader's attention to the preface's claim that 'these volumes are not presented to the public as the offspring of Mr. Sterne's pen'.[35] One reviewer censored the writer's exploitation of Sterne's 'indelicacy', while another merely complained that the continuation was 'obscene, without pathos'.[36] It was not approached by polite periodicals as an act of creative departure manipulating the genre and style of Sterne's original novella, but as a piece of 'finesse', an attempt to pass an erotic publication as a narrative by Sterne, the sentimental writer. The need of contemporary reviewers to proclaim the ridiculous impossibility that this continuation was authentic, or even recognizably Sternean, implied the danger that the unsuspecting purchaser could become duped by this anonymous commodity.

In giving these warnings, periodicals were not responding to an idle threat. While they chose to reprint or paraphrase the sentiment that these volumes were not 'presented as the offspring of Mr. Sterne's pen', they ignored the conflicting claim in the preface that an 'Editor' had 'compiled this Continuation' from Sterne's literary manuscripts.[37] The word 'compile' is from the Latin *compilare*: to pillage, rob, snatch together and carry off another person's property. The publishing history of *Yorick's Sentimental Journey Continued* also gave an air of dubious authenticity to this literary enterprise: it was often published with Sterne's *Journey*, albeit usually within the piracy of anonymous publication.[38] *The Gentleman's Magazine* emphatically stated that this continuation could not be mistaken as Sterne's work but also recognized the superficial similarity, in terms of physical size, between the original two volumes and the counterfeit continuation comprising volumes three and four of a collected edition.[39] One edition also encouraged the continuation's promotion as part of Sterne's literary career through including *A Political Romance* and a prefatory biographical sketch of Sterne; the latter was described by *The London Magazine* as 'a very entertaining morsel of biography' including details 'never before communicated to the public'.[40]

Moreover, for the Georgian reader of travel narratives, it could be difficult to differentiate between the authentic and the spurious; while 'the number of hoaxes weakened the reputation of honest travellers', this situation also 'indicated the ease with which travel books could shade into fiction'.[41] If the generic status and authorial authenticity of *Yorick's Sentimental Journey Continued* could be doubted, the same possibility also confronted the readers of *A Sentimental Journey* as a result of this textual association. For one late eighteenth-century subscription library catalogue, Sterne's *Journey* offered a problematic example of a narrative that could not be classified under 'Voyages and Travels' or 'Novels, Tales and Romances'. When faced with this genre dilemma, one option was to place Sterne's unclassifiable work under the indeterminate heading of 'Miscellanies'.[42] Both Eugenius's continuation and Sterne's original *Journey* challenged library readerships to decide if these accounts were fictional counterfeits of a travelogue or authentic accounts of a real journey.

In this atmosphere of uncertainty, there is no indisputable evidence to identify the writer behind the pseudonym of 'Eugenius'. Until the mid-twentieth century, this pseudonym had been interpreted as evidence of Hall-Stevenson's authorship through its previous use as a term of affection for him in Sterne's writing.[43] During the eighteenth century, critics playing 'the popular game of identifying fictional characters as actual people' assumed that 'Sterne had represented Hall as Eugenius, the faithful, prudent counsellor of *Tristram Shandy* and *A Sentimental Journey*'.[44] Indeed, 'it was obvious to most people how much Sterne and Hall loved one another', a fact advertised by the title of Hall-Stevenson's most commercially successful publication, *Crazy Tales*, in its titular gesture towards Sterne's 'Shandy', a word from the Yorkshire dialect meaning barmy, full of froth and levity.[45] For a proportion of the readers of *Crazy Tales*, those privileged readers aware of the 'open secret' of Hall-Stevenson's Demoniacs club at Skelton Castle as well as his relationship with Sterne, the significance of 'Eugenius' upon the second edition title page would have been obvious. And, as Mark Robson astutely notes, authorial anonymity can be 'less a matter of concealment than of an all too open secret' for authors who are 'too well known [...] to require any identification'.[46]

It is profitable to view the 1769 continuation in relation to Hall-Stevenson's personal life as a club member and a connoisseur of erotica, a lifestyle shared with Sterne throughout the 1760s. As this new, sexually promiscuous Yorick ran wild in a new journey, the reader who initially thought that '*Rochester*' was a 'mere Puritan compared to *Shandy*' would have this suspicion confirmed.[47] In the *Journey Continued*, Sterne's typical use of euphemistic metaphors, innuendo, and waggish circumlocution is matched with a roll-call of popular erotic motifs. One episode combines voyeurism, one of its 'most classic and consistent tropes', with the conventional interest in the prurience of female penitents and monks, 'a major preoccupation in a corpus of erotic anti-Catholic material during the long eighteenth century'.[48] Yorick's position as a concealed voyeur offers the reader a role model for the enjoyment of the sexual spectacle within a moment exploiting the reader's sense of 'the danger' of being discovered with an eye fixed at the 'peephole', a conventional textual strategy in Georgian erotic literature:[49]

> Meeting with a lusty Friar upon the stairs, a thought occurred to me—"Surely this man must be framed of different flesh and blood than other mortals, if, when Mademoiselle reveals all her secrets to him, he can have the resolution to withstand such an attack upon the senses."
>
> I returned, and finding a very convenient aperture in the door, planted myself to observe the fervor of the penitent's devotion.
>
> How many Ave Maria's!—how many prayers! how many ejaculations!
>
> Oh! that I had been a friar, a lusty friar! What a felicity within the pale of that holy church!
>
> Heavens! What an accident!
>
> I had always an aversion to wooden beds, from their cracking:—[50]

In one respect, this incident is a good thematic match for the original *Sentimental Journey*, where Sterne repeatedly describes Yorick's withstanding of feminine attacks upon his senses. The inquisitiveness of Sterne's character, which involves the shadowy surveillance of others to understand the mysteries of human action, is also evoked in Eugenius's surreptitious scene. In Sterne's 'THE ACT OF CHARITY. PARIS', Yorick describes the importance of secretive viewpoints for the sentimental traveller: 'the man who either disdains or fears to walk up a dark entry [...] will not do to make a good sentimental traveller [...] Nature is shy, and hates to act before spectators'.[51] His penchant for lurking in dark alleyways presents the sentimental enjoyment of emotional display as a hidden, illicit, and deviously underhand activity. But, in the continuation, Yorick's observation is presented in a new light and transformed into an overtly sexual act; the pleasure gained by Sterne's alter ego in sensuous spectatorship is purely erotic, not contaminated by sentimental feelings.

Karl Thompson's portrayal of the continuation as 'mostly re-narration and description of the events and scenes of the *Journey*, the only difference being that Yorick comments on the changes wrought by a year or two', misreads these volumes.[52] Sterne's character is transformed into a rakish pleasure-seeker who asserts 'it hath ever been a rule with me to think the goods of this world of no benefit, unless enjoyed' as Eugenius's simplification sacrifices the erotic possibilities of sexual self-constraint from the original novel.⁵³ This sexual epicure, always 'disposed for a frolic' while viewing pleasure as the greatest good, lacks the crippling self-abnegation of Sterne's character.⁵⁴ The genre of erotica demands that its heroes, like Eugenius's Yorick, have 'a quite remarkable aptitude for pleasure. They are creatures of desire, always ready [...] The chaste, the continent and the impotent are excluded from their company'.⁵⁵

We have here a textual equivalent of Hall-Stevenson's encouragement of Sterne to be 'joyful about sex'.⁵⁶ Such a strategy overlooked the significance of Yorick's moralistic posing in *A Sentimental Journey*, as well as the emphasis upon self-restraint that allows Sterne's alter ego to enjoy the physiological reactions to desire with a clean conscience. In the meeting between Yorick and the *fille de chambre*, Sterne's evocation of 'Polonius' and his self-portrayal as the promoter of a 'lesson of virtue' allow an illicit indulgence of the sensations triggered by desire, including the 'tremble' of 'every limb'. Similarly, during Yorick's 'half guilty blush' in *A Sentimental Journey*, we are told that 'virtue flies after [the blood]—not to call it back, but to make the sensation of it more delicious to the nerves'. Here, the avowal of virtue absolves and intensifies the enjoyment of the nervous sensation caused by heightened circulation.⁵⁷ While Sterne's Yorick embodies the masochistic enjoyment of the repression of desire, Eugenius's character, in the spirit of *Crazy Tales*, represents the forthright, uninhibited enjoyment of desire and sexual self-expression.

Sterne abruptly leaves *A Sentimental Journey* with coy silence after the potentially sexual incident with the *fille de chambre*; Eugenius begins his continuation by communicating Yorick's proud display of the physiological evidence of desire. This beginning exploits an awareness that the end of Sterne's second volume 'bordered "rather on sensuality than sentiment"', a point made by the *London Magazine* review of *A Sentimental Journey*.⁵⁸ After the entire inn is awakened by the screams of the *fille de chambre* in the continuation, Yorick 'jump[s] out of bed' and 'stand[s] bolt-upright close to the lady'. While twice informing the reader that he is 'standing bolt-upright', Yorick elaborates upon his act of self-display:

> [I had] most unfortunately, in my tossing and tumbling in bed for want of rest, worked off a very material button upon my black silk breeches; and by some accident the other button-hole having slipt its hold.⁵⁹

If, in *A Sentimental Journey*, Yorick's emotional response to the attractions of the feminine is located in the physiological pulsations of the arteries, Eugenius takes this delight in the pulsating movement of blood to its anatomically extreme and obscene conclusion.

Despite the attempt to develop the physiological basis of Sterne's literary sensibility, this mimic abandons a fundamental consequence of Yorick's sensitivity: emotional empathy and philanthropy. *The Monthly Review*'s complaint that this continuation had 'nothing to touch the heart' misread or deliberately ignored the narrative's primary purpose of stimulating sexual desire.⁶⁰ Certainly, Eugenius is unconcerned with Sternean displays of suffering designed to stimulate an emotional response similar to Yorick's 'burst into a flood of tears' while behaving 'as weak as a woman'.⁶¹ In one episode, Eugenius begins to narrate a conventionally sentimental scene involving the Fille de Joye's private confession to Yorick concerning her rape, by a predatory and sexually incontinent count, and her subsequent downfall into prostitution. The potential for the sentimental hero's empathy and emotional distress, as illustrated by Harley's reaction to Miss Atkins's tale of rape and abandonment in *The Man of Feeling*, is dispelled by Yorick's response.[62] In an attempt to avoid the awakening of the reader's conscience and sexual guilt, the rakish Yorick horrifically claims 'I have known an English nobleman pay fifty times the sum for such an affair, without having committed half so good [a] rape, as was committed upon you'. Chillingly for a modern reader, the act of 'rape' is merely judged in terms of having the potential to afford masculine pleasure. In this example, the arousing 'difficulty' experienced by the count, through the passionate 'opposition' from the Fille, leads Yorick to consider the rape a good one.[63] As in this response, the purpose of Eugenius's travelogue is primarily to afford sexual pleasure and amusement to such readers as frequented George Peacock's shop.

After many reprints of *Yorick's Sentimental Journey Continued*, *La Souriciere* appeared. This combination of travel narrative and explicit sexual fantasy is conveyed by a largely anonymous narrator with the pseudonym of 'Timothy Touchit', an eighteenth-century English libertine intent upon conquests during his travels through France and Austrian Flanders.[64] During his exploitation of Sterne's confidential and fragmentary first-person narrative style, complete with interruptions, digressions, and the ubiquitous dash, the narrator describes his sexual adventures as a grand tourist with a myriad of equally anonymous females including a '*Petite demoiselle*' and a '*Fille de chambre*'. Inspired by Sterne's suggestiveness, *La Souriciere* adopts the '*Hobby-Horse*' metaphor from *Tristram Shandy* to refer archly to sexual intercourse:

> Still I did not discover much ardour, which she perceived, and wisely knowing that little is gained by delay, she resolved to take *the whole business upon herself*; whereupon, she bestrode her *Hobby-horse*, and after *being secure of her seat*, jogged on till she arrived at *the point of her wishes*.[65]

This episode amplifies the bawdiness of Sterne's original passage, as the language of Uncle Toby's personal obsession with military architecture is redeployed to convey the act of intercourse. Sterne's bawdy references to the erotic heat and friction generated by the momentum of the hobby horse provided an erotic opportunity too good to miss. It was not surprising that Sterne's original description, involving the 'heated parts of the rider' created through 'much friction' in the manner of 'electrified bodies', provoked disgust in some of the first reviews of *Tristram Shandy* as they complained of Sterne's 'want of decency' through his use of 'immodest words', 'double entendre', and the 'broad hint' of sexual activity.[66] Like the reviews, Touchit's literary commentary potentially directed a new wave of Sterne's readers to the indecent insinuations of volume one.

The narrative focus in *La Souriciere* magnifies the importance of the genitalia. Like the tales of bodysnatching surrounding Yorick's death, Touchit's appropriation also involves the imaginative dissection of the literary tourist. Touchit discarded the heart with all of its literary associations; a reader of *The Beauties*, who possessed a 'heart of sensibility', would have instantly identified these associations as sympathy, pity, compassion, and the ability to evaluate personal conduct and look into the heart. This dissection by Touchit involved physiological, emotional and moral simplification, through the commodification of an individual body part in new narrative episodes. This Sternean traveller is reduced to the depiction of the phallus engaged in the act of ejaculation in a series of images that reinforces Harvey's perspective that 'erotic authors announced themselves masters of metaphor'.[67] After the satisfying attentions of one *Fille de chambre*, we are told:

> the *elevation of the Barometer* fell down to *changeable*, and I became relieved and composed.—It was a speedy, agreeable cure, and I never knew the *Mouse-trap* more serviceable than it was on this occasion.[68]

Elsewhere, the protagonist is transformed into a '*May-pole of love*', developing Tristram's playful observation on the French women's love of maypoles: 'give 'em but a May-pole, whether in May, June, July, or September—they never count the times [...] they would dance round them (and the men for company) till they were all blind'.[69] This genre where 'male genitals stood for whole male bodies' honed the potential audience for the Sternean narrative,[70] targeting a public who would have relished, rather than condemned, bawdy insinuation.

La Souriciere, like *Yorick's Sentimental Journey Continued*, reveals the facets of Sterne's narratives that were exploited by the act of erotic publication, facets condemned by the periodical press and omitted by *The Beauties*. This moral censure, along with the huge commercial success of *The Beauties*'s 'chaste' and sanitized compilation of sentimental passages, has led to a distorted perception of the value of Sterne for late eighteenth-century readers. Like the rumours concerning the accidental interment of Sterne's heart separately from the rest of his body following anatomization, *The Beauties* sought to separate his heart-rending sensibility from impolite sexual passion.[71] John Mullan remarks that sentimentalism, 'in the decades during and after publication', was 'seized on' as the 'distinctive merit' of his narratives.[72] This fails to appreciate the importance of Sterne's bawdy and erotic potential for a substantial community. While erotic writers exploited the salacious as the 'distinctive merit' of *A Sentimental Journey* and *Tristram Shandy*, the champions of sexual restraint in periodicals sought to discourage the enjoyment of narratives with sexual content. This opposition between the celebration and the condemnation of literary erotica influenced the presentation of Sternean reworkings as well as the ways in which they were consumed.

From Text to the Context of Consumption

Holland's unabashed advertisement of erotica should encourage a revision of a number of late twentieth-century generalizations about Georgian attitudes to erotic literature. Walter Kendrick in *The Secret Museum* and, more recently, Jean Marie Goulemot in *Forbidden Texts* have portrayed the erotic novel through the eyes of Samuel Pepys who, after furtively and secretly enjoying the notorious *L'ecole des Filles*, decided in a fit of guilt to burn it 'that it might not be among my books to my shame'.[73] For Goulemot, erotic texts promised the pleasures of an illicit commodity 'seized' upon 'in a sudden and furtive manner' in the 'greedy, semi-clandestine setting' of a disreputable bookshop.⁷⁴ Similarly, Tim Hitchcock's belief, that the 'largely private affair' of erotica was not for 'a crowded alehouse audience', disregards the social acceptance of such material implicit in its widespread advertisement in the communal vehicle of the daily press.⁷⁵ More recently, Vic Gatrell has correctly questioned such assumptions and argued for the revival of libertine attitudes in the late eighteenth century including permissive attitudes towards, and the public enjoyment of, erotic and satirical prints. Gatrell reproduces a myriad of persuasive images, but his view of satirical prints as documentary representations of actual behaviour neglects the fact that such material could exist as burlesque distortions of real events or social attitudes. One image, *Caricature Shop* (1801), presents the pleasure of a diverse crowd, in terms of age, gender, and race, taken in the prints displayed in the window of P. Roberts's Holborn premises. In the foreground, an infirm old man stoops with difficulty to enjoy a buxom nude.⁷⁶ Roberts's image, like Gatrell's thesis, presents visual erotica as a commodity that was publicly relished and not simply reviled. Within the late eighteenth-century context of the public advertisement and sale of erotic prints and books, it would show a lack of perspective to view the polite periodicals as representing the majority voice.

Sternean texts betray the influence of conflicting attitudes to the consumption of erotic material. These acts of mimicry promote erotica as a vehicle for gentlemanly sociability, a usage also tinged by the recognition that this material was prone to condemnation by the proponents of sexual restraint. *Crazy Tales* and *La Souriciere* celebrated erotica as a textual location for masculine fellowship, one of the key ideas of eighteenth-century politeness. These texts reinforce Harvey's idea that erotic culture did not solely constitute an 'impolite world' but instead 'had politeness at its heart, both as something to mock and as something to aspire to'.⁷⁷ A consideration of *Crazy Tales* reveals the use of impolite material for a polite purpose, and gives one perspective on the acceptable social conditions for the consumption of Sternean erotica in the 1760s.

Crazy Tales is a collection of eleven erotic stories in verse, each ascribed to a different narrator using an alias to indicate a member of the Demoniacs, Hall-Stevenson's bacchanalian club which met at his residence, Skelton Castle.⁷⁸ Each crazy tale provides evidence of the members' sexual fantasies exchanged through conversation including 'My Cousin's Tale of a Cock and a Bull' which is clearly credited to Sterne.⁷⁹ This collection gains coherence through its reliance upon three scenarios which are repeatedly employed, and sometimes combined in a single tale: the seduction of a 'Miss' along with the hoodwinking of a guardian, marital dysfunction caused by the sexual relationship between husband and wife, and the sexual antics of monks and nuns in a form of narrative labelled by Peakman as 'anti-Catholic erotica'.⁸⁰ In addition, all of these tales create fantasies to portray what sexually excites men, and causes sexual incontinence; in doing so, they often gleefully relate sexual activity which would transgress the moral and legal boundaries of twenty-first century England. For instance, 'The Governor of T★★lbury's Tale; or, the Unreasonable Complaint' describes Pierre who becomes aroused by this treatment of Jaquette, his wife:

> Who every day of his vile life,
> When he had nothing else to do,
> Thrash'd, or apply'd his wooden shoe,
> To the posteriors of his wife.
> [...]
> And every morn before he rose,
> He left her over and above
> A token of his constant love,
> Steady and constant as his blows.[81]

Jaquette successfully applies to the law to restrain her husband's violent behaviour, then he becomes impotent and 'off his mettle', leading her to request that Pierre is again allowed to 'thrash his fill'.[82] Jaquette's initial complaint is 'Unreasonable' in the world of Hall-Stevenson's imagination as her flagellatory distress merely exists as a necessary precursor to the pleasure of sexual intercourse for both marriage partners. After building a narrative upon her distress and subsequent legal 'complaint', this tale resolves conflict not through legal action, but through the mutual enjoyment of sex; *Crazy Tales* often reconciles differences through narrative endings that join bodies together. Within these tales, the behaviour motivated by desire, such as Pierre's, is never condemned by the narrator. Instead, the situations that sexually stimulate are represented as farcical, 'Laugh-at-able', and as a cause for joyful celebration, even if such a situation involves mercilessly spanking one's wife.[83]

The opening narrative, owned by Hall-Stevenson using the nom de plume of Anthony Shandy, establishes the exclusively masculine viewpoint that dominates these erotic fantasies. Unlike Sterne's professed aim 'to take in all Kinds of Readers', Hall-Stevenson targeted a rakish masculine audience. In this spirit, *Crazy Tales* communicates a graphic obsession with the 'Miss-demeanours' and 'Miss-doings' of seemingly virtuous, but impressionable and easily corruptible girls.[84] This first story, 'Anthony's Tale', describing the seduction of an adolescent Lucy by Hall-Stevenson's Captain, establishes the masculine voyeurism of female anatomy. These narratives are often concerned with the illicit enjoyment of the spectacle of the female body from a position of disguise or concealment. The Captain adopts a pretence of childish innocence which includes 'act[ing] Punch' and 'a thousand monkey tricks' in order to seduce her.[85] In the third poem, 'Miss in her Teens: Captain Shadow's Tale', the sexual predator Dick takes great pleasure in viewing his cousin's nakedness from an unseen position; the male reader is encouraged to enjoy 'peeping thro' a nick, Or thro' the key-hole'.[86] Despite such perspectives, these narratives were originally enjoyed within a community unconcerned with shame. They recall the communal exchange of erotica within seventeenth-century manuscript culture where such poetry circulated among a select coterie of readers in elite male social circles. In that tradition, poetic transcripts were 'exchanged' and 'shared with others' and, as a result, these manuscript texts were 'rarely principally "authored" by the person who had written them down'.[87] These manuscripts 'constituted the site not of private and intimate individual personal confession or sentiment but of a social exchange'.[88] With *Crazy Tales*, Hall-Stevenson positions himself within this tradition.

To promote a sense of community, the first edition of *Crazy Tales* has a lavish engraving of 'Crazy Castle', the members' nickname for Skelton Castle, as a frontispiece. This choice of image, as opposed to a portrait of the author, places the importance of belonging to a geographical location above mere self-aggrandizement. It is difficult to judge whether this frontispiece would have existed as a completely faithful or recognizable reproduction of the façade of this Castle for mid-eighteenth-century readers. For the Georgian literary detective, this engraving could have given recognizable architectural evidence of the author's proud ownership of this publication had the castle not been rebuilt to an unrecognizable extent after Hall-Stevenson's death.[89] However, a homesick Sterne, while viewing the image, affectionately claimed in a letter dated 12 August 1762:

> Oh! how I envy you all at Crazy Castle!—I could like to spend a month with you—and should return back again for the vintage.—I honour the man that has given the world an idea of our parental seat—'tis well done—I look at it ten times a day with a *quando te aspiciam?*[90]

The mere sight of this visual embodiment of masculine sociability stirred his affection for the Demoniacs.

Crazy Tales eulogizes the hedonistic lifestyle offered by the bacchanalian club, lauding friendship based upon the freedom to enjoy bawdy storytelling and salacious conversation fuelled by wine. Hall-Stevenson evokes the heady, drunken atmosphere surrounding this communal storytelling; pleasurable stories need to be uncorked through 'screwing', and eventually 'decanted', to produce narratives as 'clear' and 'bright' as fine wine.[91] In this alcoholic environment, the sharing of scandalous stories is encouraged by the liberation of the impolite tongue where members are emboldened to abandon polite, social restraint in favour of indiscreet freedom, a freedom fostered by group camaraderie and the mimicry of libertine attitudes. Consequently, *Crazy Tales* does not simply belong to the genre of erotica: this collection can also be related to eighteenth-century club literature. As Peter Clark recognizes, 'there was a large specialist literature generated by societies themselves, which sought to define and refine their distinctive image and appeal in the sociable marketplace'. This literature included 'boozing songs [...] particularly saucy or smutty ones' as an aid to rakish conversation and masculine bonding.[92] If the members of such drinking clubs provided the wine, Hall-Stevenson's publication offered to supply the 'smutty' tales and help buyers recreate the social experience of the Demoniacs. The first edition sold a lifestyle, the vicarious experience of membership to Hall-Stevenson's select and secretive society for the price of four shillings.

To view the eroticism of *Crazy Tales* as an instrument for the shameful indulgence of sexual desire in solitude would completely misunderstand his authorial purpose. Erotica promotes 'tender' masculine friendship in the privacy of a 'retreat':

> In this retreat, whilom so sweet,
>   Once TRISTRAM and his Cousin dwelt,
> They talk of CRAZY when they meet,
>   As if their tender hearts would melt.[93]

To foster an understanding of Georgian erotica as a form of communal recreation, Peakman speculates that readings from Cleland's *Memoirs* in manuscript form could have been one type of entertainment for the secretive libertine club, 'Beggar's Benison and Merryland', in 1730s Anstruther in Scotland.[94] The consumption of *Crazy Tales* in a comparable society of close friendship would have influenced the members' experience of this poetry; the location of reading and 'the company the reader may keep undoubtedly change the nature of that reading'.[95] The atmosphere of drunken bravado and disorderly lewdness surely encouraged frank responses to these accounts of sexual conquest. The material could not be indiscriminately displayed in general society, and that in itself strengthened group identity.

His bacchanalian club has been related by historians to Sir Francis Dashwood's scandalous fraternity at Medmenham Abbey. Stories of Dashwood's 'allegedly depraved society of anti-clerical libertines who dressed up as monks and held secret meetings where they debauched local virgins' have become part of eighteenth-century folklore.[96] Hall-Stevenson's association with the aristocratic founder of the mid-eighteenth-century 'Hell-Fire Club', now legendary for speculation concerning its delight in sexual deviance and promiscuity, also potentially found expression in his creation of the Demoniacs. According to Donald McCormick, 'there is evidence that Dashwood was consulted and asked for his advice on the rituals which [Hall-Stevenson] should adopt'.[97] Hall-Stevenson's club has been dismissed as a pale imitation of the fabulous debauchery of Dashwood's scandalous fraternity, but such a relationship is difficult to ascertain as modern critical accounts of both private clubs and their activities involve supposition.[98] Even the name given to Skelton's members, the 'Demoniacs', involves speculation; it is only found in one letter by Sterne from 1761.[99] Despite such mystery, *Crazy Tales* nonetheless gives an insight into the prurient preoccupations of the members' drunken anecdotes and conversation. Within Hall-Stevenson's mid-century library, a focal living and entertaining room, the boisterous enjoyment of his extensive collection of erotica perhaps sparked such conversation.[100]

Away from the privacy of Skelton Castle, the anonymity of the first edition of *Crazy Tales* showed Hall-Stevenson's reluctance to own his poetry in the public and commercial environment of the bookseller's shop. It is not surprising that the anonymity of his early publications led to confusion surrounding the exact identity of the writer. When his *Two Lyric Epistles* appeared, speculations concerning the author of this scurrilously bawdy piece included both Sterne and Garrick.[101] In *Crazy Tales*, the waggish 'Author's DEDICATION to Himself', and the use of the pseudonym 'A.S.', mischievously presented the text as unfit to own or dedicate. Even the location of *Crazy Tales*'s publication was only indicated as 'London' without the printer's name and address to aid buyers or legal prosecutions. In spite of the availability of erotica in a shop like Peacock's, the illusion of secrecy was an important facet of this genre. Erotic content was commonly advertised by this lack of accurate title page information; Georgian erotica was 'invariably disguised behind false authors, publishers, dates and places of publication', hinting at the forbidden literary pleasures within.[102]

After the appearance of three completely anonymous London editions, two leading publishers in 1780 exploited the financial potential of *Crazy Tales*: J. Dodsley and T. Becket. When Sterne was searching for a publisher for the first two volumes of *Tristram Shandy*, he was advised to 'settle only for the best — send it to Dodsley'.[103] Had these figures been aware of the commercial demand for *Crazy Tales* during Sterne's lifetime, Hall-Stevenson's poetry would have sat side by side with copies of the first four volumes of *Tristram Shandy* in Dodsley's Pall-Mall rooms while also competing for room with volumes five to nine of *Tristram Shandy* in Becket's shop on the Strand. This stamp of respectability, provided by these publishers' names, was unthinkable for the original printer. It is difficult to gauge whether commercial patronage by these two booksellers signified a growing social tolerance of erotica, as a freely available commodity, as the 1760s gave way to the '70s and '80s. There is apparently no evidence of erotic publications by the Dodsley business other than those authored by Hall-Stevenson, a situation that perhaps relates to the remembrance of Robert as a man who conscientiously 'preserved the strictest integrity' and respectability.[104]

Despite the abandonment of authorship, the grand 1762 folio presented erotica as a commodity for proud display befitting a genteel, masculine author and consumer. Traditionally, such a large format as the folio was 'reserved for serious works that were religious or philosophical rather than literary' or 'for prestige editions that enshrined a literary work'.[105] According to one review, the showy, 'pompous form' of the folio was unsuitably lavish and extravagant for exhibiting such a 'paultry Publication' as Hall-Stevenson's inferior, obscene verse.[106] The periodical press were concerned with the printing of Hall-Stevenson's immodest obscenity within a format that encouraged the reader to cherish, display, and exhibit — albeit only realistically possible within a close-knit masculine group such as the Demoniacs.

Sexually explicit writing was enjoyed under the guise of aristocratic refinement in the confines of a club, but it risked condemnation in other social situations and forms of communication that lacked relative sophistication. The boundaries sketched by the voices of polite society, in terms of the restraints upon the declaration of sexual terms, were touched upon by Cleland's criticism of *Tristram Shandy*. His comment illustrates that the uncontrolled use and display (partial or not) of terms relating to sexual anatomy could encounter moral disgust, even from the author of the *Memoirs*. When Cleland took umbrage at Sterne's use of asterisks to represent a four-letter word, he asked him: 'If you had a pupil who wrote c— on a wall, would not you flog him?' Before drawing conclusions about Cleland's remark, it is necessary to note that Boswell's papers record a partial conversation at second hand, many years after the event; his entry from April 1779 postdates Sterne's death by eleven years. Nonetheless, Cleland's condemnation of such a hint, as appears in the sixth chapter of the second volume of *Tristram Shandy*, is revealing as is Sterne's mortification and subsequent refusal to forgive him. Cleland's comment was offensive through its lack of discrimination in his reduction of Sterne's arch, textual clues, open to interpretation in a novelistic form, to a crude scrawling of a word, in full, for everyone to see. But, Cleland's analogy with a child's scrawl also ignored the importance of bawdy humour as a sign of elite culture (as celebrated by Hall-Stevenson's group). While Bosch dismisses Sterne's employment of bawdy typography as unoriginal through citing early eighteenth-century literature, the value of such typographical play for Sterne was exactly its unoriginality. Skelton's rakish enjoyment of prurient humour from an aristocratic past can be illustrated by Hall-Stevenson's use of the same visual joke in *Two Lyric Epistles* which addresses 'the Grown Gentlewomen, The Misses of ★★★★'.[107] In their club, rakish humour, with precedents from literary history, provided socially legitimate amusement that conformed to established forms of behaviour and encouraged sociability; these social values were ignored by Cleland's scathing portrayal of Sterne's indecorous humour as a cause of readerly embarrassment in the mid-century.

His question had additional power to hurt because Cleland failed to acknowledge that the means were as important as the message. Aesthetic style was as important as the form of entertainment for the Shandy cousins since the shared values of the Demoniacs encouraged refinement, not simply sexual liberation. In its presentation of sexual material in a stately, aesthetically pleasing object for select gatherings, *Crazy Tales* exists as a forerunner for Richard Payne Knight's *An Account of the Remains of the Worship of Priapus* (1786). Knight's visually grandiose folio was 'printed in limited numbers for a specifically private male audience; only eighty copies were to be circulated for members of the Dilettanti Society'.[108] He included plates that combined the aesthetic pleasure involved in the discovery of an antique Roman past with the erotic pleasure provided by images of sexual organs and activity. For Knight (like Hall-Stevenson) aesthetic appreciation was inseparable from an enjoyment of the sexual, with the book existing as an object of beauty for an appreciative aristocratic audience. Such taste was later satirized by Rowlandson's caricature, *Connoisseurs* (1799), where he depicts the intense interest of an elderly group of aristocratic rakes in a picture of a female nude; their appraisal merely reveals the real stimulus for their fascination, the sexual. This point is emphasized by Rowlandson's related drawing entitled *Cunnyseurs* (undated), another illustration of his love of puns, in which the painting has been replaced by a real woman.[109]

As the last erotic reworking of Sterne in the eighteenth century, *La Souriciere* highlights the issues surrounding the possible readerships, social contexts, and purposes of such material. Despite the duodecimo format which seems tailored for private, clandestine consumption, *La Souriciere* promoted the reading of erotica as a communal act. The introduction places the consumer within a like-minded public; it encourages masculine fellowship and fraternity despite the titular promise to provide 'divertisement for both sexes'. Its presentation as 'A LITERARY OLIO, that will be happy to *pass through many hands*' is not simply a waggish innuendo referring to the encouragement of masturbation by the act of reading; the image of '*many hands*' also implies a community created by the circulation of the narrative.[110] 'A LITERARY OLIO', the literary equivalent of a mixed dish of stewed meat, evoked the pleasures of the stew through wordplay while also conveying the impression of feasting and hospitality as the erotic fare is passed from hand to hand.

To imply that the consumer is part of a larger audience participating in a communal act of erotic spectatorship, *La Souriciere* exploits theatrical metaphors. Sexual activity is a 'performance' and an 'exhibit[ion]' suitable for public display in the theatre.[111]

The preface declares that 'I must not discover the plot of my play in the first scene. —My dancing-bears and flying-dragons, shall be exhibited in due time'.[112] This image of spectacular entertainment, enjoyed publicly, is clearly incompatible with the depiction of erotic reading as a furtive pleasure dependent upon concealment (as discussed earlier in the chapter). But the author's theatrical analogy is ill-suited to portray the consumption of *La Souriciere*. While the price of admission was the sole restriction upon the enjoyment of pantomime, the financial cost of purchase was not the only constraint upon the enjoyment of *La Souriciere*. Within this duodecimo format implying financial affordability, linguistic complexity discourages all except an educated and bilingual readership, an audience familiar with celebrated fine art who would have appreciated the comparisons of feminine beauty with the 'delicacy of *Titian*, the brilliancy of *Guido*, and the fire of *Raphael*'.[113] In addition, sexual acts are expressed using euphemisms based upon French phraseology: '*transport d'Amour*', '*Une conversation particuliere*' and '*LE TOUCHER-GALANT*', leading to sexual satisfaction and 'the *declination* of the *point-principal*'.[114]

La Souriciere can be placed in a line of development involving changes in the format of Sternean erotica over the last four decades of the century: the imposing folio of *Crazy Tales* was replaced by the discreet pocketbooks of the 1780s and '90s as illustrated by *La Souriciere*, the 1783 publication of *Crazy Tales* 'in a neat Pocket Volume' for '2s. 6d.', and the erotic 1785 version of *Tristram Shandy* with similar dimensions.[115] The use of modest formats for printing encouraged readers to consume books on the move and carry them into a wide variety of diverse social settings as 'publishers began to assure customers [that] pocket-books could be read at the hairdressers, in the carriage, by the billiards table, or at the racecourse'.[116] With Sternean erotica size matters, but its significance can be difficult to interpret as changes in format provide ambiguous evidence of changes in consumption. A duodecimo, for example, could either indicate a portable book to be openly consumed, or a commodity designed to be easily secreted upon a bashful reader. Either way, the use of this format towards the end of the century saw Sternean erotica set free from the confines of personal libraries and display cases. Considering its physical dimensions, *La Souriciere* could have been used as a portable guide for pleasure seekers in need of guidance upon Flanders's eighteenth-century tourist routes. Easily accommodated by the commodious pockets of a Georgian frock-coat, it encourages the reader to follow Touchit's footsteps with his book in hand.

In terms of the relationship between format and purpose, an analogy can be made between *La Souriciere* and *Harris's List of Covent Garden Ladies; or, New Atlantis for the Year 1761* (1761).[117] Just as Harris's directory of prostitutes gave directions to readers in their pursuit of sexually available women, including the street names where these women could be found, Touchit identifies Continental locations for sexual satisfaction, although these locations are less specific than in Harris's guide. *Harris's List*, published annually between 1757 and 1795, was contained in a 'six-by-four-inch volume' that, according to Hallie Rubenhold, allowed it to be carried by London's men about town. Despite being updated annually and constantly changed in terms of content and style, *Harris's List* always retained its original format, the duodecimo.[118] Size creates a book with a particular purpose in mind, rather than an attempt to cater for a readership with modest spending power through the use of a cheap format. After all, the guide includes information for a wide variety of customers, in terms of the money available to them, in its advertisement of prostitutes from those whose price was 'an affordable five shillings to the exclusive "banknotes only"'.[119] *Harris's List* was primarily designed to enable readers to consult it during their wanderings around Covent Garden, and it anticipates Touchit's diminutive book which similarly allowed curious tourists to read about locations offering sexual intrigue while travelling.

Touchit's guidance of the traveller towards bodily pleasure instead of intellectual stimulation is comparable with Sterne's 'delight in living women' in *A Sentimental Journey* and his disregard for 'the more obvious aspects of heritage' including Continental topography and architecture.[120] This narrative preoccupation with the opposite sex in both *A Sentimental Journey* and *La Souriciere* mirrors one motivation for travel within a section of grand tourists during this period. Touchit's creation of his guide commercially developed an awareness that sexual desire provided one intense impetus for travel upon the tour; travel provided 'a major opportunity for sexual adventure', with tourists 'generally young, healthy and wealthy and poorly, if at all, supervised'.[121] For the wealthy contemporaries of Touchit, it would have been easily possible to recreate his journey. By the late eighteenth century, the Low Countries had become a well-worn European thoroughfare and 'a goal in themselves' for British travellers: 'after Paris and Italy, they offered the third most important group of places' visited by such tourists.[122] Touchit's sexual adventure follows one standard and accessible post route from Ostend to Paris via Bruges, Brussels and Valenciennes; it is a route which, for the reader knowledgeable of European geography and the location of Toby's military misfortunes, takes Touchit close to Namur.[123]

As with Eugenius's adventures, the relation of sexual fantasy as part of real, day to day life in actual locations worked to intensify the erotic charge of *La Souriciere* for sedentary armchair explorers and dynamic tourists alike. Like the 1769 continuation, which placed Yorick's adventures in precise locations down to the nearest 'range of shrubbery', *La Souriciere* combined sexual exploits with the topographical details commonly found in travel narratives.[124] Touchit firmly places sexual opportunities within the specific locale of Valenciennes:

> By *Saint George*, it was an odd adventure, and the devil must have been in the young creature, or she might have perceived [...] the *magnitude of the May-pole of love* [...] In my opinion it must have been a *painful pleasure* to her, and it was a trick I had never been played by an *English Mouse-trap*; but I have since been informed it is a *French fashion*. [...] I arose greatly refreshed;—joined the ladies at breakfast;—and took a hasty view of the City.—*Valenciennes* stands on the rivers *Scheld* and *Rouelle*, over which there are many bridges with houses upon them. It is built upon the ascent of a hill, in an oblong form, and on the North-West side, greatly resembles the South-West prospect of the *City of Oxford*.—This city is encompassed with a wall, strong ramparts and a formidable Citadel.[125]

Here, 'adventure' encompasses both geographical and sexual exploration. Sexual fantasy is conveyed by the '*painful pleasure*' of '*French fashion*', designed to stimulate the reader's imagination, within a landscape clearly constructed using concrete details and features in the style of eighteenth-century travel guides to mainland Europe, such as Thomas Nugent's *The Grand Tour* (1756) or Joseph Marshall's *Travels through Holland, Flanders, Germany, Denmark, Sweden [...] and Poland* (1772). The narrative correctly situates the city upon the '*Scheld*' and '*Rouelle*' rivers, but Touchit's description of the altitude of Valenciennes is not wholly accurate, suggesting a narrative written using a rudimentary map, instead of from memory. The conscientiously factual and painstakingly detailed account by Nugent places Valenciennes in a valley consisting wholly of a lowland region under constant threat of flooding.[126]

These inaccuracies question the potential of Touchit's account to direct the movements of travellers across a physical landscape, not simply a sexual one. This uncertainty surrounding the primary purpose of *La Souriciere* is amplified by the lack of critical consensus concerning the exact influence of travel guides upon the eighteenth-century tourist. Scott Rice asserts that 'guide-book information' existed as 'pocket tutors' for 'future tourists'; Jeremy Black has an alternative perspective:

> As it is by no means clear what travel literature if any tourists used or read, references generally being sparse or to the 'guide', it is difficult to assess what type they preferred and what effect, if any, it had.[127]

The difficulty of assessing the intended purpose of guides and their effect upon readerships is complicated by the multifarious content of these publications which often included 'reality and fiction, autobiography and narration, scientific and subjective data'. This hybridity (which contributed to the classification of Sterne's *Journey* under the heading of 'Miscellanies' by one London subscription library) can also partly account for the success of this genre. Eighteenth-century guides, encompassing varying degrees of fictional entertainment and factual instruction, engaged a wide reading public 'from the light-headed perusers of adventure stories to the meticulous collector of geographical books';[128] this engagement of diverse readerships, though, prevents definite conclusions on their purpose and audience.

Nonetheless, like Touchit's narrative, the other texts considered in this chapter also give valuable glimpses into the act of reading Sternean erotica across a span of time from the 1760s to the 1790s. With the ability to provoke moral outrage, these commodities also encouraged the sociable, communal enjoyment of sexually explicit print, albeit potentially between close, like-minded individuals. Just as Sterne actively encouraged bacchanalian sociability at Skelton, the erotic reinterpretation of his narratives also promoted sociable gatherings as his risqué literary style was commercially exploited to cater for club members in textual celebrations of storytelling, entertainment, and hospitality. Of course, outside of bacchanalian clubs, the consumption of prurient material by other readers did not always mean the enjoyment of it. Hall-Stevenson possessed an ability to shock and outrage contemporary morality; correspondents to the literary periodicals and daily newspapers portrayed his creative efforts as unspeakable obscenity, material unfit for polite consumption. As both a poet and a self-styled gentleman, he assaulted the boundaries of acceptability for the display and distribution of erotic verse. He was someone who challenged the restrictions of the code of politeness, a literary radical who tested the acceptability of sexually explicit material in print.

The confrontation caused by his style of poetry in *The Public Advertiser* provides one final insight into the admissibility of sexual content in open publication with no restrictions except availability and financial cost. On 5 September 1778, this newspaper created outrage through the publication of Hall-Stevenson's brand of inflammatory obscenity in verses entitled 'COUNTER EPISTLES from BRIGHT-HELMSTONE, NUMBER I'.[129] This episode centres upon a poem that can not be firmly attributed to Hall-Stevenson in the absence of other evidence, since the writer assumes the pseudonym of '*The Author of* CRAZY TALES' which is suggestive of his authorship but not conclusive proof. Without overlooking this possibility, the relevance of 'COUNTER EPISTLES' in this discussion of Sternean erotica is not solely dependent upon its potential as biographical material on this mimic. This piece, as well as the subsequent debate it generated, is also important for providing evidence of the contrasting Georgian attitudes to the writing and reading of erotica, whether Sternean or not. The incident involving 'Crazy Hall' identifies material in a London newspaper that caused offence and provides a useful conclusion to this chapter, through drawing together the antagonistic social values at the heart of erotic consumption in the 1770s.

Obscenity Made Public

This satire on Methodist worship at Brighthelmstone combined a contempt for religion with a love of lecherous fantasy, a combination which was earlier employed in a number of *Crazy Tales*, including 'My Cousin's Tale of a Cock and a Bull'.[130] 'COUNTER EPISTLES' satirized the meetings at the first chapel opened by Selina Hastings (Countess of Huntingdon) in 1761 within the grounds of her Brighton residence on the North Street; this flagship chapel was the first of more than sixty places of Methodist worship associated with Lady Huntingdon at her death in 1791. In this prurient poem, the prominent advocate of Methodism appears thinly disguised as the 'Countess of Grace' presiding over lascivious acts of worship involving 'Lady Bell S—' who cuckolds the jealous husband, 'Sir John'. This piece evoked the lurid rumours about Methodist love-feasts which titillated late eighteenth-century society. These scandals, concerning Methodist preachers sexually exploiting impressionable female members of the congregation, were not uncommon. Indeed, the founders of Methodism, John and Charles Wesley, gained disreputable reputations for inappropriate liaisons, both emotional and sexual: one contemporary in 1740 called the brothers 'dangerous snares to many young women'.[131] For such women, 'the fragile line between discipleship and amorousness' became indistinguishable when Methodist ministers presented sexual desire as 'evidence of sanctified love'. In the period that this poem appeared, the scandalous reputation of Lady Huntingdon's drawing room services 'attracted "scented beaus" hoping to see a young wench in a religious frenzy'.[132] As 'COUNTER EPISTLES' associates an erotic fantasy of sexual conquest with such sites of worship, this piece may have further increased male curiosity and attendance at Methodist chapels immediately after its publication. There was also a dangerous potential for libel through the presentation of the Brighthelmstone chapel as a site of lascivious voyeurism and enjoyment for the man about town.

The poet presents Methodist devotion as inseparable from the satisfaction of sexual desire as the moral laxity of this sect panders to the debauched and abandoned. After directly addressing an imaginary reader as 'DEAR SIR', the poet invites this male reader to engage with the following fantasy:

> First, then, observe those Ladies who church love,
> Are mighty demure, and are fond of a grove—
> And as it would happen, one night in the dark,
> Lady Bell from her church was o'erta'en by her spark.
> Alas, what a tale! oh wond'rous to tell you,
> For a *toil* it was that charm'd Lady Belly!
> And who is to blame, when from church, if they can,
> They'll chear their thrill'd souls by the help of a man.
> [...]
> But without a derision, sans shame I may say it,
> Tho' sweet the repast, Lady Bell must betray it.
> Thus food for the soul, when sought with devotion,
> And mix'd with precision with animal lotion,
> Will answer two *ends*, if the *facts* we don't smother,
> 'Twill serve god on one hand, and man on t'other.
> [...]
> Come do, do pray now, my bless'd Lady Belly;
> No person can know it—here, down in this field;
> So there I must leave them—you guess what 'twill yield.

Crazy Tales attempts to titillate his newspaper readership through the presentation of sexual acts as hidden and secretive, typical of the depiction of bodies and desire 'through illusions of concealment and distance' in the genre of Georgian erotica.[133] This account departs once from arch-innuendo for a moment of vivid imagery. While describing her physical and sexual '*toil*', he claims that the 'food for the soul [...] sought with devotion' is 'mix'd with precision with animal lotion', a reference to Methodist worship that also slyly evokes the fluidity of intercourse. In a final allusion to her sexual career, he satirizes the field preaching of Methodism, pointing to the potential of obscure, rural locations for encouraging immoral behaviour.

The *Advertiser* gave this text a huge readership in a period when the estimated sales of this newspaper fluctuated between 3000 and 4500. In addition, newspaper reading was 'a form of communal activity which could extend far beyond the limits of the literate, or indeed, the purchasers of newspapers'.[134] The presentation of erotic material in the *Advertiser*, enjoyed at street corners, taverns, coffee houses, and polite tea tables, clearly challenges the modern critical perception of erotica as material enjoyed secretly in the century. The communal consumption of 'COUNTER EPISTLES' was implied by one writer to the *Advertiser* who described his 'daily Custom' of allowing his 'eldest Son' to read 'aloud your Paper of that Day, for the Benefit of the Company then present'.[135] It is interesting to speculate what reactions, possibly including shock, embarrassment, stifled laughter, or lascivious enjoyment, were provoked at the family's breakfast table. Unsurprisingly, the publication provoked outrage. One reader, under the pseudonym of 'A DETESTER *of ill-natur'd* SATIRE', stirred a protracted dispute on the pages of the *Advertiser* between the poet of the offending piece and the offended reader.[136]

The poet had to defend himself against the charges of creating 'Trash', 'obscene Writing' and 'a loose and filthy Poem'. The printer and proprietor Henry Sampson Woodfall immediately apologized in the edition containing the first complaint, distanced himself from this erotic satire, and admitted the 'Justice' of these criticisms of verses 'inserted through Mistake'. Woodfall now decided that such erotic poetry was unacceptable content for newspaper circulation and a dangerous challenge to the social boundary between the newsworthy and the salacious. Given the potential for libel, it is not surprising that Woodfall adopted this position. In the period, 'libel' did not simply signify the modern-day meaning of a defamatory publication against a specific individual through writing or pictures. Eighteenth-century publishers could also be painfully aware of the alternative offence involving the production of an obscene, blasphemous, or seditious publication capable of threatening the morality of society as a whole. Woodfall, who famously announced that 'he had been *fined* by the House of Lords; *confined* by the House of Commons; *fined and confined* by the court of the king's bench and indicted at the Old Bailey', should have been very conscious of this.[137] His potential adversary, the Countess, was an infamously fearsome opponent whose displeasure could be 'dignified but terrifying'. Modern biographers have emphasized her capacity to assume an autocratic attitude that included a sour, domineering, and formidable personality prone to violent outbursts of anger.[138] Yet, the attack in the *Advertiser* was not conspicuously unusual or remarkable in a climate of anti-Methodist feeling. As Boyd Stanley Schlenther has argued, 'with her increasingly exuberant and public activities during the 1760s and '70s, it was hardly to be expected that she could avoid the full virulence of flowing satirical pens'.[139]

The critical backlash against 'COUNTER EPISTLES' was deeply concerned with the potential for libel (in both interpretations of the term), even if recognizable legal terminology was not used in the consequent debate. The first letter addressed to Crazy Tales claimed that 'it is possible [Lady Bell S—] may be a fictitious Character; and if so, some other of the Sex may be vilified whose initial Letters of her Name agree with the Writer's Description'. But the poem was not blatantly topical: when Crazy Tales began by asking 'DEAR Sir, have you heard of the Countess of Grace, / Who built a new methodist-house at this place?' he was referring to events from seventeen years earlier. The inclusion of at least one recognizable contemporary within a specific location could nevertheless signal his enjoyment of a recent aristocratic scandal that is now forgotten. His choice of aliases for the protagonists both safely obscured and recklessly offered the possibility of the detection of real people. Consequently, his defensive point, 'If there were any Satyr in my Lines, it was general' and 'intended originally only to raise an innocent Laugh', seems disingenuous.

The literary promiscuity caused, according to the Detester, by the poet's 'Vanity to appear in Print' contrasts with the clandestine anonymity prized by both correspondents. Paradoxically, in this debate, both writers engaged in a public contest while retaining secret identities; this strategy was reminiscent of, and publicized, Hall-Stevenson's partial concealment upon the pages of *Crazy Tales* years earlier. The unwillingness of the Detester to identify himself caused the poet to complain that such an unnamed and unidentifiable adversary enjoyed 'throw[ing] Dirt in the Dark' during an 'Attack in Ambush'. The desire of the poet to conclude the dispute as a private affair, through requesting the Detester to leave his name and address at the printing house, demonstrates the danger of self-identification in such an open quarrel on this controversial subject.

Hannah Barker, on the political contributions by eighteenth-century newspaper readers, claimed that anonymity 'allowed for the contribution of those either so lowly they ought not to presume to rise, or so high that they should not have sunk, to involve themselves in public debate'.[140] If we assume that Crazy Tales was Hall-Stevenson, a land-owning gentleman courting moral and social infamy, his pseudonym did not aim at a protective blanket anonymity. His recognizable literary alias, '*The Author of* CRAZY TALES', existed as an act of esoteric self-display in the select network of his friendships. He was known as 'Crazy Hall' in the 1760s to both close and slight associates; this was recorded by Boswell, whose slight acquaintance with him did not involve membership to the social intimacy of the bacchanalian clubs at Skelton and Medmenham Abbey.

Eventually, the confrontation in the *Advertiser* developed into a smear campaign over social status. The poet's response to the accusation of 'a shameful Display of Poetry' was to assert his right to the title of 'gentleman' and imply his social superiority over the Detester. He commented that:

> If the Writer [...] be a *Gentleman*, he will, after what I have already said to him, either send his Name and Address to your House, or cease to dedicate any other Sentiment on my Lines to your Paper.

He asked for informers among the readership and promised to pay him 'a personal Visit' if 'informed where at Chelsea or elsewhere to apply to the *Detester of ill-natur'd Satyr*'. For the increasingly self-conscious erotic poet, the public self-display involved in conducting a personal quarrel in a newspaper was inappropriate conduct for a 'gentleman' accustomed to settling disputes in discreet one-to-one privacy. Only when the Detester nervously pleads to 'leave the Field of Paper War intirely open to the Author of *Crazy Tales*' can his combative opponent charitably admit 'I think from his Manner of Writing he is the Gentleman' while also reasserting 'I have so much of the Gentleman in me'. The need to reclaim the status of a 'gentleman' indicates that the Detester's reaction had the potential to endanger the poet's self-conscious assumption of that title. While occupying a position of partial disguise and concealment, the poet failed to admit explicitly that a gentleman who was also a writer of newspaper erotica could exist as a contradiction in the late 1770s, a period when the proponents of politeness expressed support for sexual self-restraint and personal modesty as two qualities of a gentleman. These efforts to civilize male manners led to 'the decline (but not disappearance) of violence', according to Robert Shoemaker, as well as 'a new concern with inner virtue' from the mid-century onwards.[141] The Detester's unwillingness to confront the poet in person was possibly an assertion of polite masculinity based upon personal self-control.

The debate displays the clash of two cultural trends in the development of masculinity towards the end of the century. Within one trend, 'high libertinism's trickledown effect' involved the promotion and exploitation of 'self-aware sexual freedom' for 'new commercial purposes within the sphere of print'.[142] Hall-Stevenson's rakish, sexually explicit verse, reminiscent of the celebration of promiscuity by elite masculinity in the seventeenth century, was commercially exploited in this period to entertain readerships, as Holland was well aware. In contrast, literary libertinism was opposed by voices championing forms of masculinity based upon the ethics of polite self-restraint, ethics that condemned displays of sexuality and promoted self-control, both emotional and sexual. In this conflict, polite periodicals continued to exert moral pressure against the authorship and consumption of risqué material. *The Monthly Review*, which had condemned Hall-Stevenson's verse, maintained their moral position through the denouncement of 'indecent' print in 1773. One reviewer claimed: 'no man should write a novel, or any book of entertainment, which a gentleman cannot read aloud to a company of ladies'.[143] Their criticisms attacked illicit, clandestine publications consumed by men, but never publicly read aloud by polite gentlemen in mixed company. In response to the moral threat posed by the pleasures of erotica, the *Review* sought to regulate the private reading habits of its subscribers. Like the writers of this periodical, one admirer of Sterne in the 1780s sought to create a publication that could be read aloud in mixed company. Like the *Review*, Combe sought to educate his readers; to achieve this, he used the unlikely source of Sterne's epistles.

Notes to Chapter 4

1. Quotation on the emergence of this genre from Peakman, *Mighty Lewd Books*, p. 166.
2. *The World and Fashionable Advertiser*, 20 March 1787.
3. Harvey, p. 3.
4. Gillray's image, while offering titillation, also existed as another advertisement for Holland's business. At this sale of English courtesans at Madras, where exotic buyers examine their breasts and legs, the auctioneer is stood on a box of birch-rods while beside a box of books containing *Female Flagellants* and *Madame Birchini's Dance*. For a discussion of Gillray's image see, for example, Peakman, *Mighty Lewd Books*, pp. 12–14; and Gatrell, *City of Laughter*, pp. 333–34.
5. Quotation from Berg and Clifford, p. 146.
6. Two images from the 1771 [1785?] edition of *The Life and Opinions of Tristram Shandy* are reproduced in Peakman, *Mighty Lewd Books*, p. 120. Gerard, p. 182 gives 1785 as the real date of publication which would provide chronological proximity to Holland's advertisement.
7. Quotation from Baines and Rogers, p. 291. This tradition linking sexual and geographical exploration is discussed in Peakman, *Mighty Lewd Books*, pp. 93–125, who lists Roger Pheuquewell, *A New Description of Merryland* (London: J. Leake and E. Curll, 1741) and *Merryland Displayed; or, Plagiarism, Ignorance, and Impudence* (London: E. Curll, 1741).
8. Largier, p. 22.
9. On 'the display of blood' as an 'essential ingredient' in flagellation literature, see Peakman, *Mighty Lewd Books*, pp. 177–78.
10. In *A Sentimental Journey*, p. 124 Sterne asks 'If nature has so wove her web of kindness, that some threads of love and desire are entangled with the piece—must the whole web be rent in drawing them out?—Whip me such stoics, great governor of nature! said I to myself'.
11. Peakman, *Mighty Lewd Books*, p. 182 quotes one illustrative passage from the *Exhibition of Female Flagellants*: 'Flirtilla, who was about to be spanked by Lady Caroline, "idolized Lady Caroline's hand and arm, could not bear to see it hold the rod without the ornaments of pearls"'.
12. Peakman discusses the significance of gloves in *Mighty Lewd Books*, pp. 182–83.
13. Sterne, *A Sentimental Journey*, pp. 20, 25, 71, 74, and 121–22.

14. On the dates of flagellation literature, see Peakman, *Mighty Lewd Books*, pp. 161–86; and Peakman, *Lascivious Bodies*, pp. 236–54.
15. Discussion of Rowlandson's 1788 print from Gatrell, *City of Laughter*, p. 445. This print, reproduced by Gatrell, adopted the title of Mackenzie's 1771 novel, *The Man of Feeling*.
16. Gerard's appendix (pp. 199, 213) notes that Rowlandson's illustrations graced Tegg's 1809 edition of *A Sentimental Journey* and his 1809 edition of *The Beauties of Sterne*.
17. To give only one example, the unpaginated appendix to Cash's *Laurence Sterne: The Early and Middle Years* prints Patch's caricature (plate VII), an image frequently reproduced in studies of Sterne. Although Patch is often cited as an influence upon Rowlandson's early work — as in Hayes, p. 31 — I am not claiming that Patch's portrait influenced Rowlandson's image. Nevertheless, the similarities between the two faces potentially adds extra significance to *A Man of Feeling* for Sterneans.
18. On Aretino, see Peakman, *Mighty Lewd Books*, p. 15; and Kearney, pp. 24–26.
19. *Boswell: Laird of Auchinleck*, p. 76. As Cash acknowledges in *Laurence Sterne: The Later Years*, p. 92 this meeting between Cleland and Sterne can not be dated precisely.
20. Advertisements from Peacock and Holland's establishment at No. 66, Drury Lane can be found in the following newspapers: *The Morning Herald and Daily Advertiser*, 4 February 1785, 11 October 1786, 8 December 1786; *The Gazetteer and New Daily Advertiser*, 15 June 1785; *The World and Fashionable Advertiser*, 7 February 1787, 20 March 1787, 4 November 1788; and *Stuart's Star and Evening Advertiser*, 27 February 1789.
21. *Yorick's Sentimental Journey Continued*, British Library catalogue number C.123.fff.7.
22. Information taken from Bosch, pp. 286–93 and Watts, p. 245 with the addition of two other titles: *Continuation of Yorick's Sentimental Journey* (1788) and *A Sentimental Journey: Intended as a Sequel to Mr. Sterne's through Italy, Switzerland, and France. By Mr. Shandy* (1793).
23. Three electronic databases (ESTC, ECCO, and the British Library catalogue) give evidence of *Crazy Tales* appearing in the following years: 1762, 1764, 1769, 1780, 1783, 1785, and 1795. *Yorick's Sentimental Journey Continued* appeared in the following years: 1769, 1774, 1782, 1784, 1790, 1791, 1792, 1794, 1795, and 1796.
24. *Miss C--Y's Cabinet of Curiosities*, p. 15.
25. *The Monthly Review*, 26 (June 1762), p. 453.
26. *Miss C--Y's Cabinet of Curiosities*, p. 29. Biographical details on Ann Catley in Highfill et al., III: pp. 107–15 roughly correspond with the information for 'Miss C--Y'. The differences between the two accounts can be explained by Highfill et al., the editors of the *Biographical Dictionary*, p. 107: 'Ann Catley became, even during her lifetime, the subject of numerous memoirs which must be approached with caution because of their mixture of fact and fiction. Even the more dependable ones [...] sometimes err gravely'.
27. Cleland, 1999 edn, p. xxii.
28. See, in order of their appearance in this chapter, *The Critical Review*, 14 (June 1795), p. 238; *The Monthly Review*, 16 (January 1795), p. 119; *The Critical Review*, 27 (May 1769), p. 390; *The Gentleman's Magazine*, 39 (August 1769), p. 398; *The Monthly Review*, 26 (June 1762), p. 454; and *The Critical Review*, 13 (June 1762), p. 480.
29. Ferguson, p. 7.
30. Ibid., p. 8.
31. *The Gentleman's Magazine*, 39 (August 1769), p. 398; and 39 (July 1769), p. 366.
32. See, for example, *Derby Mercury*, 22 April 1874, p. 7; and *The Western Mail*, 14 April 1874, p. 6.
33. Ross, pp. 117, 376–77. The main source for Ross's claims about Sterne is Kuist.
34. For two examples of the moral criticism of Sterne's fiction in the late eighteenth century, see Foster's *The Boarding School; or, Lessons of a Preceptress to Her Pupils* (1798) and Bates's *A Chinese Fragment* (1786), both in Howes, *Sterne: The Critical Heritage*, p. 279.
35. See *The Monthly Review*, 40 (May 1769), p. 428; and *The Gentleman's Magazine*, 39 (August 1769), p. 398.
36. *The London Magazine*, 38 (June 1769), p. 323; *The Gentleman's Magazine*, 39 (August 1769), p. 398.
37. Compare *The Monthly Review*, 40 (May 1769), p. 428 and *The Gentleman's Magazine*, 39 (August 1769), p. 398 with the preface of *Yorick's Sentimental Journey Continued*, III: p. iii.

38. The first edition of *Yorick's Sentimental Journey Continued* (London: S. Bladon, 1769) was published as volumes three and four of Sterne's complete travelogue. I follow these volume numbers in subsequent references.
39. *The Gentleman's Magazine*, 39 (August 1769), p. 398.
40. *The London Magazine*, 38 (June 1769), p. 323.
41. Curley, p. 38.
42. *Catalogue of the London and Westminster Circulating Library*, p. 78.
43. Hall-Stevenson's authorship of *Yorick's Sentimental Journey Continued* had been widely accepted until two late twentieth-century accounts attempted to discredit this authorship using scant evidence. Lodwick Hartley's bid to disclaim Hall-Stevenson's accountability has subsequently been faithfully accepted by later biographers. See Hartley's '*Yorick's Sentimental Journey Continued*: A Reconsideration of the Authorship' and the acceptance of his claims by Cash in *Laurence Sterne: The Later Years*, p. 331, and Turner, p. 101.
44. Quotation from Cash, *Laurence Sterne: The Early and Middle Years*, p. 53. Also see Cash, *Laurence Sterne: The Later Years*, pp. 47, 216; and Ross, p. 42.
45. Quotation from Cash, *Laurence Sterne: The Later Years*, p. 47.
46. Robson, p. 357.
47. *The Grand Magazine*, 3 (April 1760), p. 195.
48. Quotations on the generic conventions of erotica from Pease, p. 7 and Peakman, *Mighty Lewd Books*, p. 126.
49. Peakman, *Mighty Lewd Books*, pp. 158–59. A famous and infamous example of the erotic employment of the peephole motif can be found in Cleland, p. 157.
50. *Yorick's Sentimental Journey Continued*, IV: pp. 52–53.
51. Sterne, *A Sentimental Journey*, p. 141.
52. K. F. Thompson, p. 319.
53. *Yorick's Sentimental Journey Continued*, III: p. 76.
54. Ibid., III: p. 78.
55. Goulemot, p. 72.
56. Cash, 'Sterne, Hall-Stevenson, Libertinism and *A Sentimental Journey*', p. 302.
57. Sterne, *A Sentimental Journey*, pp. 87, 121–22.
58. Werner, p. 25.
59. *Yorick's Sentimental Journey Continued*, III: pp. 4–6.
60. *The Monthly Review*, 40 (May 1769), p. 428.
61. Sterne, *A Sentimental Journey*, p. 27.
62. See Mackenzie, pp. 109–33.
63. *Yorick's Sentimental Journey Continued*, III: pp. 141–42.
64. The fictive pseudonym of 'Timothy Touchit' upon the title page existed as a guarantee of the erotic quality of the publication and immediately signalled the intentions of the text to the prospective purchaser.
65. *La Souriciere*, II: pp. 89–90. Throughout the publication, such euphemisms are italicized to highlight and signpost the sexual content of the narrative and aid apprehension.
66. Sterne, *Tristram Shandy*, p. 86.
67. Harvey, p. 23.
68. *La Souriciere*, II: pp. 5–6.
69. *La Souriciere*, II: p. 43; and Sterne, *Tristram Shandy*, pp. 640–41.
70. Quotation from Harvey, p. 126.
71. Brant, p. 100 repeats the anecdote about Sterne's heart as fact.
72. Mullan, p. 152.
73. *The Diary of Samuel Pepys*, vol. IX: *1668–69*, p. 59.
74. Goulemot, p. 80.
75. Hitchcock, p. 17.
76. *Caricature Shop* is reproduced in Gatrell, p. 211.
77. Harvey, p. 75.
78. For descriptions of Hall-Stevenson's 'Demoniacs', see Cash, *Laurence Sterne: The Early and Middle Years*, pp. 184–95 and *Laurence Sterne: The Later Years*, pp. 45, 99; and also Ross, pp. 104–05.

79. Hall-Stevenson, *Crazy Tales*, pp. 16–29.
80. Peakman, *Mighty Lewd Books*, pp. 126–60.
81. Hall-Stevenson, *Crazy Tales*, p. 105.
82. Ibid., pp. 107–08.
83. The phrase 'Laugh-at-able' is from Sterne's description of *Tristram Shandy* in a letter '*To Robert Dodsley*' dated 23 May 1759, which can be found in Sterne, *The Letters, Part 1*, p. 80.
84. Hall-Stevenson, *Crazy Tales*, p. 7. The phrase 'to take in all Kinds of Readers' is from Sterne's letter '*To Thomas Becket*' dated 3 September 1767 which can be found in *The Letters, Part 2*, p. 616.
85. Hall-Stevenson, *Crazy Tales*, p. 9.
86. 'Miss in Her Teens: Captain Shadow's Tale' appears in *Crazy Tales*, pp. 30–36. Quotation from p. 30.
87. Moulton, p. 37.
88. Ibid., p. 38.
89. For further details, see Cash, *Laurence Sterne: The Early and Middle Years*, p. 182.
90. Sterne, *The Letters, Part 1*, p. 286.
91. Hall-Stevenson, *Crazy Tales*, p. 19.
92. P. Clark, pp. 262, 227.
93. Hall-Stevenson, *Crazy Tales*, p. 4.
94. Peakman, *Mighty Lewd Books*, pp. 28–29.
95. Raven, Small, and Tadmor, p. 12.
96. Peakman, *Mighty Lewd Books*, p. 32. She also raises the speculative possibility that Sterne 'might have been a visitor to Dashwood's gatherings' (p. 119).
97. McCormick, p. 25.
98. Largely speculative accounts of Dashwood's mysterious 'Hell-Fire Club' can be found in Geoffrey Ashe's sensational *The Hell-Fire Clubs* (2000); Daniel P. Mannix's *The Hell-Fire Club* (1962); and Louis C. Jones's conservative *Clubs of the Georgian Rakes* (1942).
99. Cash, 'Sterne, Hall-Stevenson, Libertinism and *A Sentimental Journey*', p. 299.
100. It is impossible to write with any confidence on the possible content of Hall-Stevenson's personal library at Skelton. Before attempts to document his library, 'the wind was whistling through the broken windows and swinging doors of derelict Skelton Castle, and Hall-Stevenson's books had been dispersed' (Cash, *Laurence Sterne: The Early and Middle Years*, pp. 194–95).
101. Ross, p. 251.
102. Kearney, p. 9.
103. Cash, *Laurence Sterne: The Early and Middle Years*, p. 278. Here, 'Dodsley' refers to Robert who handed the business to his brother James on retirement in 1759. The first London edition of volumes one to four of *Tristram Shandy* was published by 'R. and J. Dodsley'.
104. Solomon, p. 256.
105. Genette, *Paratexts*, p. 17.
106. *The Monthly Review*, 26 (June 1762), p. 454.
107. Bosch, pp. 102, 106.
108. Quotation from Peakman, *Mighty Lewd Books*, pp. 32–33.
109. The discovery of Rowlandson's *Cunnyseurs*, and its relationship to *Connoisseurs*, is made by Mudge, pp. 236–37.
110. *La Souriciere*, I: p. vi.
111. Ibid., I: p. 73.
112. Ibid., I: p. 3.
113. Ibid., II: p. 87.
114. Ibid., I: pp. 39, 45; and II: p. 45.
115. An advertisement for this edition of *Crazy Tales* appeared in the folio edition of Hall-Stevenson's *Moral Tales: A Christmas Night's Entertainment. By Lady* ******* (London: T. Becket, 1783). Also see *The Life and Opinions of Tristram Shandy, Gentleman* (Amsterdam [London?]: P. van Slaukenberg, 1771 [1785?]). It is worth noting that, despite this trend towards smaller formats for Sternean erotica, Hall-Stevenson's erotic publications were always published first in the folio format, perhaps indicating his control over the initial appearance of his work, and his intention that his poetry should be showcased within a lavish first edition. See, for example,

Two Lyric Epistles (1760), *Crazy Tales* (1762) which was subsequently reprinted in the octavo and duodecimo formats, and *Moral Tales* (1783).

116. Raven, p. 52.
117. Of course, there is no relationship between this publication and the manager of Covent Garden theatre, Thomas Harris. For an account of the creation of *Harris's List*, see Rubenhold.
118. Rubenhold, pp. 131, 306, and 315. Despite estimated sales of 8000 copies annually, Rubenhold, p. 315 acknowledges that 'only volumes from nine years (1761, 1764, 1773, 1774, 1779, 1788, 1789, 1790, 1793) have evaded the wear and the censure of time to be retained in public collections', all in the duodecimo format.
119. Ibid., p. 133.
120. Analysis of Sterne's narrative from K. E. Smith, pp. 20–21.
121. Black, *The British Abroad*, p. 189.
122. Ibid., p. 56.
123. For the standard eighteenth-century post routes through the Netherlands, see Nugent, I: pp. 235, 249, 274. He claims that Namur is only 'thirty-five [miles] south-east of *Brussels*' (I: p. 310).
124. In one erotic anecdote, Yorick gives very precise directions: 'On the left-hand walk from the Louvre is a range of shrubbery, that runs parallel to the wall, at about six feet distance, and which in summer, when the leaves are fully expanded, forms a kind of retreat; behind which, obscenities of any species may be committed, unobserved by the company in the Gardens. In winter and spring, everything performed behind this shrubbery is as much exposed as if done in any other part of the Thuilleries' (*Yorick's Sentimental Journey Continued*, IV: pp. 72–73).
125. *La Souriciere*, II: pp. 43–46.
126. Nugent, I: p. 240.
127. Rice, p. 211, and Black, 'Tourism and Cultural Challenge', p. 198.
128. Ogée, p. 35.
129. This poem was first published in *The Morning Chronicle and London Advertiser* on the previous day, 4 September 1778.
130. Hall-Stevenson, *Crazy Tales*, pp. 16–29.
131. Schlenther, p. 136.
132. Quotations from Schlenther, pp. 134, 140, 137.
133. Harvey, p. 20.
134. Barker, pp. 29–31. For sales figures, see D'Archenholz, p. 42.
135. *The Public Advertiser*, 14 September 1778.
136. After *The Public Advertiser* published 'Counter Epistles from Bright-Helmstone' on 5 September 1778, correspondence relating to this piece appeared on the following dates: 10 September, 14 September, 19 September, 2 October, 9 October, and 16 October 1778.
137. Nichols, I: p. 301.
138. Langford, p. 275.
139. Schlenther, p. 120.
140. Barker, p. 38.
141. Shoemaker, 'Reforming Male Manners', p. 149. On the relationship between the assertion of masculinity and violence, including the decline of the latter as the eighteenth century progressed, also see Foyster, pp. 151–66.
142. Cryle and O'Connell, p. 6.
143. *The Monthly Review*, 48 (February 1773), p. 129.

CHAPTER 5

William Combe, Esq., Sterne's 'Dear Boy'

As a man of means in the early 1760s, Combe was eager to gain access to Hall-Stevenson's bacchanalian group. In a letter dated 13 November 1764, Sterne told Hall-Stevenson about a message from 'C—' who was 'ambitious of being better acquainted with you; and longs from his soul for a sight of you in your own castle'.[1] At this time, Combe was unfamiliar with the novelist's network of friendships at Skelton; he had, after all, only become acquainted with Sterne earlier in the year while at Paris.[2] An embarrassed Sterne felt the need to apologize to Hall-Stevenson for introducing this interloper: 'I cannot do otherwise, than bring him with me—nor can I gallop away and leave him an empty house [...] as he comes half express to see me'.[3] Later in life, Combe would nostalgically recall Skelton through committing to paper Sterne's declaration, 'I love you, and *Hall* says you are a lad of promise', to celebrate and possibly exaggerate his past relationship with 'the Lord of *Crazy*'.[4]

Combe's enjoyment of their company was the result of a vast change in his fortunes. He was able to escape, for a time, his modest merchant background after the inheritance of an estimated £2500 from his father's estate in 1763 and an additional £2000 from his guardian's estate in 1766.[5] Through this new-found wealth, the obscure ironmonger's son financed an eye-catching lifestyle of aristocratic impersonation within the elite circles of Georgian society. According to Harlan Hamilton, Combe 'lived in a most princely style' and 'kept two carriages, several horses, and a large retinue of servants' which earned him the 'appellation of "Count Combe"'.[6] The exhaustion of his funds led to his humiliating separation from London society as he 'scrambled for a bare living' in France, then the West Midlands, and Wales from 1769 to 1773.[7] Eventually, he suffered the inevitable fate of confinement in the King's Bench prison for debt throughout the summer of 1786.[8] His fall from grace was so complete that when he died in 1823, *The Sun* newspaper presented his life as a morality tale: 'The Life of Mr. Coombe, if impartially written, would be pregnant' with 'instruction'.[9]

Combe's social downfall provides the key to understanding his production of thirty-nine epistles purporting to be the *Original Letters of the Late Reverend Mr. Laurence Sterne* (1788). In this publication, he attempted to rescue his own reputation and Sterne's character at the same time. Combe is not a disreputable bankrupt, but a 'dear boy', the intimate friend of a Sterne who is complaisant and sentimental rather than the scurrilous and licentious figure he had become in the press. This refashioning of Sterne was self-serving: as a result of this flattering portrayal, Combe could gain credit from his past association. As part of the public rehabilitation of the novelist to create an appropriate tutor for the younger man, Sterne's epistolary reflections address negative aspects of his posthumous personal reputation. His admiration of Archbishop Richard Sterne (?1596–1683), for example, refashions the author into a modest, spiritual character who implies that accusations of immorality have a questionable basis: 'I have not half his virtues, if report speaks true of us both, which, for his sake, I hope it does—and for my own, I hope it does not'.[10] In another instance dated 9 September 1765, Sterne expresses anxiety concerning the care of his family after a problem involving the transfer of funds to them in France; his commentary, full of good intentions, provides an apologetic gloss upon subsequent events, namely the notorious financial embarrassments of his widow and daughter caused by the death of the spendthrift author.[11] Within this associational world, even Hall-Stevenson's character is rescued to reflect positively upon Combe. As if to oppose the infamous image of the poet constructed by the periodical reviewers, Sterne describes Hall-Stevenson as a man of 'great humanity' who 'feels' sentimental subjects. Instead of criticizing him for a thoughtless lack of morality and decency in his poetry, Sterne declares, 'Nay, I am acquainted with several, who cannot be persuaded but that he is a very insensible, hard-hearted man, which I, who have known him long, and known him well, assure you he is not'.[12]

Lewis Perry Curtis rejected all but three of these letters as forgeries, a position adjusted by the editors of the 2009 Florida edition of the *Letters*, Melvyn New and Peter de Voogd, who increased the amount of Combe's text judged to be authentic and accepted 'small portions' of three other epistles.[13] Curtis approached the *Original Letters* as 'overpaintings' created by Combe, who 'split up a letter or two in his possession and by copious additions eked out a profitable series'. These elaborations 'are marked', according to the Florida editors, '(and identifiable) by his lavish use of passages from Sterne's published writings'.[14] Many of Combe's letters have been identified using the concept of 'forgery', but this term has not been used to explain his purpose; in this respect, forgery as a criminal act offers an interesting analogy. To gain financial credit and secure a loan, forged bonds appropriated the identity of a third party to underwrite or guarantee the trustworthy character, social connections, and solvency of the bearer. Such bonds 'involved no immediate transfer of funds; rather it aided efforts to secure a loan [...] With the right name on it, and presented by a creditworthy person, it offered access to vast sums of money'.[15] While reaping the financial rewards of publication, Combe similarly appropriated Sterne's name to persuade the reader of his virtuous character and his social credibility as a well-connected figure. Just as eighteenth-century trials attempted to unmask the corrupt 'social ambitions' and aspirations of the forger, this chapter applies the term forgery to highlight Combe's evasion of the blacksmith's hearth and the manual labour of the smithy.[16]

As a literary forger, Combe was a repeat offender: in 1775, he had produced *Sterne's Letters to His Friends on Various Occasions*.[17] Eight of these twelve letters are regarded as inventions, with the remaining four included, with editorial changes, in the Florida edition.[18] Every letter provides a different perspective upon Sterne's personality, but each collection by Combe as a whole creates a different emphasis with regard to Sterne's relationship to the ideal of politeness. In 1775, Sterne freely expresses his rakishly impolite impulses; in 1788, he is a sentimental hero who cultivates polite correspondence and provides moral guidance. Aside from two brief sections where sentimentality hints at sensuality, the remaining two hundred and twelve pages of the *Original Letters* maintain a polished epistolary address characterized by emotional calm, complaisance, and polite propriety.[19] These two collections also reveal Combe's attitude to these different Sternes, in terms of his willingness to associate, in print, with representations of the author's masculinity. The 1775 anthology lacks Combe's self-promotion as the author's intimate friend, a relationship that provides many of the situations in the *Original Letters*. Combe's self-display as the addressee in 1788 contrasts with his complete textual disassociation from the anonymous 1775 epistles with the forger's careful cultivation of self-image, through the selection of associates, clearly apparent. His aspirations were dependent upon the presentation of Sterne as fit company for the polite gentility which he hoped to attract through publication.

Consequently, this situation encourages an analysis of the *Original Letters* as both autobiography and Sternean biography, with Combe's self-portrayal achieved through the novelist's acts of addressing and apostrophizing. Although only four of these letters are explicitly addressed to 'W. C. Esq.', Combe encourages the reader to assume that other correspondence was sent to this recipient of the opening epistle. To reinforce this impression, until page 192 no other correspondent is identified except 'W. C. Esq., W. C—. Esq., W— C—, Esq.' and '— —, Esq.' combined with the use of a consistent tone and form of address. Moreover, phrases initially addressed to him reverberate within later epistles, keeping the original recipient at the forefront of the reader's mind.[20] In letters I to VI, Sterne desperately solicits the visit of 'W. C. Esq.' to Coxwold and expresses his intense desire for the appearance of 'my dear boy' and the resumption of closeness, an intimacy frustratingly delayed by Combe's injuries sustained upon the road.[21] In a period when the enjoyment of leisure partly defined social status, Combe's self-depiction as a figure preoccupied with social visits represented an escapist fantasy to bolster his claim to gentlemanly status:[22]

> I am safe arrived at my bower—and I trust that you have no longer any doubt about coming to embower it with me. Having, for six months together, been running at the ring of pleasure, you will find that repose here which, all young as you are, you ought to want. We will be witty, or classical, or sentimental, as it shall please you best.[23]

This passage combines polite complaisance, to 'please you best', with private intimacy and a retreat from worldly affairs.[24] It includes Sterne's willingness to modify his personality to suit Combe's mood and assist conversation, emphasizing an ability to be 'sentimental' at the expense of any potentially impolite attempt to be 'witty'. The closeness seems to be based upon mutual dependence. Combe provides friendship and creative inspiration (to the extent that Sterne complains 'If you don't come soon, I shall set about another volume of Tristram without you') and the famous author reciprocates with professions of intense attachment and the offer of guidance:[25]

> If you do not come soon to me, I shall take the wings of some fine morning and fly to you; but I should rather have you here; for I wish to have you alone;

and if you will let me be a *Mentor* to you for one little month, I will be content
—and you shall be a *Mentor* to me the rest of the year; or, if you will, the rest
of my days [...] I will be your surgeon, or your nurse; and warm your verjuice
every evening, and bathe your sprain with it.[26]

The language of friendship borders upon amatory infatuation and echoes the intensity of the sentimental lover. In the Restoration and early eighteenth century, 'literary men's letters to each other used the same figures of desire as they did to their mistresses' to communicate mutual esteem and admiration.[27] Combe's style, while being sentimental, also incorporates this formal mode of aristocratic address, a language discussed in Raymond Stephanson's analysis of familiar epistles between male friends in the decades before the *Original Letters*. For Stephanson, 'there existed a *public* discourse which encouraged (predominantly heterosexual men) to imagine their friendships with men in ways similar to their experience of affection for wives or female lovers'.[28] This type of address would have been apt for Combe, the socially ambitious figure who fondly remembered Hall-Stevenson's society, a society based upon aristocratic forms of sociability.

Combe also displayed his former relationships with aristocratic figures such as Baron Conyngham, Francis Pierpoint Burton (d. 1787), and Viscount John Spencer (1734–1783).[29] However, this attempt to maintain the title of 'Esq.', through the public celebration of connections, also forced Combe to acknowledge that authorial boasts undermined claims to gentlemanliness. The desire to conceal is evident in the partial and cryptic references to himself and to Thomas Scrope (1723–1792), a living aristocratic figure who is only referred to as 'S—' despite being represented as a close friend.[30] Prior to the publication of the *Original Letters*, the first appearance of this epistle about '*Scroop*' in *The Daily Universal Register* spelled out his name while omitting the reference to Combe.[31] This refusal to name both parties of a friendship at any one time could indicate Combe's genteel unwillingness to be identified by a former member of the Demoniacs. In contrast, Combe was willing to identify explicitly a number of former companions who only existed in the memory of the fashionable eighteenth-century world. Despite being named, the deceased figures of Burton, Spencer, Hall-Stevenson, and 'the late *Lord Mulgrave*' could not verify or expose his braggadocio.[32] Combe's cautious approach echoed the sentiment of one correspondent to *The Morning Herald and Daily Advertiser* who pointed out that 'gentlemen' of the 'highest good-breeding' expertly practised 'the art of politeness' which was dependent upon the careful 'concealment' of 'superiority, that he may not be painful' to 'unsuitable companions' or 'inferiors'.[33] This late eighteenth-century statement amplifies Carter's belief that polite gentlemen were expected to be unconcerned with competing.[34] For Combe, superiority was partly based upon the social standing of friends and associates as well as the ability to gain admission to select circles; his literary boast of past connections, which smacked of vanity and self-regard, threatened to explode his right to gentility.

The employment of a publication to elevate one's social standing was problematic in other ways. An association with the vulgar press was by and large avoided by genteel authors throughout the century who favoured anonymity.[35] As one writer in a 'paper war' with Combe commented, a gentleman of discretion and 'sensibility' in the 1770s would 'look upon it as a horrid thing' to find his name conspicuously 'stuck up' in a book advertisement 'at Charing Cross' for the perusal and entertainment of passing shoppers.[36] The financial necessity of publication for an impoverished Combe also potentially compromised his social aspirations and gentlemanly pretensions. Throughout his career, he 'wished to identify himself as a gentleman rather than as a professional writer who wrote for sordid cash considerations. That is why, though he never attached his name to a title page, he was not above printing it in the subscription lists of his own books'.[37]

Throughout 1777 and 1778, the anonymity of Combe's moralistic tracts addressed to Georgiana Cavendish (Duchess of Devonshire), provoked suspicions concerning his social standing.[38] His unsolicited advice in a mixed tone of reproach and deference, concerning the Duchess's lifestyle and 'her slavish devotion to fashion', encouraged one reply, *A Letter to Her Grace the Duchess of D. Answered Cursorily, by Democritus* (1777). This pamphlet interpreted Combe's anonymity as an indication of his social worthlessness and commercial opportunism, to the extent that his adversary made the following complaint:

> Your shape is so very questionable, that I can't tell how to introduce myself to you. I cannot pretend to examine you upon gentleman-like interrogatories, for fear I should be guilty of needless propriety.[39]

After rejecting Combe's pretensions, this writer portrays his opponent as a self-important social outcast whose desperation for an association with the 'ultra-fashionable' Georgiana has led to his presumptuous self-appointment as an adviser to the Devonshire House Circle.[40] Combe's comments are interpreted as the ramblings of a fantasist who longs for a friendship with the unapproachable leader of aristocratic society:

> But after all, sir, perhaps your letter may prove to have been addressed to a lady you never saw in your life---to one whose real character you never heard; and to one whose Merit, consequently, you can be no judge of [...] go to the *Haymarket* the first time the Duchess of D. goes to the Opera---observe her attentively---peruse her minutely.[41]

Combe's social self-importance would have been wounded by the view that his relationship would never develop beyond the admiration of distant spectatorship at the theatre. Such envious distress had the potential to be especially acute at a time when some of his former acquaintances, including Garrick, were part of the Duchess's social circle. His frustration, caused by the inability to re-enter fashionable circles, was betrayed by his criticism of the financial extravagance and excessive 'splendor' of her society. In his disparagement of 'the power of external appearance', that allows any man to 'bear the title of a Gentleman' who 'dresses well' with the 'tinsel of foppery', Combe championed character against the seductiveness of superficial dress.[42]

Despite implying that magnificent appearances had a powerful influence upon others, Combe's earlier relationship with Sterne acknowledged that acceptance within aristocratic society was dependent upon more than such personal splendour. While Combe took advantage of Sterne's familiarity with the elite to gain introductions to restricted circles at Skelton and elsewhere, Sterne's encouragement of their friendship allowed him to call upon the diplomatic skills of the socialite. Sterne, who was liable to cause offence while outrageously entertaining polite society, turned to Combe's tactfulness to avoid rejection as a *persona non grata* and effect reconciliations. Shaun Regan has suggested that Sterne's acceptance by the 'brilliant throng' was brittle and dependent upon the favours of his social superiors; as an amplification of this idea of Sterne's social vulnerability, Lichtenburg's diary entry for 25 February 1775 includes a revealing comment from the son of the first Baron Walsingham:[43]

> Mr. de Grey told me that Yorick was a very tiresome visitor. He would frequently wait on people at 9 o'clock in the morning and scarcely ever leave before 9 o'clock in the evening. When they went out he went with them and then came back with them. He was very poor.[44]

For de Grey, Sterne was 'very poor' and deficient, both financially and socially: he was a man whose poverty led him to impose upon and abuse people's hospitality, while being without the social grace to know when he had outstayed his welcome. He was an interloper who tenaciously monopolized the attentions of other people, someone who was tolerated rather than embraced as a witty companion. Sterne, as a figure from the past, was an easy target for malicious gossip, yet de Grey's condescending judgement on him powerfully depicts an author who was far from being welcomed and treated as a social equal everywhere in aristocratic society.

As with Sterne, Combe's presence was not assured by the superiority of birth, a factor emphasized by the playful mockery of the title of 'Count'. In spite of that, his ability to masquerade as nobility and his talent for acquiring advantageous friendships were beneficial to Sterne. In June 1765, Sterne called upon Combe's helpful influence to preserve the friendship and indulgence of mutual acquaintances. Sterne responded to a rumour, that he had 'ridiculed' Burton and his 'Irish friends at Bath for an hour together', by calling upon Combe's diplomacy, requesting him to communicate his esteem and respect to prevent any further antagonism. This request for help is a rare example of a genuine piece of correspondence in the *Original Letters*:[45]

> Read *Burton* this letter if you have an opportunity, and assure him of my most cordial esteem and respect for him and all his social excellencies: and whisper something kind and gentle for me, as you well know how, to my fair countrywomen; and let not an unmerited prejudice or displeasure against me remain any longer in their tender bosoms.—When you get into disgrace of any kind, be assured that I will do as much for you.[46]

Even when placing trust in Combe as his representative and peacemaker, Sterne was still concerned that his words should persuade Burton through the act of reading this letter. In a final attempt to control the meeting between the two men and solicit Combe's best efforts, the author emphasizes the idea of mutual dependency and promises 'When you get into disgrace of any kind, be assured that I will do as much for you'. Sterne's apology, presenting the novelist as a potentially impolite, yet apologetic figure, also conveys Combe's past involvement in representing the author. Over twenty years after the incident between Sterne and Burton, Combe again sought to influence the perception of Sterne's character, this time through an act of publication. Once again, as in the 1760s, the depiction of Sterne as a polite, moral figure was dependent upon the words of Combe, just as the perception of Combe as a suitable companion in elite circles was reliant upon the words of Sterne.

Throughout the *Original Letters*, Combe portrays the personal epistle as a form of character reference, a suitable vehicle to express the best qualities of an individual and 'a means of qualifying for polite society'.[47] In this spirit, Sterne describes the effectiveness of one of Combe's letters, presenting it as a text to be proudly read to stimulate conversation about the writer:

> I happened to have it ['your last letter'] in my pocket yesterday morning when I breakfasted with Mrs. M————; and, for want of something so good of my own, I read the whole of your letter to her [...] she desired to read it herself, and then she entreated me not to delay the earliest opportunity to present *you* to her breakfast-table, and the mistress of it to you [...] I really begin to think I shall get some credit by you.[48]

Like La Fleur's billet-doux in the *Journey*, the content of a letter is circulated to gain social favour.[49] Both Combe and Sterne gain 'credit' from the former's letter, giving the latter an opportunity to display his expert ability at reading an epistle aloud, 'an important and ingratiating social skill'.[50] This use of the term 'credit' equates the advantages of a pleasing character, as displayed by an epistle, with the benefits of wealth; this coupling of the financial and the personal is also present in 'commerce' in late eighteenth-century usage, a word encompassing both communication, as in the interchange of letters, and monetary exchange.

But, if Combe's aim was to gain recognition from an elite readership, the *Original Letters* would have solicited the wrong readers; just as he aspired to be a gentleman, his letters were aimed at an aspirational audience. The duodecimo size presented these letters as instruction for consumers with modest spending power, a collection, moreover, in a format not designed to guarantee the longevity of the author's claim to fame. As seen in Chapter Four, the pocketbook was not simply a portable commodity to be enjoyed in a variety of locations; it was also an ephemeral one. The sum required for binding, to extend the life of this publication, was disproportionate to the cost of the actual printed sheets. Without this financial layout, the paper binding of a duodecimo would have lasted only one or two readings.[51] In contrast to the slight expense of three shillings for the *Original Letters*, the standard trade price for binding these dimensions in the 1760s was seven shillings and six pence.[52] Of course, even eighteenth-century books purchased as bound commodities were perishable items and they 'may only have been sufficient to stand a few readings before the book would have to be discarded or rebound', though they were 'still most commonly advertised sewn in paper or boards at the end of the century'.[53] In one similarity with the daily newspapers which first reproduced many of Combe's epistles, the *Original Letters* was a commodity to be consumed and then discarded by a diverse audience including the financially inconsequential.[54]

Nonetheless, Combe's obituaries, printed by English newspapers both in London and the provinces, provide evidence that he successfully kept alive memories of his glittering past in the public consciousness. The day after his death, *The Times* asserted that he was a 'gentleman' who 'had become known' to 'so many people in every rank of society' which, while posthumously awarding Combe the title that he craved throughout his life, also euphemistically gestured towards the wildly vacillating fortunes of their former employee.[55] Fittingly, considering Combe's life, these memories of the author jostled for space with insolvency notices, advertisements for house auctions, and lists of bankrupts.[56] *The Leeds Mercury* and *The Newcastle Courant* also remembered Combe as 'well known in fashionable life' and, like the *Original Letters*, communicated his progression from socialite to author, especially his authorship of 'instructive works, and moral works' for readers who may 'derive instruction and delight from the inculcations of the moralist'.[57]

As implied by these provincial newspapers, Combe's relatively affordable publications exploited the popularity of conduct literature with socially ambitious readers. The explosion of interest in guides on the attainment of gentlemanliness through behaviour can be traced to the transformation of Chesterfield's 1774 letters into anthologies of accomplishments for a middle- and lower-class readership.[58] Handbooks on polite deportment, like the *Original Letters*, represented the cultivation of sociability and advantageous friendships as a way of achieving gentility. Accordingly, 'the qualifications and marks of a real gentleman [did] not consist in elegant mansions' or 'a numerous retinue of servile attendants'; instead, the fostering of 'all manner of good company' defined the bona-fide *'compleat gentleman'*.[59] Instructional literature, like *An Essay on Politeness [...] By a Young Gentleman* (1775) and *Pleasing Reflections on Life and Manners* (1788), was purely theoretical; Combe presented the principles of politeness in action within epistolary conversation between two friends.

Carter and Ellis have argued that the promise of gentlemanly status for all, along with the integration of all social classes through the adoption of modish refinement, was a commercial strategy. For Carter, the promise of acceptance by the elite existed as a widespread fantasy that generated a variety of educational and leisure commodities to exploit aspirational purchasers. Just as guides to politeness were attractive for this readership through the emphasis upon 'good character, not just on means', venues for sociability seductively promised the 'egalitarian mixing' of all ranks capable of a certain style of behaviour. The success of venues like Vauxhall and Ranelagh pleasure gardens depended upon their 'dual reputation for accessibility and exclusivity' involving both the welcoming and exclusion of socially unattractive figures.[60] Similarly, Ellis in *The Coffee-House: A Cultural History* proposes that the 'ideal of a polite coffee-house', involving accessibility, openness and indiscriminate social mixing, was a literary fabrication initially popularized by *The Spectator*. In his view, this notable venue of eighteenth-century sociability was 'stratified, with very different kinds of establishment serving very different social classes' as the coffee-house sociability of Queen Anne's reign became atomized into 'distinct and separate institutions for the leisured elite and the working class'.[61] Their historical perspectives undermine the fundamental idea of uninhibited sociability sold by Combe, with his literary ideal of class by association becoming authorial wishfulness offering glimpses into social surroundings inaccessible to the readership primarily solicited by the *Original Letters*. If so, the buyers who understood the references to Combe would have also identified a trailblazing, short-lived exception to the rule. Despite the scepticism of Carter and Ellis, Combe's career is evidence of his ability to befriend aristocrats, albeit only when in possession of financial resources, an ability that later fuelled his literary imagination. Whether or not his readers would be able to follow Combe's example, the idea that favourable relationships could be gained through the development of conversational skills was still attractive for these consumers.

Another appropriation of Sterne's literary fame, *Sterne's Witticisms; or, Yorick's Convivial Jester* (1782), solicited readers using exactly that sentiment. The title page promised 'pleasing' and 'smart Repartees' for 'The Amusement of Convivial Assemblies' and promoted this collection of jests as a conversational prop with material for purchasers who wished to gain the approval and esteem of polite mixed company. The help offered to inept conversationalists is further explained by another publication advertised within the *Witticisms* which promised 'HELPS for SHORT MEMORIES, Consisting of Maxims, Rules, proverbial Sayings', all 'selected from the best Authors'.[62] In contrast to Clark's proposal that the art of conversation in masculine eighteenth-century clubs was stifled by the studied rehearsal of material and advanced by 'spontaneity' and 'free-wheeling' exchanges, these anthologies advocated the contrived recital of 'the best authors' to guarantee social success.[63]

The frontispiece of this collection of anecdotes, concerning such diverse celebrity figures as Hogarth, Garrick, Foote, and Chesterfield, depicts Sterne in clerical dress surrounded by the adoration of a genteel crowd (see Fig. 5.1). The author commands their attention through 'reading jokes aloud from the very book the reader is holding' while 'the subscription "Yorick in Clover" suggests that buyers can enjoy similar social success if they purchase this book'.[64] Recalling Sterne's enjoyment of applause in the 1760s, it implied that the purchaser could impersonate the author's alter ego Yorick and appropriate Sterne's conversational wit. Both *Sterne's Witticisms* and the *Original Letters* followed a comparable method and purpose in their use of Sterne's literary legacy to achieve social self-promotion, for the reader and the author respectively. As a social outsider in the 1780s, Combe would have been part of the audience solicited by the *Witticisms*, an anthology including sketches of famous people and celebrity gossip for the modest cost of one shilling.

The frontispiece of the *Witticisms*, however, was aimed at a broader audience, also encompassing those readers interested in Sterne's risqué and ribald wit. Barbara Benedict's description of 'the adoring dog, the urn, the flask of wine, the natural setting, and the smiles of the audience', as an indication of a 'sentimental context', fails to notice the significance of Sterne's mischievous pose and expression as well as the mixed responses to his performance.[65] While the exercise of politeness was partly dependent upon the ability to engage with pleasing and inoffensive conversation which avoided subjects with the potential to inflame or offend, Sterne's wit has instead attracted the intimate and lascivious gaze of one female figure who leans towards him, and created the embarrassed bashfulness of another who attempts concealment behind a fan. This image incorporates Sterne's reputation for both storytelling and salaciousness, and the *Witticisms* returns on a number of occasions

Fig. 5.1. 'Yorick in Clover', the frontispiece to
Sterne's Witticisms; or, Yorick's Convivial Jester (1782).
© British Library Board. British Library shelfmark: 12316.bb.31

to topics concerning beds and bedrooms, appropriately so for a publication that wished to be placed in the same authorial canon as *Tristram Shandy*. There is even a gesture towards the novel's preoccupation with the science of reproduction through a report on Dr. James Graham and his novel invention of the 'celestial bed' as an aid to procreation at '*the Temple of Hymen*'. Graham's crusade to 'restore fertility and bliss to married couples' attracted such notoriety that he was forced to abandon this project three years after beginning in 1780.[66] The description of his bed is representative of the *Witticisms* in its use of coy suggestiveness to encourage the lascivious imagination of the purchaser:

> many persons have expressed a wish to know in what respect the celestial beds differ from all others [...] what is called the *sacking* of other beds, is here composed of *India rubbers*, whose elasticity is most astonishing, and causes a motion progressive and retrograde.[67]

The Impolite Sterne and Combe's Dissociation

For the image-conscious forger, this link between Sterne and risqué material was unwelcome, as illustrated by Combe's first collection, *Various Occasions*. This publication depicts Sterne in ways incompatible with the polite and sentimental correspondent of the *Original Letters* and, consequently, lacks Combe's celebration of a friendship with him. Despite the prefatory point that the 1775 letters 'reflect honour on the author in every capacity, and place him in the most pleasing point of view', this collection presents, for eyes such as Combe's, injurious aspects of Sterne's personal character.[68] He appears as rakishly masculine, but far from gentlemanly, when compared to the models of behaviour promoted by the proponents of late-century politeness. Combe presents an unrepentant libertine; one of these letters even anticipates the visual satire from the engraving of the *Witticisms* by claiming that 'sentimental prudes' may be offended by his willingness to display the 'heart' with 'its caprices' and 'wantonness'; 'if so', Sterne claims, 'let them put their fans before their faces'.[69]

Through an appeal to open honesty as a 'man who hides nothing, who varnishes nothing', Combe's self-righteous Sterne attempted to transform the accusations of unrestrained and unchaste behaviour into a moral crusade against the supporters of polite self-restraint.[70] Sterne's response to the charge of indecency championed the uninhibited, unaffected expression of desire in defiance of 'disguise' and self-repression which, he maintained, was 'the fashion'.[71] In doing so, he played upon contemporary anxieties surrounding politeness generated by the publication of Chesterfield's letters in the previous year, letters which advocated performative social personae built upon concealment, dissimulation, and 'calculation' in contrast to 'the primacy of unaffected feeling'.[72] Tapping into the eighteenth-century 'counter-culture of anti-civility', Sterne's support of healthy displays of manly desire targeted Chesterfield's refined gentleman who was susceptible to charges of corruption and personal dishonesty.[73]

Sterne as a licentious and opportunistic seducer of women would have undoubtedly reinforced the late eighteenth-century opinion of polite commentators that he was an undesirable companion for a woman of delicacy. One letter with the potential to create this impression was his erotic epistle to the 'Bluestocking' Elizabeth Vesey (?1715–1791), who he probably met in London during December 1761.[74] The 1895 discovery of an autograph version in Sterne's hand, while providing an indication of its genuineness, provides no evidence that this epistle was sent. Cash suggests that such a personally compromising letter was subject to Sterne's self-censorship: 'the most ribald letter [he] ever wrote' was far too risqué to be sent to such a slight acquaintance.[75] New and de Voogd also raise the possibility that Combe and Sterne 'worked jointly' to create the original text 'for their own amusement', 'a Shandean letter that took added piquancy from being addressed to a woman who would have been appalled to receive it'.[76] If so, this purely private epistolary fantasy was transformed into a very public one in 1775. In this letter, Sterne's confession that his 'acquaintance' with 'Mrs. V — —' is 'so short' is followed by his rakishly suggestive attempt to seduce, culminating in a sexual reverie involving the pleasure of touch:

> That you are graceful, elegant, and desirable, &c. &c.—every common beholder who can stare at you [...] can easily find out—but that you are sensible, gentle and tender, and from one end to the other of you full of the sweetest tones and modulations, requires a deeper research.—You are a system of harmonic vibrations—the softest and best attuned of all instruments.[77]

After assuming an air of polite gentility, through the use of such polished compliments as 'graceful, elegant' and 'sensible, gentle' to temper his sly suggestiveness, Sterne expresses his desire to engage in the 'deeper research' of her personal qualities, a typically Shandean double entendre; this hinting at sexual intercourse is anticipated by Sterne's evocation of her physical body: 'from one end to the other of you'. In the context of such a risqué letter, even the reference to the 'modulations' of her singing voice stimulates images of the erotic 'easy and insensible swell' of physical female beauty 'about the neck and breasts' during vocalization, a representation of beauty which interested Burke.[78] Sterne completes his provocative description by immodestly admitting 'I would give away my other cassoc to touch you—But in giving my last rag of priesthood for that pleasure, I should be left naked'.[79]

Sterne's willingness to attempt the lewd seduction of a slight acquaintance presented the late eighteenth-century reader with a potentially controversial image of masculinity as developing conceptions of polite gentility encompassed emotional 'self-regulation' and the suppression of offensive displays of passion, sexual or otherwise.[80] Just as Crazy Tales championed aristocratic forms of literary rakishness in The Public Advertiser and provoked criticism of his verse, Combe's promotion of Sterne three years earlier was similarly insensitive to developments in contemporary morality concerning appropriate behaviour for a gentleman. As illustrated by the frontispiece of the Witticisms, risqué conversation could be indulged in some public gatherings, a circumstance included by Carter in his biographical sketch of Boswell's penchant for 'coarse raillery'. Boswell's refusal to refrain from such behaviour in the 1770s indicated 'the pleasurableness of rule breaking in polite company from which, in view of [his] social standing and the tolerance of his wife and companions, he was scarcely in danger of being ostracised'.[81] That his behaviour gained a level of acceptance in polite mixed society because of his 'social standing' is an important qualification for understanding Combe's refusal to forge an association with *Various Occasions*. With the loss of social connections, and without financial independence or gentlemanly lineage, Combe's claim for gentlemanly status could only be based upon meritorious personal character. As displays of impolite behaviour by figures without status could reinforce a contemptuous opinion of them, the ambitious Combe attempted to distance himself from this version of Sterne, a version exhibiting lasciviousness, followed by impetuously violent impulses in a later epistle.

Combe would have been aware, after the commercial success of Chesterfield's *Letters*, that only the 'vulgar man' grows 'angry and testy', while the 'man of fashion' never 'suspects' that he is 'slighted'.[82] While this publication encouraged controversy and provoked criticism including Johnson's famous comment that Chesterfield taught 'the morals of a whore and the manners of a dancing master', its emphasis upon emotional restraint, as befitting the winsome character of nobility, still gained substantial recognition and approval from Combe's competitors, the writers of late-century guides to gentlemanly politeness for an aspirational audience. Typically, *Pleasing Reflections on Life and Manners*, in the spirit of Chesterfield's teachings, insisted that the polite gentleman who 'never descends to engage in disputes and quarrels' gained the reward of a social 'passport' to 'all manner of good company'.[83] Captain 'Tyger' Roche and George 'Fighting' Fitzgerald, 'two of the most notorious duellists of the period', realized that a reputation for dangerous passion and violent behaviour created fear and harmed acceptance within elite society.[84]

In one letter from *Various Occasions* with the ability to provoke this disquiet, Sterne relates his paternal affection for the daughterly Harriot which is transformed into unrestrained 'rage' after her 'vile seduction' and abandonment. Like Sterne in the 'Maria' episodes, Combe employs the sentimental figure of the tearful, deserted female; unlike Sterne, he includes an explosive burst of anger in response to this desertion:

> The news of affliction flies—I heard it, and posted to ****, where forgetting my character [...] I saw him in his retreat—I flew out of the chaise—caught him by the collar—and in a tumult of passion—demanded:—sure, if anger is excusable, it must be when it is exerted by a detestation of vice [...] Vengeance! [...] Distracted with my rage—I charged him with his crime—exploded his baseness—condemned his villany—while coward guilt sat on his sullen brow, and, like a criminal conscious of his deed, tremblingly pronounced his fear [...] His humiliation struck me—'twas the only means he could have contrived to assuage my anger.[85]

The acceptability of these actions at the end of the century, for a specific social group, is difficult to determine. V. G. Kiernan has indicated that the defence of another's reputation would not have proscribed violent conduct for a gentleman; but, to disregard the formal codes of the duel in favour of rash and wild action would have been perceived as improper. These formalities prevented the destructiveness of sudden anger and gave limits upon the location, duration, and method of violent expression, a set of constraints ignored by Sterne's spontaneous outburst. Using a distinction which appears simplistic when applied to the variety of possible responses to anger, Kiernan states that 'gentlemen could not retaliate with crude physical force', only 'with decorum and dignity' unlike 'the noisy plebeians'.[86]

Markku Peltonen reinforced this approach to class, proposing that a 'tarnished reputation' demanded 'a proper counterattack' with the duel as 'the only polite response to an impolite word or deed, and thus the only proper means of restoring gentlemanly civility'.[87] In a more balanced view, Shoemaker similarly asserted that duellists came from 'the nobility, gentry and military' with those lower down the social scale settling disputes with their fists, but he also recognized that the practice of boxing on streets was known to resolve quarrels among the upper class, although such behaviour 'appears to have declined' significantly by the 1770s.[88]

Neat generalizations about gentlemanly attitudes would fail to accommodate the range of possible reactions to Sterne's epistolary behaviour, but Combe's opinion is clear from his absence. For someone in his position, a literary relationship with this depiction of violent conduct had the potential to reinforce the perception that men without status brawl, while gentlemen duel. In addition, this letter fails to gratify Combe's social pretensions through disregarding one facet of polite gentility identified by Michèle Cohen concerning 'proper conduct' in speech and the 'discipline of the tongue'.[89] Sterne's frantically violent voice clearly displays a loss of control, a disregard for thoughtful self-discipline, and a lack of concern for the sensibilities of the addressee. Possibly, Combe's passage on Sterne's rage was intended to portray the novelist as a figure of intense sensibility, governed by the acute and heightened experience of emotion leading to his position as a moral crusader and champion of feminine virtue. Indeed, his radical reaction to the fate of this Maria figure becomes a means to a conventional, sentimental end as Sterne's anger melts into a desire to console Harriot, once she has retired 'to some corner of the world' to 'weep out the remainder of her days in sorrow'.[90]

In a number of ways, this forgery is typically Sternean. Combe's awareness of Sterne's penchant for dramatic self-fashioning, as well as his appreciation of Garrick's influence upon the novelist's epistolary style, adds authenticity to this voice. Following the actor's performances, the emotional intensity of Sterne's rage is communicated through a collection of choreographed physical actions, including 'posted, flew, caught, demanded, charged'. Combe's use of the Sternean dash, to divide the narrative into this series of short and discrete movements, communicates the frantic intensity of Sterne's actions while creating a series of separate emotional moments or tableaux, reminiscent of Drury Lane spectacles. On the other hand, this letter represents a complete and radical transformation of Sterne's epistolary character. Its content, including Sterne's spectacular loss of temper, his breathless demand for 'Vengeance!', and the resort to a reckless tussle, is not comparable with any other judgement about his personality or, indeed, any other epistle which has been authenticated by Curtis, or New and de Voogd.[91] In the twentieth-century flurry of Sternean biography and criticism, the slender, consumptive cleric has never been labelled as a street brawler. But, even if Sterne scholars quickly discount the authenticity of the majority of the letters on *Various Occasions* as well as their potential to provide biographical insights, newspaper advertisements could still confidently report:

> ☞ Though the contents of these volumes neither interfere with, or form any Part of a Work advertised to be compiling by Mrs. Medalle, Daughter of the

late Mr. Sterne, yet the Public may be assured of their AUTHENTICITY; the whole being transcribed from the Original Manuscripts of the Author.⁹²

This assertion, both publicly removing Combe's responsibility for this impolite publication and promising genuine insights into the novelist's character, potentially influenced contemporary readers. The bookseller's recognition of Medalle's collection, in the attempt to distance her letters from his, also emphasized the selective nature of epistolary anthologies. If nothing else, the disregard shown to the 'Harriot' letter by Medalle's compilation illustrates that the anthologizing of Sterne was (and still is) a subjective and temporal project, a line drawn in the sand. As time passes and one anthology is replaced by another, the mass of available material is again redivided into the legitimate and illegitimate. The exclusion of this letter by New and de Voogd's Florida edition, like their inclusion of the entire 'Burton' letter in response to Curtis's shortened version in *Letters of Laurence Sterne* (1935), highlights that the selection of Sternean epistles within a collection not only recreates Sterne's literary heritage, but also reshapes his character as well as the reader's potential interpretation of his epistolary persona.⁹³

Unsurprisingly, Combe's 1775 epistles were approached as misbegotten and in need of severe editorial reduction by *The Beauties*. Under the title of 'SEDUCTION', this anthology printed a short, moralistic extract from Combe's letter XI relating Sterne's distress after the seduction of Harriot:

> How abandoned is that heart which bulges the tear of innocence, and is the cause—the fatal cause of overwhelming the spotless soul and plunging the yet-untainted mind into a sea of sorrow and repentance—Though born to protect the fair, does not man act the part of a Demon?—first alluring by his temptations, and then triumphing in his victory—when villainy gets the ascendency it seldom leaves the wretch 'till it has thoroughly polluted him.⁹⁴

Combe's epistle gave a new, startling revelation about Sterne's private character; *The Beauties* instead chose an excerpt consistent with its representation of the author as a deeply moral figure of philanthropic virtue and sentimental refinement. To sustain the consistent editorial portrayal of the quintessential Sterne for the polite 'CHASTE lovers of literature', this compilation disregarded Combe's sensational insight into the author's character. In an opportunity lost, the abridgement represented him in a typical pose reminiscent of the *Journey*, weeping over the tears of innocence from the fallen Harriot. While this study has questioned Mullan's opinion that Sterne's sentimentalism was the distinctive merit of his legacy for the majority of eighteenth-century readers, the editorial decisions in *The Beauties* supported such one-dimensional appreciation. Unlike *The Beauties*, Combe's two epistolary collections, taken as a whole, provide a mercurial, heteroclite portrayal, one which is inconsistent in relation to the model of late eighteenth-century politeness: Sterne is fatherly and predatory, protective and rakish, complaisant and splenetic, sociable and hostile. To employ the analogy with anatomical articulation again, Sterne is recreated using fragments (in Combe's case, epistolary extracts) lacking symmetry and points of connection, producing a very eccentric skeleton.

Masculine Fellowship

In the 1770s and 80s, the society loved by Combe and Hall-Stevenson had become a ghostly one from the recent past. While masculine clubs still thrived, Combe's letters and the reprints of *Crazy Tales* existed as textual nostalgia, the remembrance of personal connections and literary fellowships within a particular community that had disappeared years before. After *Crazy Tales* had celebrated belonging to the Demoniacs, Combe similarly promoted an aristocratic group from the same period while also attempting to reassert his place within the world. To engage distinct and diverse readerships, both writers creatively reworked Sterne's literary heritage, recreating the camaraderie and loyalty within the select society that connected all three authors. Hall-Stevenson and Combe's recording of a relationship with Sterne was tempered by their gentlemanly defence of privacy, exploiting anonymity to avoid the complete exposure of their alliance with him, and thereby revealing the limits of an association in print. As a consequence, *Crazy Tales* and Combe's *Original Letters* exist as intimate, personal testimonies to friendship as well as impersonal publications for general sale. Hall-Stevenson and Combe's willingness to publicize an acquaintance with Sterne was partly dependent upon their perception of him as fulfilling an ideal of masculinity. Whereas Hall-Stevenson's celebration of a friendship with the obscene storyteller enabled his self-fashioning as a model of rakish libertinism, Combe's self-promotion as the author's acquaintance in 1788 depended upon Sterne's attainment of an ideal involving polite complaisance.

Combe's display of intimacy with Sterne in 1788 recorded that 'unlimited confidence' was a 'very dangerous business'.[95] As an illustration of this sentiment, such dangerous business, according to *Yorick's Sentimental Journey Continued*, spawned this outrageously bawdy conclusion to Sterne's travels: 'the intimacy which subsisted between Mr. Sterne and the Editor', it was claimed, 'gave the latter frequent occasion of hearing him relate the most remarkable incidents of the latter part of his last journey [...] as to be able to commit them to paper'.[96] Whether true or not, Sterne's unguarded storytelling with friends is given as one reason for the creation of this continuation and the very public connection of his authorial identity with a scandalous tale. The pleasure of closeness brought the threat of personal betrayal and exposure, a threat which was realized in some measure by the publications of both Hall-Stevenson and Combe. *Crazy Tales* divulged facets of Sterne's bacchanalian lifestyle that flouted a number of the restrictions of politeness, and Combe's 1775 epistles similarly recalled companionship and imagined impolite aspects of Sterne's private character. Even though the publications by both men provided indelicate portrayals of him, these texts nevertheless addressed the threat of Sterne being 'eternally misunderstood' and 'eternally misrepresented by ignorance'.[97] In contrast to the editorial selection of *The Beauties*, Combe's allegedly faithful and trustworthy depiction of Sterne in *Various Occasions* would have appeared unabridged, uncensored, and whole, if not completely wholesome.

Combe's presentation of Sterne also revealed the personal qualities that encouraged or inhibited masculine fellowship. Friendship, for Combe, was facilitated by the late eighteenth-century ideal of polite, gentlemanly behaviour including a talent for pleasing conversation, self-discipline in speech and action, and the affectionate care and reciprocal consideration of others.[98] Within the letters, Sterne's relationship to these qualities resulted in either Combe's celebration or rejection of a textual link to him in a culture involving guilt or merit through association. The beneficial construction of Sterne's voice in relation to politeness in 1788 allowed Combe to grasp at the title of gentleman through the portrayal of his privileged admission into Sterne's good company, recorded by letters exploring aspects of masculine intimacy. Such an assertion of gentlemanliness followed late eighteenth-century discourses on social refinement that emphasized the importance of a 'good character', not simply 'means', for men who desired the public display of 'Esq.' after their name.[99]

Notes to Chapter 5

1. Sterne, *The Letters, Part 1*, p. 395; the editorial commentary interprets 'C—' as 'very probably William Combe', p. 396. Hamilton, *Doctor Syntax*, p. 21 claims 'the identification with Combe is not certain, but no one has seriously doubted it'.
2. Hamilton, *Doctor Syntax*, p. 20.
3. Sterne, *The Letters, Part 1*, p. 395.
4. *Original Letters of the Late Reverend Mr. Laurence Sterne; Never Before Published*, pp. 34, 54.
5. Dates and figures of inheritance from Hamilton, *Doctor Syntax*, pp. 15, 17. Figures from Berg suggest that Combe's inheritance would have financially allied him, for a finite period, with the social elite. According to Berg, p. 208 'the metropolis, though the centre for elite expenditure, could claim in 1798 to have only 2–3 per cent of its population in the upper income bracket, that is with average incomes of £200 a year'.
6. Hamilton, *Doctor Syntax*, pp. vii, 25.
7. Ibid., p. 27.
8. For an account of Combe's conspicuous consumption and eventual bankruptcy, see Hamilton, *Doctor Syntax*, pp. 18–26.
9. *The Sun*, 19 June 1823.
10. *Original Letters*, p. 26.
11. Ibid., pp. 81–83. On the financial embarrassment of Sterne's widow and daughter shortly after his death, see Cash, *Laurence Sterne: The Later Years*, pp. 335–39; and Ross, pp. 420–21.
12. *Original Letters*, pp. 65–66.
13. Sterne, *The Letters, Part 1*, pp. 369–74 includes one letter with a version having previously appeared in the *Original Letters*; Sterne, *The Letters, Part 2*, pp. 430–35 and 445–47 includes two letters with this same history. For details of the additional extracts deemed to be authentic, see the editorial commentary by New and de Voogd in *The Letters, Part 1*, p. li.
14. See Sterne, *The Letters, Part 1*, p. 372, and Curtis. Combe's method of forgery is also discussed by Hamilton, 'William Combe and the *Original Letters of the Late Reverend Mr. Laurence Sterne*', pp. 420–29.
15. Andrew and McGowan, p. 140.
16. See Groom, *The Forger's Shadow*, p. 70, and the etymology of 'forgery' from p. 48.
17. For details of Combe's authorship of this collection, see Hamilton, *Doctor Syntax*, pp. 46–48.
18. For the letters included in the Florida edition, see Sterne, *The Letters, Part 1*, pp. 122–27; and Sterne, *The Letters, Part 2*, pp. 491–96, 645–49, and 703–05.
19. See the *Original Letters*, pp. 4, 205–07.
20. For example, compare letters I and III which are addressed to 'W. C. Esq.' with letter XVIII 'To ——', p. 96.
21. Only letters I, III, and V are explicitly addressed to 'W. C. Esq.'; however, I to VI follow a clear narrative sequence to imply one recipient.
22. On the enjoyment of leisure as a marker of gentility, see W. D. Smith, p. 32.
23. *Original Letters*, pp. 1–2.

24. The importance of complaisance is discussed by Carter, pp. 63–64.
25. *Original Letters*, p. 16.
26. Ibid., pp. 19, 21.
27. Brant, p. 50.
28. Stephanson, p. 159.
29. These figures are mentioned in the *Original Letters*, pp. 39, 54. Burton is discussed in Sterne, *The Letters*, Part 2, p. 432; while Spencer is described by Cash, *Laurence Sterne: The Later Years*, pp. 81–82, 108, 226–27, and 292, who also portrays his relationship with Sterne.
30. *Original Letters*, pp. 9–14. For biographical details on Thomas Scrope, including his relationship with the Demoniacs, see Cash, *Laurence Sterne: The Early and Middle Years*, pp. 187–88.
31. Hamilton, 'William Combe and the *Original Letters*', p. 426.
32. Hall appears in the *Original Letters*, pp. 33–35, 53–56, and 58; the deceased Lord Mulgrave is mentioned on p. 96.
33. *The Morning Herald and Daily Advertiser*, 17 August 1781.
34. Carter, p. 63.
35. Barchas, p. 70.
36. *A Letter to Her Grace the Duchess of D. Answered Cursorily, by Democritus*, p. 4. While offering no reasons or evidence, ECCO has followed the ESTC and attributed this anonymous pamphlet to Combe.
37. Hamilton, *Doctor Syntax*, p. 4.
38. Combe is attributed with the following anonymous publications: *The First of April; or, The Triumphs of Folly: A Poem. Dedicated to a Celebrated Duchess* (1777); *A Letter to Her Grace the Duchess of Devonshire* (1777); and *An Interesting Letter to the Duchess of Devonshire* (1778). See Hamilton, *Doctor Syntax*, pp. 308, 310, and 313.
39. *A Letter to Her Grace the Duchess of D. Answered Cursorily, by Democritus*, p. 3.
40. For pertinent descriptions of the Duchess, see Foreman, pp. 49–50.
41. *A Letter to Her Grace the Duchess of D. Answered Cursorily, by Democritus*, pp. 13–14.
42. *An Interesting Letter to the Duchess of Devonshire*, pp. 94–95.
43. Regan, p. 142.
44. Translation from Lichtenberg, *Lichtenberg's Visits to England*, p. 118. The original German text can be found in Lichtenberg, *London-Tagebuch*, p. 71: 'Mr. de Grey erzählt mir, daß Yorick ein sehr plagender Besucher gewesen ist. Er kam öffters zu Leuten um 9 des Morgens und verließ sie alsdann selten vor 9 des Abends, wenn sie ausgiengen so gieng er mit aus und kam mit ihnen zurück. Er war sehr arm'.
45. I have followed the editorial judgement of the Florida editors who have included this letter in Sterne, *The Letters*, Part 2, pp. 430–31.
46. *Original Letters*, pp. 42–43.
47. Brant, p. 16.
48. *Original Letters*, pp. 169–70. This extract, like the previous one, illustrates the proposition of Bannet, p. 47 that 'the expectation in the eighteenth century was still that letters would be read aloud to family, friends and acquaintance, and/or shown around, to give everyone something to talk about'.
49. See Sterne, *A Sentimental Journey*, pp. 61–64.
50. Bannet, p. 47.
51. Harvey, p. 38.
52. For the cost of the *Original Letters*, see Hamilton, 'William Combe and the *Original Letters*', p. 424.
53. Harvey, p. 38.
54. For details of the publication of Combe's letters in *The Daily Universal Register* and *The Times*, see Hamilton, 'William Combe and the *Original Letters*', pp. 422–24.
55. *The Times*, 20 June 1823, p. 4.
56. See, for example, the appearance of Combe's obituary on the final page of *The Leeds Mercury*, 17 July 1824.
57. The obituary notice '*from the* BRITISH TRAVELLER' appeared in both newspapers on 17 July 1824.

58. The inclusion of *Letters Written by the Late Right Honourable Philip Dormer Stanhope* within anthologies is discussed by Davidson, p. 12.
59. See Harris, pp. 28–29; and *Pleasing Reflections on Life and Manners with Essays, Characters & Poems, Moral & Entertaining*, pp. 229–30.
60. Carter, pp. 17–19, 37–39.
61. Ellis, *The Coffee-House*, pp. 196, 212, and 214. To support this idea of social exclusiveness Ellis, p. 214 cites White's Chocolate House which transformed open coffee rooms into a gentleman's club with the strict regulation of admission.
62. *Sterne's Witticisms*, p. i.
63. Clark, pp. 229–30.
64. Benedict, *Making the Modern Reader*, p. 180.
65. Ibid., p. 180.
66. Langford, p. 639.
67. *Sterne's Witticisms*, pp. 18–20 (p. 20).
68. *Various Occasions*, p. ii. A large advertisement in *The London Chronicle*, 27 June 1775, claimed that 'in these letters the wit, humour, and benevolence, which so strongly mark Mr. Sterne's character are displayed to great advantage' before reproducing three of the letters from this collection.
69. *Various Occasions*, pp. 32–33.
70. Ibid., p. 34.
71. Ibid., pp. 32–33.
72. On the Chesterfield controversy, see Davidson, pp. 57–58; and Langford, p. 586.
73. Carter, p. 135.
74. In Sterne, *The Letters, Part 2*, p. 495 New and de Voogd provide a possible context for their meeting: 'On December 30, 1761, she was in Reynolds's studio when the Earl of Bath was sitting for his portrait. The occasion had been organized by Elizabeth Montagu, who had also invited Sterne to be there'. In Combe's 1775 collection, Vesey's name is abbreviated to 'Mrs. V — —'.
75. See Cash, *Laurence Sterne: The Later Years*, pp. 25–27.
76. Sterne, *The Letters, Part 1*, p. xlix.
77. *Various Occasions*, p. 46.
78. Burke, *A Philosophical Enquiry*, 1st edn, p. 100. Leppert, p. 30 has discussed 'the relation of music to sensuality' and the erotic potential of the act of singing upon the masculine gaze.
79. *Various Occasions*, pp. 46–47.
80. Carter, pp. 64–66 and 73–74.
81. Ibid., p. 195.
82. *Letters Written by the Late Right Honourable Philip Dormer Stanhope*, p. 463.
83. *Pleasing Reflections on Life and Manners*, pp. 229–30.
84. Langford, p. 589 notes that Captain Roche 'stood as a candidate at the famous Middlesex contest between Wilkes and Luttrell, when he achieved the distinction of registering no votes at all' while George Fitzgerald's application for membership to Brookes's Club was 'blackballed by every member', but 'none would tell him for fear of having to fight'.
85. *Various Occasions*, pp. 58–60.
86. Kiernan, p. 136.
87. Peltonen, p. 304.
88. Shoemaker, *The London Mob*, pp. 194, 211.
89. Cohen, p. 45.
90. *Various Occasions*, p. 61.
91. *Letters of Laurence Sterne*, ed. by L. P. Curtis, 1935 edn.
92. *The Morning Chronicle and London Advertiser*, 25 August 1775 and 30 November 1775. Reference is made to *Letters of the Late Rev. Mr. Laurence Sterne, to His Most Intimate Friends [...] Written by Himself. And Published by His Daughter, Mrs. Medalle*. In Sterne, *The Letters, Part 1*, New and de Voogd, pp. xlviii–xlix note that Combe's collection appeared on 12 July 1775 and Medalle's collection shortly afterwards on 25 October 1775.
93. Compare Sterne, *The Letters, Part 2*, pp. 430–31 with Curtis's *Letters of Laurence Sterne*, pp. 250–51. In response to Curtis's version of this letter, New and de Voogd state: 'we have also included

the final paragraph, no more or less suspect than the rest of the letter, which does seem to be derived — however corrupted — from a Sterne text', p. 432.
94. *Various Occasions*, pp. 54–55; and *The Beauties of Sterne*, 7th edn, p. 251. Here, the extract from *The Beauties* is quoted in its entirety. Another anthology, *Gleanings from the Works of Laurence Sterne*, also reproduced this extract on p. 185.
95. *Original Letters*, p. 10.
96. *Yorick's Sentimental Journey Continued*, 1st edn, III: pp. iv-v.
97. *Original Letters*, p. 137.
98. Carter, p. 21 claims that 'the most frequently considered element of politeness' was 'the display of generosity and accommodation to one's companions'.
99. Ibid., p. 19.

CODA

Tristram Shandy and Fooling Around

Sternean mimicry did not end with the eighteenth century. The desire to appropriate Sterne, to create new forms of entertainment, continues into the twenty-first century as illustrated by Michael Winterbottom's film adaptation of *Tristram Shandy*.[1] However, *A Cock and Bull Story* (2005) is not simply a screen version of Sterne's novel; it also self-consciously reflects upon the process of composition through a behind-the-scenes account of the film's creation. Just as Sterne's novel is partly about the writing of a novel, *A Cock and Bull Story* is, to a certain degree, about the making of a film.[2] Winterbottom's self-reflexive adaptation of Sterne's narrative encompasses, albeit unknowingly, many of the characteristics displayed by the mimicry considered in this study. Steve Coogan's first appearance as Tristram introduces this art:

> Groucho Marx once said that the trouble with writing a book about yourself is you can't fool around. Why not? People fool around with themselves all the time. I'm Tristram Shandy. The main character in this story. The leading role [...] There are those who say this is a cock and bull story. That's the bull *[gestures towards the animal in the field]*, my father's bull and I'll show you the cock in a minute *[laughs]*.

Like Coogan, Georgian impersonators fooled around with themselves in numerous ways. In the act of appropriation, these writers played around with identity and fashioned new identities, for themselves and Sterne. To become Sterne involved writing a book about yourself, with such literary self-fashioning dependent upon the depiction of the famous novelist. Sternean impersonations enabled flattering self-promotion and self-portrayal, embodying views of masculinity and championing opinions on the qualities of a gentleman. In one example, Hall-Stevenson's model of masculinity involved the rakish expression of sexual desire through acts of bawdy storytelling and the adoption of Shandean personae. In the employment of these characters to afford sexual pleasure to himself and others, his mimicry provides a point of comparison with Coogan's innuendo linking performances of Sterne with people's tendency to 'fool around with themselves'.

This interest in Sternean obscenity and prurience represents one tradition in the creative manipulation of Sterne which originated in the eighteenth century. In a film that Hall-Stevenson would have relished, Tristram's opening speech anticipates Winterbottom's portrayal of Sterne's novel through the selection of salacious narrative incidents. While not entirely eschewing sentimental scenes, *A Cock and Bull Story* celebrates bawdy episodes from *Tristram Shandy* such as the timing of Walter's sexual intercourse with his wife (I. i-iv); Tristram's near castration by the falling sash window (V. xvii); *Phutatorius*'s misfortune with the hot chestnut (IV. xxvii); and, in the words of New, 'one dreadfully silly bit with a rubber womb that calls to mind the dregs of Benny Hill's bad taste'.³ As in *Crazy Tales*, Wilson's 'low comedy', *La Souriciere*, and Combe's *Various Occasions*, this filmic reworking gestures emphatically towards Sterne's preoccupation with the body and its sexual physiology, a representation of the narrative that highlights the delight in rude and lewd storytelling. Like Harris's version of *Tristram Shandy*, Coogan's bawdy statement exploits the promise of self-exposure; in both of these entertainments, Sterne's novel is associated with the outrageous display of sexual anatomy to create humour.

Further parallels can be made between this film version and the eighteenth-century mimicry of Sterne. In *A Cock and Bull Story*, the competing lead roles perform numerous characters to showcase their talent, gain the camera's attention, and solicit the audience's laughter. Consequently, Coogan masquerades as Tristram, Walter, and a filmic version of himself, the actor with a comic reputation and celebrity baggage. The supporting actor Rob Brydon impersonates an array of characters including Uncle Toby, Al Pacino, Roger Moore, and even Coogan. In a battle of egos between these two performers, mimicry represents rival forms of self-promotion to showcase ability, a principle that also motivated Sterne's public performances as well as the literary efforts of Hall-Stevenson and Combe. While in different historical periods and media, the *Original Letters* and Winterbottom's film suggest that impersonation is driven, to an extent, by the desire for applause and recognition, like Sterne's desire to be '*famous*' not simply '*fed*'.⁴ In literary disguises, both Hall-Stevenson and Combe tentatively sought fame through the display of semi-fictional personalities and lifestyles involving the celebration of an ideal view of themselves. As a result, it is important to appreciate their texts as exuberant affirmations of selfhood, not as inferior, throwaway publications written by anonymous hacks starving in garrets, a collection of prejudices that have been associated with eighteenth-century Sterneana in modern literary criticism.

While Coogan and Brydon compete and produce a variety of characters, the film questions the possibility of the role effacing the actor's personality, albeit the contrived personalities offered for the entertainment of a cinema audience. At one point, Coogan's on-screen change of role, from Tristram to Walter, asks this question:

> When I was born, my father was four years older than I am now. So given the family resemblance, I felt I should portray him as well as myself *[dons a wig and enters the next scene as Walter]*.

In a gesture towards the artificiality of life on film, he playfully implies that performative identities can be worn or discarded as easily as a wig. In contrast to Coogan's view of the dispensability of character, Brydon repeatedly claims that Coogan's personality will always be seen as inseparable from his famous alter ego, Alan Partridge, an opinion acknowledged by Coogan's annoyance, to Brydon's satisfaction.⁵ The interrogation of the boundary between performer and part was encouraged by Winterbottom through his request that Coogan should 'blur the differences' between the characters of Tristram, Walter, and the film version of himself; consequently, one reviewer was forced to concede that 'you can never tell where being ends and acting begins'.[6] Similarly, Sterne's attempts to embody his narrative characters, and 'Shandy it away' in society, confused the extent to which the personae of Tristram and Yorick were merely fictions, or projections of his personality. Georgian commentators who were willing to condemn Sterne as an erotomaniac, unfit for polite company, approached his personal identity as an extension of his bawdy performances in print; this perspective upon him was compounded by the publication of erotic reworkings of his fiction.

The possibility that a role could affect the public's view of the player was an eighteenth-century phenomenon. As Wilson discovered, role-play and mimicry impacted upon the perception of an actor with public opinion fuelled by hostile newspaper reports. Like Wilson before him, Coogan expresses anger at a poor review that fails to distinguish between the role and the actor's actual personality. In a scene that was removed from the film's final edit, he reacts to being described as 'an obnoxious Steve Coogan'; it is 'as if I'm obnoxious rather than the character' complains the comic.[7] The 'Coogan' character in *A Cock and Bull Story* is partly the performance of 'an unflattering caricature taken from the British tabloids: a self-absorbed, arrogant, insecure womaniser', as if to illustrate the power of the press to mould opinion and popularize a collection of uncomplimentary ideas about an actor's off-stage character, a danger encountered by Wilson in the aftermath of his appearance as Mrs. Peachum.[8]

In their approach to the dramatization of *Tristram Shandy*, both Harris and Winterbottom exploit the celebrity of one key performer. Harris's attempt to encourage laughter through the audience's awareness of Wilson's reputation, and their recognition of his unsuitability for the role of Toby, bears comparison with Winterbottom's attempt to play upon the public image of Coogan for comic effect to the extent that the screenplay was written around the leading actor. Just as 'Coogan is the star and subject of the film', Wilson was the star and subject of the stage version in the moments that gestured towards his theatrical misdemeanours.[9] As a result of Winterbottom's focus upon his actors at the expense of Sterne's narrative characters, this reflexive comedy can fail with audiences lacking knowledge of the popular culture and immediate context surrounding the film: 'much of an American's disappointment with this film', New claimed, is that the main actors are 'relatively unknown on this side of the Atlantic', yet 'much of the film seems to depend on an intimate knowledge of their film and TV careers, their tabloid existence, their relationship to one another'.[10] It is testimony to Harris's confidence in Wilson's widespread popularity and infamy among London theatregoers that he was willing to gamble the success of the production upon an audience's familiarity with his employee's tempestuous life and recent theatrical career; a similar gamble is taken by the film version, with mixed results.

In drawing conclusions about the creative process of Sternean mimicry, it is useful to make comparisons between Winterbottom's film and eighteenth-century literary appropriations since numerous links exist between these different forms of mimicry from different centuries. Just as Winterbottom's film-making suggests that 'the reason we tell stories of the past is *not* to recreate' but rather 'to illustrate our *human connections*' with them, the authors in this study illustrate that Sternean narratives deserve to be retold because they encourage personal identification and a recognition that the reader shares characteristics with Sterne's personae.[11] In another parallel, the Sternean entertainments considered in this study often reflect or portray the situations surrounding their creation, the environments normally behind closed doors and, consequently, unseen. Like Hall-Stevenson's self-conscious portrayal of the club which produced his erotic tales, *A Cock and Bull Story* foregrounds the locale of movie production including a fanciful depiction of a group and their friendships. Ultimately, the Georgian versions of Sterne encourage a consideration of literary context and its relationship to the mimic's self-fashioning as these publications were clearly shaped by the environments surrounding their conception and production. While *Crazy Tales* was modelled upon the storytelling practices at Skelton, the *Original Letters* existed as a response to Combe's experience of poverty 'within the rules'. Similarly, Harris's bawdy production of MacNally's afterpiece was influenced by the expectations of theatregoers who watched performances from the Covent Garden gallery.

While noting these correspondences, I am not claiming that Winterbottom researched the work of MacNally, Hall-Stevenson, or Combe. Nonetheless, these similarities represent a consensus, shared by all of the Sternean impostors considered in this book, about the value of becoming Sterne. The adoption of Sterne's personae offered a myriad of possibilities for the mimic: the freedom to indulge in impolite, bawdy humour and sexual fantasy; the potential to escape social constraints and become someone else through the playful refashioning of personality; the opportunity for self-promotion and the showcasing of talent; the celebration of friendship; and, finally, the ability to earn money. For the Sternean bodysnatcher, these possibilities proved irresistible.

Notes to the Coda

1. *A Cock and Bull Story*, dir. by Michael Winterbottom (BBC Films, 2005).
2. There are many examples of Sterne's authorial reflections on the problems of composition in *Tristram Shandy*; such reflection begins in volume one, chapter fourteen where Tristram bemoans his rate of progress: 'In short, there is no end of it;-----for my own part, I declare I have been at it these six weeks, making all the speed I possibly could,—and am not yet born'. Such a statement can be compared with the advertisement of *A Cock and Bull Story* as the 'making [of] a film within a film'.
3. New, p. 581.
4. The phrase 'I wrote not to be *fed*, but to be *famous*' is from a letter dated 30 January 1760 to an unknown addressee. See Sterne, *The Letters, Part 1*, p. 116.
5. Coogan had expanded the role of Alan Partridge from radio vignettes in 1991 to the BBC television series *Knowing Me, Knowing You with Alan Partridge* (1994) and *I'm Alan Partridge* (1997 and 2002).
6. Spencer, p. 17; see also French's 'A Shaggy Dog Story with Legs' in *The Observer: The Observer Review*, 22 January 2006, p. 16.
7. This episode, entitled 'Deleted Scenes: Poor Notices', can be found as an extra upon the 2006 Lionsgate DVD.
8. Quotation from Foley-Dawson, p. 149.
9. Quotation from Spencer, p. 14.
10. New, p. 580.
11. Quotation from Foley-Dawson, p. 151.

BIBLIOGRAPHY

1. Primary Sources

1.1 Newspapers and Periodicals

Critical Review, 13 (June 1762), 475–80; 27 (May 1769), 390; 14 (June 1795), 238
Derby Mercury, 14 April 1874, 6; 22 April 1874, 7
European Magazine and London Review, 2 (November 1782), 325–28
Gazetteer and New Daily Advertiser, 3 May 1783, 15 June 1785, unpaginated
Gentleman's Magazine, 39 (July 1769), 366; 39 (August 1769), 398
Grand Magazine, 3 (April 1760), 194–98
Ipswich Journal, 10 August 1844, unpaginated
Leeds Mercury, 17 July 1824, unpaginated
Liverpool Mercury, 28 October 1882, 7
London Chronicle, 27 June 1775, unpaginated
London Evening Post, 10 January 1782, unpaginated
London Magazine, 38 (June 1769), 323
Monthly Review, 26 (June 1762), 451–54; 40 (May 1769), 428; 48 (February 1773), 129; 69 (December 1783), 439; 16 (January 1795), 119
Morning Chronicle and London Advertiser, 25 August 1775, 30 November 1775, 4 September 1778, 15 September 1781, 28 April 1783, 21 January 1784, unpaginated
Morning Herald and Daily Advertiser, 17–31 August 1781, 5 August 1782, 28 April 1783, 20 February 1784, 4 February 1785, 11 October 1786, 8 December 1786, unpaginated
Morning Post and Daily Advertiser, 5 August 1782, 13 May 1783, unpaginated
Newcastle Courant, 17 July 1824, unpaginated
Observer, Observer Review section, 22 January 2006, 16
Pall Mall Gazette, 26 April 1867, 13; 3 February 1891, 6
Parker's General Advertiser and Morning Intelligencer, 28 April 1783, 5 May 1783, unpaginated
Public Advertiser, 20 July 1767, 24 March 1769, 5 September 1778, 10 September 1778, 14 September 1778, 19 September 1778, 2 October 1778, 9 October 1778, 16 October 1778, 9 August 1781, 24 September 1782, 28 April 1783, 29 April 1783, 13 May 1783, unpaginated
Punch; or, The London Charivari, 1 June 1867, 2
Royal Female Magazine, 1 (February 1760), 56
Stuart's Star and Evening Advertiser, 27 February 1789, unpaginated
Sun, 19 June 1823, unpaginated
Times, 20 June 1823, 4; 29 January 1867, 4; 5 June 1969, 1
Universal Magazine of Knowledge and Pleasure, 26 (April 1760), 189–90
Western Mail, 14 April 1874, 6
Whitehall-Evening Post, 26 April 1783–29 April 1783, unpaginated
Willis's Current Notes (1854), 31
World and Fashionable Advertiser, 7 February 1787, 20 March 1787, 4 November 1788, unpaginated

1.2 Prints

Caricature Shop (London: P. Roberts, 1801)
GILLRAY, JAMES, *A Sale of English-Beauties in the East Indies* (London: W. Holland, 1786)
RAVENET, SIMON FRANÇOIS, *Mr. Garrick and Miss Bellamy in the Characters of Romeo and Juliet* (London: B. Wilson, 1753)
ROWLANDSON, THOMAS, *Connoisseurs* (London: Fores, 1799)
—— *The Man of Feeling* (London: William Holland, 1788)
—— *A Man of Feeling* (London: Thomas Tegg, 1811)

1.3 Books and Pamphlets

BAKER, DAVID ERSKINE, ISAAC REED, and STEPHEN JONES, *Biographia Dramatica; or, A Companion to the Playhouse*, 3 vols (London: Longman, 1812)
The Beauties of Sterne [...] Selected for the Heart of Sensibility, 1st edn (London: T. Davies, J. Ridley, W. Flexney, J. Sewel, and G. Kearsley, 1782)
The Beauties of Sterne [...] Selected for the Heart of Sensibility, 7th edn (London: G. Kearsley, 1783)
The Beauties of Sterne [...] Selected for the Heart of Sensibility, 11th edn (Boston, MA: printed by John W. Folsom, for Daniel Brewer of Taunton, 1793)
BOSWELL, JAMES, *The Life of Samuel Johnson, LL.D.*, 2 vols (London: Henry Baldwin for Charles Dilly, 1791)
Boswell: Laird of Auchinleck, 1778–1782, ed. by J. W. Reed and F. A. Pottle (London: McGraw-Hill, 1977)
BURKE, EDMUND, *A Philosophical Enquiry into the Origin of our Ideas of the Sublime and Beautiful*, 1st edn (London: R. and J. Dodsley, 1757)
—— *A Philosophical Enquiry into the Origin of our Ideas of the Sublime and Beautiful*, 2nd edn (London: R. and J. Dodsley, 1759)
Candid and Impartial Strictures on the Performers Belonging to Drury-Lane, Covent-Garden and the Haymarket Theatres (London: Martin and Bain, 1795)
Catalogue of the London and Westminster Circulating Library (London: David Ogilvy and Son, 1797)
CHURCHILL, CHARLES, *The Rosciad*, 1st edn (London: W. Flexney, 1761)
CLELAND, JOHN, *Memoirs of a Woman of Pleasure* (London: G. Fenton, 1749)
—— *Memoirs of a Woman of Pleasure*, ed. by Peter Sabor (Oxford: Oxford University Press, 1999)
Continuation of Yorick's Sentimental Journey (London: printed for the author, at the Literary-Press, 1788)
CUMBERLAND, RICHARD, *The West Indian: A Comedy. As it is Performed at the Theatre Royal in Drury Lane* (London: W. Griffin, 1771)
D'ARCHENHOLZ, M., *A Picture of England* (London: [n. pub.], 1791)
DAVIES, THOMAS, *Memoirs of the Life of David Garrick Interspersed with Characters and Anecdotes of his Theatrical Contemporaries*, 2 vols (London: printed for the author, 1780)
The Diary of Samuel Pepys, vol. IX: 1668–69, ed. by Robert Latham and William Matthews (Berkeley: University of California Press, 1976)
Extracts from the Tristram Shandy and Sentimental Journey of Law. Sterne, M. A. (Ludlow: George Nicholson, 1799)
The First of April; or, The Triumphs of Folly: A Poem. Dedicated to a Celebrated Duchess (London: J. Bew, 1777)
FITZPATRICK, THADDEUS, *An Enquiry into the Real Merit of a Certain Popular Performer* (London: M. Thrush, 1760)
FOOTE, SAMUEL, and ARTHUR MURPHY, *Plays by Samuel Foote and Arthur Murphy*, ed. by George Taylor (Cambridge: Cambridge University Press, 1984)

Foster, Hannah Webster, *The Boarding School; or, Lessons of a Preceptress to her Pupils* (Boston, MA: I. Thomas and E. T. Andrews, 1798)
Gamelin, Jacques, *Nouveau recueil d'ostéologie et de myologie* (Toulouse: J. F. Desclassan, 1779)
Gay, John, *The Beggar's Opera* (London: J. Watts, 1728)
Gilliland, Thomas, *The Dramatic Mirror: Containing the History of the Stage from the Earliest Period to the Present Time*, 2 vols (London: C. Chapple, 1808)
Gleanings from the Works of Laurence Sterne (London: C. Whittingham, 1796)
Hall-Stevenson, John, *Crazy Tales* (London: [n. pub.], 1762)
—— *Moral Tales: A Christmas Night's Entertainment. By Lady* ******* (London: T. Becket, 1783)
—— *Two Lyric Epistles: One to My Cousin Shandy, on his Coming to Town; and the Other to the Grown Gentlewomen, the Misses of* **** (London: R. and J. Dodsley, 1760)
Harris, John, *An Essay on Politeness; wherein the Benefits Arising from and the Necessity of Being Polite are Clearly Proved, by a Young Gentleman* (London: B. Law, 1775)
Harris's List of Covent-Garden Ladies; or, New Atlantis for the Year 1761 (London: H. Ranger, 1761)
Haslewood, Joseph, *The Secret History of the Green Room: Containing Authentic and Entertaining Memoirs of the Actors and Actresses in the Three Theatres Royal*, 3rd edn, 2 vols (London: H. D. Symmonds, 1793)
An Interesting Letter to the Duchess of Devonshire (London: J. Bew, 1778)
Johnson, Samuel, *A Dictionary of the English Language*, 2 vols, 2nd edn (London: J. Knapton, C. Hitch and L. Hawes, A. Millar, R. and J. Dodsley, and M. and T. Longman, 1755–56)
Joineriana; or, The Book of Scraps, 2 vols (London: [n. pub.], 1772)
Knight, Richard Payne, *An Account of the Remains of the Worship of Priapus* (London: T. Spilsbury, 1786)
The Letters of David Garrick, ed. by D. M. Little and G. M. Kahrl, 3 vols (London: Oxford University Press, 1963)
Letters of Laurence Sterne, ed. by L. P. Curtis (Oxford: Clarendon Press, 1935)
Letters of the Late Rev. Mr. Laurence Sterne, to His Most Intimate Friends [...] Written by Himself. And Published by His Daughter, Mrs. Medalle, 3 vols (London: T. Becket, 1775)
Letters Written by the Late Right Honourable Philip Dormer Stanhope, Earl of Chesterfield, to His Son, Philip Stanhope, Esq., 4 vols (London: J. Dodsley, 1774)
A Letter to Her Grace the Duchess of D. Answered Cursorily, by Democritus (London: R. Baldwin, 1777)
A Letter to Her Grace the Duchess of Devonshire (London: Fielding and Walker, 1777)
Lichtenberg, Georg Christoph, *Gesammelte Werke*, ed. by W. Grenzmann, 2 vols (Frankfurt-am-Main: Holle, 1949)
—— *Lichtenberg's Visits to England*, trans. by M. L. Mare and W. H. Quarrell (Oxford: Clarendon Press, 1938)
—— *London-Tagebuch, September 1774 bis April 1775*, ed. by H. L. Gumbert (Hildesheim: Gerstenberg, 1979)
—— *Werke*, ed. by C. Brinitzer (Hamburg: Hoffmann und Campe, 1967)
Lyser, Michael, *The Art of Dissecting the Human Body, in a Plain, Easy, and Compendious Method*, trans. by G. Thomson (London: Joseph Davidson, 1740)
MacDonald, John, *Travels in Various Parts of Europe, Asia, and Africa, during a Series of Thirty Years and Upwards* (London: printed for the author, and sold by J. Forbes, 1790)
Mackenzie, Henry, *The Man of Feeling* (London: T. Cadell, 1771)
Macklin, Charles, *A New Comedy: Love a-al-a-Mode* (London: [n. pub.], 1779)
MacNally, Leonard, *Sentimental Excursions to Windsor and Other Places* (London: J. Walker, 1781)
—— *Tristram Shandy: A Sentimental, Shandean Bagatelle*, 2nd edn (London: S. Bladon, 1783)

Maria; or, The Generous Rustic (London: T. Cadell, 1784)
Maria; or, The Vicarage. A Novel in Two Volumes (London: Hookham and Carpenter, 1796)
MARSHALL, JOSEPH, *Travels through Holland, Flanders, Germany, Denmark, Sweden [...] and Poland* (London: J. Almon, 1772)
The Memoirs of Richard Cumberland (London: Lackington, Allen, & Co., 1806)
The Memoirs of Richard Cumberland, ed. by Richard J. Dircks (New York: AMS Press, 2002)
Merryland Displayed; or, Plagiarism, Ignorance, and Impudence (London: E. Curll, 1741)
The Miscellaneous Works of Charles Collignon (Cambridge: F. Hodson. Sold by J. & J. Merrill, 1786)
Miss C--Y's Cabinet of Curiosities; or, The Green-Room Broke Open. By Tristram Shandy, Gent. (Utopia [London(?)]: William Whirligig, 1765)
The Narrative Companion and Entertaining Moralist (London: Joseph Wenman, 1789)
A New Description of Merryland (London: J. Leake and E. Curll, 1741)
NICHOLS, JOHN, *Literary Anecdotes of the Eighteenth Century*, 9 vols (London: Nichols, Son and Bentley, 1812–15)
NICHOLSON, GEORGE, *Extracts from the Tristram Shandy and Sentimental Journey of Law. Sterne, M. A.* (Ludlow: printed and sold by George Nicholson, 1799)
NUGENT, THOMAS, *The Grand Tour; or, A Journey through the Netherlands, Germany, Italy and France*, 4 vols (London: D. Browne, A. Millar, G. Hawkins, W. Johnston, P. Davey, and B. Law, 1756)
'One of Uncle Toby's Illegitimate Children', *Sentiments on the Death of the Sentimental Yorick* (London: Staples Steare, 1768)
Original Letters of the Late Reverend Mr. Laurence Sterne; Never Before Published (London: Logographic Press, 1788)
OULTON, W. C., *The History of the Theatres of London [...] from the Year 1771 to 1795*, 2 vols (London: Martin and Bain, 1796)
PARSONS, PHILIP, *Dialogues of the Dead with the Living* (London: N. Conant, 1779)
The Plays of David Garrick, vol. IV, Garrick's Adaptations of Shakespeare, 1759–1773, ed. by H. W. Pedicord and F. L. Bergmann (Carbondale: Southern Illinois University Press, 1981)
Pleasing Reflections on Life and Manners with Essays, Characters & Poems, Moral & Entertaining; Principally Selected from Fugitive Publications (London: S. Hooper, 1788)
The Polite Companion; or, Wit a-la-Mode (London: G. Kearsly, 1760)
PRIOR, SIR JAMES, *Life of Edmond Malone, Editor of Shakespeare, with Selections from His Manuscript Anecdotes* (London: Smith, Elder & Co., 1860)
The Prose Epitome; or, Elegant Extracts Abridged (London: C. Dilly, 1791)
A Scotsman's Remarks on the Farce of Love a la Mode, Scene by Scene (London: J. Burd, 1760)
A Sentimental Journey: Intended as a Sequel to Mr. Sterne's through Italy, Switzerland, and France, by Mr. Shandy (Southampton: T. Baker and S. Crowder, 1793)
SHAKESPEARE, WILLIAM, *Hamlet, Prince of Denmark*, ed. by P. Edwards (Cambridge: Cambridge University Press, 2007)
—— *Hamlet, Prince of Denmark: A Tragedy* (London: J. and P. Knapton, T. Longman, C. Hitch, 1751)
—— *Hamlet, Prince of Denmark: A Tragedy. As it is Now Acted at the Theatres Royal, in Drury-Lane, and Covent-Garden* (London: Hawes and Co., B. Dodd, J. Rivington, S. Crowder, T. Longman, 1763)
—— *Romeo and Juliet. By Shakespear. With some Alterations, and an Additional Scene: As it is Performed at the Theatre-Royal in Drury-Lane* (London: J. and R. Tonson and S. Draper, 1748)
—— *Romeo and Juliet by Shakespear; with Alterations and an Additional Scene by D. Garrick. As it is Performed at the Theatre-Royal in Drury Lane* (London: [n. pub.], 1766)
—— *The Works of Mr. William Shakespear* (London: John Osborn, 1747)

SHERIDAN, THOMAS, *A Course of Lectures on Elocution* (Dublin: Samuel Whyte, of the English Grammar School, 1764)
SMOLLETT, TOBIAS, *The Adventures of Peregrine Pickle* (London: printed for the author and sold by D. Wilson, 1751)
La Souriciere: The Mouse-Trap. A Facetious and Sentimental Excursion through Part of Austrian Flanders and France. Being a Divertisement for Both Sexes, by Timothy Touchit, Esq. (London: J. Parsons, 1794)
The Spectator, ed. by D. F. Bond (Oxford: Clarendon Press, 1965)
STERNE, LAURENCE, *The Letters, Part 1: 1739–1764*, ed. by M. New and P. de Voogd (Gainesville: University Press of Florida, 2009)
—— *The Letters, Part 2: 1765–1768*, ed. by M. New and P. de Voogd (Gainesville: University Press of Florida, 2009)
—— *The Life and Opinions of Tristram Shandy, Gentleman* (Amsterdam [London?]: P. Van Slaukenberg, 1771 [1785?])
—— *The Life and Opinions of Tristram Shandy, Gentleman*, ed. by M. New and J. New (Gainesville: University Press of Florida, 1978)
—— *A Sentimental Journey through France and Italy and Continuation of the Bramine's Journal*, ed. by M. New and W. G. Day (Gainesville: University Press of Florida, 2002)
—— *The Works of Laurence Stern*, 5 vols (London: [n. pub.], 1769)
—— *The Works of Laurence Sterne. Complete in Eight Volumes* (London: the proprietors, 1790)
Sterne's Letters to His Friends on Various Occasions (London: G. Kearsly and J. Johnson, 1775)
Sterne's Maria: A Pathetic Story with an Account of Her Death at the Castle of Valesine (London: R. Rusted, 1800)
Sterne's Witticisms; or, Yorick's Convivial Jester (London: A. Milne, 1782)
The Theatrical Campaign, for MDCCLXVI and MDCCLXVII (London: S. Bladon, 1767)
Theophilus Cibber to David Garrick, Esq., with Dissertations on Theatrical Subjects (London: W. Reeves and J. Phipps, 1759)
THOMPSON, GEORGE, *A Sentimental Tour, Collected from a Variety of Occurrences, from Newbiggin, near Penrith, Cumberland to London* (Penrith: Anthony Soulby, 1798)
WILLIAMS, DAVID, *A Letter to David Garrick, Esq.* (London: S. Bladon, 1772)
The Works of the Late Aaron Hill, Esq., 4 vols (London: printed for the benefit of the family, 1753)
Yorick's Sentimental Journey Continued, 1st edn (London: S. Bladon, 1769)
Yorick's Sentimental Journey Continued, 3rd edn (London: J. Bew, 1774)

1.4 Film

A Cock and Bull Story, dir. by Michael Winterbottom (BBC Films, 2005)

2. Secondary Sources

ANDREW, DONNA T. and RANDALL MCGOWEN, *The Perreaus and Mrs. Rudd: Forgery and Betrayal in Eighteenth-Century London* (London: University of California Press, 2001)

APPLETON, WILLIAM W., *Charles Macklin: An Actor's Life* (London: Oxford University Press, 1961)

ASFOUR, LANA, *Laurence Sterne in France: A Reception History, 1760–1800* (London: Continuum, 2008)

ASHE, GEOFFREY, *The Hell-Fire Clubs: A History of Anti-Morality*, rev. edn (Stroud: Sutton Publishing, 2000)

AUBURN, MARK S., 'Theatre in the Age of Garrick and Sheridan', in *Sheridan Studies*, ed. by J. Morwood and D. Crane (Cambridge: Cambridge University Press, 1995), 7–46

BAINES, PAUL, *The House of Forgery in Eighteenth-Century Britain* (Aldershot: Ashgate, 1999)

—— and PAT ROGERS, *Edmund Curll: Bookseller* (Oxford: Oxford University Press, 2007)

BANDRY, ANNE, 'Imitations of *Tristram Shandy*', in *Critical Essays on Laurence Sterne*, ed. by M. New (New York: G. K. Hall, 1998), 39–52

BANNET, EVE TAVOR, *Empire of Letters: Letter Manuals and Transatlantic Correspondence, 1688–1820* (Cambridge: Cambridge University Press, 2005)

BARCHAS, JANINE, *Graphic Design, Print Culture, and the Eighteenth-Century Novel* (Cambridge: Cambridge University Press, 2003)

BARKER, HANNAH, *Newspapers, Politics and Public Opinion in Late Eighteenth-Century England* (Oxford: Clarendon Press, 1998)

BARKER-BENFIELD, G. J., *The Culture of Sensibility: Sex and Society in Eighteenth-Century Britain* (London: University of Chicago Press, 1992)

BAUGH, CHRISTOPHER, *Garrick and Loutherbourg* (Cambridge: Chadwyck-Healey, 1990)

—— 'Philippe James de Loutherbourg and the Early Pictorial Theatre: Some Aspects of its Cultural Context', in *The Theatrical Space*, ed. by J. Redmond (Cambridge: Cambridge University Press, 1987), 99–128

BENEDETTI, JEAN, *David Garrick and the Birth of Modern Theatre* (London: Methuen, 2001)

BENEDICT, BARBARA M., *Framing Feeling: Sentiment and Style in English Prose Fiction, 1745–1800* (New York: AMS Press, 1994)

—— *Making the Modern Reader: Cultural Mediation in Early Modern Literary Anthologies* (Princeton, NJ: Princeton University Press, 1996)

BERG, MAXINE, *Luxury and Pleasure in Eighteenth-Century Britain* (Oxford: Oxford University Press, 2005)

—— and HELEN CLIFFORD, 'Selling Consumption in the Eighteenth Century: Advertising and the Trade Card in Britain and France', *Cultural & Social History*, 4 (2007), 145–70

BLACK, JEREMY, *The British Abroad: The Grand Tour in the Eighteenth Century* (New York: St. Martin's Press, 1992)

—— 'Tourism and Cultural Challenge: The Changing Scene of the Eighteenth Century', in *English Literature and the Wider World* (London: Ashfield Press, 1990-), I: *All Before Them, 1660–1780*, ed. by John McVeagh (1990), 185–202

BLACKWELL, MARK, 'Hackwork: It-Narratives and Iteration', in *The Secret Life of Things: Animals, Objects, and It-Narratives in Eighteenth-Century England*, ed. by M. Blackwell (Lewisburg: Bucknell University Press, 2007), 187–217

BOSCH, RENÉ, *Labyrinth of Digressions: Tristram Shandy as Perceived and Influenced by Sterne's Early Imitators*, trans. by P. Verhoeff (Amsterdam: Rodopi, 2007)

BRANT, CLARE, *Eighteenth-Century Letters and British Culture* (Basingstoke: Palgrave Macmillan, 2006)

BREWER, DAVID A., *The Afterlife of Character, 1726–1825* (Philadelphia: University of Pennsylvania Press, 2005)

BRIGGS, PETER M., 'Laurence Sterne and Literary Celebrity in 1760', in *Laurence Sterne's Tristram Shandy: A Casebook*, ed. by T. Keymer (Oxford: Oxford University Press, 2006), 79–107
BURNIM, KALMAN A., *David Garrick: Director* (Carbondale: Southern Illinois University Press, 1973)
BUTLER, MARILYN, *Romantics, Rebels, and Reactionaries: English Literature and its Background, 1760–1830* (Oxford: Oxford University Press, 1981)
CAINES, MICHAEL, ed., *Lives of Shakespearean Actors, Part I: David Garrick, Charles Macklin, and Margaret Woffington by their Contemporaries* (London: Pickering & Chatto, 2008)
CARTER, PHILIP, *Men and the Emergence of Polite Society: Britain, 1660–1800* (London: Longman, 2001)
CASH, ARTHUR H., *Laurence Sterne: The Early and Middle Years* (London: Methuen, 1975)
—— *Laurence Sterne: The Later Years* (London: Methuen, 1986)
—— 'Sterne, Hall, Libertinism, and *A Sentimental Journey*', *The Age of Johnson: A Scholarly Annual*, 12 (2001), 291–327
CLARK, PETER, *British Clubs and Societies, 1580–1800: The Origins of an Associational World* (Oxford: Clarendon Press, 2000)
CLARK, WILLIAM SMITH, *The Irish Stage in the County Towns, 1720 to 1800* (Oxford: Clarendon Press, 1965)
CLERY, E. J., *The Rise of Supernatural Fiction, 1762–1800* (Cambridge: Cambridge University Press, 1995)
COHEN, MICHÈLE, *Fashioning Masculinity: National Identity and Language in the Eighteenth Century* (London: Routledge, 1996)
COLLEY, LINDA, *Captives: Britain, Empire, and the World, 1600–1850* (London: Pimlico, 2003)
COPELAND, NANCY, 'The Sentimentality of Garrick's *Romeo and Juliet*', *Restoration and 18th Century Theatre Research*, 4 (1989), 1–13
CRUISE, JAMES, *Governing Consumption: Needs and Wants, Suspended Characters, and the 'Origins' of Eighteenth-Century English Novels* (Lewisburg: Bucknell University Press, 1999)
CRYLE, PETER and LISA O'CONNELL, 'Sex, Liberty and Licence in the Eighteenth Century', in P. Cryle and L. O'Connell, eds., *Libertine Enlightenment: Sex, Liberty, and Licence in the Eighteenth Century* (Basingstoke: Palgrave Macmillan, 2004), 1–14
CUNNINGHAM, VANESSA, *Shakespeare and Garrick* (Cambridge: Cambridge University Press, 2008)
CURLEY, THOMAS M., *Samuel Johnson and the Age of Travel* (Athens: University of Georgia Press, 1976)
CURTIS, LEWIS PERRY, 'Forged Letters of Laurence Sterne', *PMLA*, 50 (1935), 1076–1106
DAVIDSON, JENNY, *Hypocrisy and the Politics of Politeness: Manners and Morals from Locke to Austen* (Cambridge: Cambridge University Press, 2004)
DAY, W. G., *Laurence Sterne. A Sentimental Journey: A Bibliographical Catalogue of Editions Spanning Nearly Two and a Half Centuries* (York: Spelman, 2005)
DESCARGUES, MADELEINE, '*Tristram Shandy* and the Appositeness of War', *The Shandean*, 12 (2001), 63–77
DE VOOGD, PETER, 'The Letters of Laurence Sterne', *The Shandean*, 4 (1992), 181–95
—— '*Tristram Shandy* as Aesthetic Object', in *Laurence Sterne's Tristram Shandy: A Casebook*, ed. by T. Keymer (Oxford: Oxford University Press, 2006), 108–19
—— 'Uncle Toby, Laurence Sterne and the Siege of Limerick', *Dutch Quarterly Review of Anglo-American Letters*, 18 (1988), 199–208
DONOGHUE, FRANK, *The Fame Machine: Book Reviewing and Eighteenth-Century Literary Careers* (Stanford: Stanford University Press, 1996)
EGMOND, FLORIKE, 'Execution, Dissection, Pain and Infamy — A Morphological Investigation', in *Bodily Extremities: Preoccupations with the Human Body in Early Modern European Culture*, ed. by F. Egmond and R. Zwijnenberg (Aldershot: Ashgate, 2003), 92–127

ELLIS, MARKMAN, *The Coffee-House: A Cultural History* (London: Phoenix, 2005)
—— *The Politics of Sensibility: Race, Gender, and Commerce in the Sentimental Novel* (Cambridge: Cambridge University Press, 1996)
ENGLERT, HILARY JANE, 'Occupying Works: Animated Objects and Literary Property', in *The Secret Life of Things: Animals, Objects, and It-Narratives in Eighteenth-Century England*, ed. by M. Blackwell (Lewisburg: Bucknell University Press, 2007), 218–41
ERICKSON, ROBERT A., *Mother Midnight: Birth, Sex, and Fate in Eighteenth-Century Fiction (Defoe, Richardson, and Sterne)* (New York: AMS Press, 1986)
FEATHER, JOHN, *Publishing, Piracy, and Politics: An Historical Study of Copyright in Britain* (London: Mansell, 1994)
FERGUSON, FRANCES, *Pornography, the Theory: What Utilitarianism Did to Action* (London: University of Chicago Press, 2004)
FITZSIMMONS, LINDA and ARTHUR W. MCDONALD, eds, *The Yorkshire Stage* (London: The Scarecrow Press, 1989)
FLINT, CHRISTOPHER, 'The Eighteenth-Century Novel and Print Culture: A Proposed Modesty', in *A Companion to the Eighteenth-Century English Novel and Culture*, ed. by P. R. Backscheider and C. Ingrassia (Oxford: Blackwell, 2005), 343–64
FOLEY-DAWSON, D'ARCY, '24 Hour Party People and A Cock and Bull Story', *The Shandean*, 18 (2007), 148–55
FOREMAN, AMANDA, *Georgiana: Duchess of Devonshire* (London: HarperCollins, 1998)
FOYSTER, ELIZABETH, 'Boys will be Boys? Manhood and Aggression, 1660–1800', in *English Masculinities, 1660–1800*, ed. by T. Hitchcock and M. Cohen (London: Longman, 1999), 151–66
GATRELL, VIC, *City of Laughter: Sex and Satire in Eighteenth-Century London* (London: Atlantic Books, 2006)
—— *The Hanging Tree: Execution and the English People, 1770–1868* (Oxford: Oxford University Press, 1994)
GENETTE, GERARD, *Palimpsests: Literature in the Second Degree*, trans. by C. Newman and C. Doubinsky (London: University of Nebraska Press, 1997)
—— *Paratexts: Thresholds of Interpretation*, trans. by J. E. Lewin (Cambridge: Cambridge University Press, 1997)
GERARD, W. B., *Laurence Sterne and the Visual Imagination* (Aldershot: Ashgate, 2006)
GORING, PAUL, '"John Bull, pit, box, and gallery, said No!": Charles Macklin and the Limits of Ethnic Resistance on the Eighteenth-Century London Stage', *Representations*, 79 (2002), 61–81
GOULEMOT, JEAN MARIE, *Forbidden Texts: Erotic Literature and its Readers in Eighteenth-Century France*, trans. by J. Simpson (Oxford: Polity Press, 1994)
GRIFFIN, ROBERT J., 'Anonymity and Authorship', *New Literary History*, 30 (1999), 877–95
GROOM, NICK, *The Forger's Shadow: How Forgery Changed the Course of Literature* (London: Picador, 2002)
—— 'Forgery, Plagiarism, Imitation, Pegleggery', in *Plagiarism in Early Modern England*, ed. by P. Kewes (Basingstoke: Palgrave Macmillan, 2003), 74–89
HAFTER, RONALD, 'Garrick and *Tristram Shandy*', *SEL: Studies in English Literature, 1500–1900*, 7 (1967), 475–89
HAMILTON, HARLAN W., *Doctor Syntax: A Silhouette of William Combe, Esq.* (London: Chatto and Windus, 1969)
—— 'William Combe and the *Original Letters of the Late Reverend Mr. Laurence Sterne* (1788)', *PMLA*, 82 (1967), 420–29
HARE, ARNOLD, ed., *Theatre Royal Bath: A Calendar of Performances at the Orchard Street Theatre, 1750–1805* (Bath: Kingsmead Press, 1977)
HARRIES, ELIZABETH WANNING, *The Unfinished Manner: Essays on the Fragment in the Later Eighteenth Century* (London: University Press of Virginia, 1994)

HARTLEY, LODWICK, 'Laurence Sterne and the Eighteenth-Century Stage', *Papers on Language and Literature*, 4 (1968), 144–57
—— 'Sterne's Eugenius as Indiscreet Author: The Literary Career of John Hall-Stevenson', *PMLA*, 86 (1971), 428–55
—— '*Yorick's Sentimental Journey Continued*: A Reconsideration of the Authorship', *South Atlantic Quarterly*, 70 (1971), 180–90
HARVEY, KAREN, *Reading Sex in the Eighteenth Century: Bodies and Gender in English Erotic Culture* (Cambridge: Cambridge University Press, 2004)
HAWLEY, JUDITH, 'The Anatomy of *Tristram Shandy*', in *Literature and Medicine during the Eighteenth Century*, ed. by M. M. Roberts and R. Porter (London: Routledge, 1993), 84–100
HAYES, JOHN, *Rowlandson: Watercolours and Drawings* (London: Phaidon, 1972)
HIGHFILL, PHILIP H., KALMAN A. BURNIM and EDWARD A. LANGHANS, *A Biographical Dictionary of Actors, Actresses, Musicians, Dancers, Managers and Other Stage Personnel in London, 1660–1800*, 16 vols (Carbondale: Southern Illinois University Press, 1973–1993), I (1973), V (1978), VII (1982), VIII (1982), X (1984), XI (1987), XIII (1991), XVI (1993)
HITCHCOCK, TIM, *English Sexualities, 1700–1800* (London: Macmillan, 1997)
HOGAN, CHARLES BEECHER, ed., *The London Stage, Part 5: 1776–1800* (Carbondale: Southern Illinois University Press, 1968)
HOLLAND, PETER and MICHAEL PATTERSON, 'Eighteenth-Century Theatre', in *The Oxford Illustrated History of the Theatre*, ed. by J. R. Brown (Oxford: Oxford University Press, 2001), 255–98
HOWES, ALAN B., *Yorick and the Critics: Sterne's Reputation in England, 1760–1868* (New Haven: Yale University Press, 1958)
—— ed., *Sterne: The Critical Heritage* (London: Routledge and Kegan Paul, 1974)
HUNTER, J. PAUL, 'From Typology to Type: Agents of Change in Eighteenth-Century English Texts', in *Cultural Artifacts and the Production of Meaning: the Page, the Image, and the Body*, ed. by M. J. M. Ezell and K. O'Brien O'Keeffe (Ann Arbor: University of Michigan Press, 1994), 41–69
JONES, LOUIS C., *Clubs of the Georgian Rakes* (New York: Columbia University Press, 1942)
KEARNEY, PATRICK J., *A History of Erotic Literature* (London: Macmillan, 1982)
KENDRICK, WALTER, *The Secret Museum: Pornography in Modern Culture* (London: University of California Press, 1987)
KERNAN, ALVIN, *Printing Technology, Letters and Samuel Johnson* (Princeton, NJ: Princeton University Press, 1987)
KEWES, PAULINA, 'Historicizing Plagiarism', in *Plagiarism in Early Modern England*, ed. by P. Kewes (Basingstoke: Palgrave Macmillan, 2003), 1–18
KEYMER, THOMAS, *Sterne, the Moderns, and the Novel* (Oxford: Oxford University Press, 2002)
KIERNAN, V. G., *The Duel in European History: Honour and the Reign of Aristocracy* (Oxford: Oxford University Press, 1988)
KINSERVIK, MATTHEW J., *Disciplining Satire: The Censorship of Satiric Comedy on the Eighteenth-Century London Stage* (Lewisburg: Bucknell University Press, 2002)
KUIST, JAMES M., 'New Light on Sterne: An Old Man's Recollections of the Young Vicar', *PMLA*, 80 (1965), 549–53
LANGFORD, PAUL, *A Polite and Commercial People: England, 1727–1783* (Oxford: Oxford University Press, 1989)
LANHAM, RICHARD A., *Tristram Shandy: The Games of Pleasure* (London: University of California Press, 1973)
LARGIER, NIKLAUS, *In Praise of the Whip: A Cultural History of Arousal*, trans. by G. Harman (New York: Zone Books, 2007)

LAWLOR, CLARK, 'Consuming Time: Narrative and Disease in *Tristram Shandy*', *Yearbook of English Studies*, 30 (2000), 46–59

LEE, SIDNEY, ed., *Dictionary of National Biography* (London: Smith, Elder and Co., 1898)

LEPPERT, RICHARD, *Music and Image: Domesticity, Ideology, and Social Function* (Cambridge: Cambridge University Press, 1998)

LYNCH, DEIDRE, 'Personal Effects and Sentimental Fictions', in *The Secret Life of Things: Animals, Objects, and It-Narratives in Eighteenth-Century England*, ed. by M. Blackwell (Lewisburg: Bucknell University Press, 2007), 63–91

MADOFF, MARK S., '"They caught fire at each other": Laurence Sterne's Journal of the Pulse of Sensibility', in *Sensibility in Transformation: Creative Resistance to Sentiment from the Augustans to the Romantics*, ed. by S. McMillen Conger (London: Associated University Presses, 1990), 43–62

MANNIX, DANIEL P., *The Hell-Fire Club* (London: New English Library, 1962)

MARSHALL, TIM, *Murdering to Dissect: Grave-Robbing, Frankenstein and the Anatomy Literature* (Manchester: Manchester University Press, 1995)

MATTHEW, H. C. G., and B. HARRISON, eds, *Oxford Dictionary of National Biography* (Oxford: Oxford University Press, 2004)

MAYO, R. D., *The English Novel in the Magazines, 1740–1815* (London: Oxford University Press, 1965)

MAZELLA, DAVID, '"Be wary, sir, when you imitate him": The Perils of Didacticism in *Tristram Shandy*', *Studies in the Novel*, 31 (1999), 152–77

MCCORMICK, DONALD, *The Hell-Fire Club* (London: Jarrolds, 1958)

MCINTYRE, IAN, *Garrick* (Harmondsworth: Penguin, 1999)

MCLOUGHLIN, T. O., *Contesting Ireland: Irish Voices Against England in the Eighteenth Century* (Dublin: Four Courts Press, 1999)

MCMASTER, JULIET, '"Uncrystalized flesh and blood": The Body in *Tristram Shandy*', in *Laurence Sterne*, ed. by M. Walsh (London: Longman, 2002), 95–111

MILHOUS, JUDITH, 'Company Management', in *The London Theatre World, 1660–1800*, ed. by R. D. Hume (Carbondale: Southern Illinois University Press, 1980), 1–34

MONKMAN, KENNETH and W. G. DAY, 'The Skull', *The Shandean*, 10 (1998), 45–79

MOODY, JANE, *Illegitimate Theatre in London, 1770–1840* (Cambridge: Cambridge University Press, 2000)

MORASH, CHRISTOPHER, *A History of Irish Theatre, 1601–2000* (Cambridge: Cambridge University Press, 2002)

MOSS, ROGER B., 'Sterne's Punctuation', *Eighteenth-Century Studies*, 15 (1982), 179–200

MOULTON, IAN FREDERICK, *Before Pornography: Erotic Writing in Early Modern England* (Oxford: Oxford University Press, 2000)

MUDGE, BRADFORD K., *The Whore's Story: Women, Pornography, and the British Novel, 1684–1830* (Oxford: Oxford University Press, 2000)

MULLAN, JOHN, *Sentiment and Sociability: The Language of Feeling in the Eighteenth Century* (Oxford: Oxford University Press, 1988)

NAGLE, CHRISTOPHER C., *Sexuality and the Culture of Sensibility in the British Romantic Era* (Basingstoke: Palgrave Macmillan, 2007)

NEW, MELVYN, 'Tristram Shandy: A Cock and Bull Story', *Eighteenth-Century Studies*, 39 (2006), 579–81

NEWBOULD, M.-C., 'Shandying it Away: Sterne's Theatricality', *The Shandean*, 18 (2007), 156–70

NICOLL, ALLARDYCE, *The Garrick Stage: Theatres and Audience in the Eighteenth Century* (Manchester: Manchester University Press, 1980)

O'BRIEN, JOHN, 'Harlequin Britain: Eighteenth-Century Pantomime and the Cultural Location of Entertainments', *Theatre Journal*, 50 (1998), 489–510

——— *Harlequin Britain: Pantomime and Entertainment, 1690–1760* (Baltimore and London: Johns Hopkins University Press, 2004)
OGÉE, FRÉDÉRIC, 'Channelling Emotions: Travel and Literary Creation in Smollett and Sterne', *Studies on Voltaire and the Eighteenth Century*, 292 (1991), 27–42
OYA, REIKO, *Representing Shakespearean Tragedy: Garrick, the Kembles, and Kean* (Cambridge: Cambridge University Press, 2007)
PEAKMAN, JULIE, *Lascivious Bodies: A Sexual History of the Eighteenth Century* (London: Atlantic Books, 2004)
——— *Mighty Lewd Books: The Development of Pornography in Eighteenth-Century England* (Basingstoke: Palgrave Macmillan, 2003)
PEASE, ALLISON, *Modernism, Mass Culture, and the Aesthetics of Obscenity* (Cambridge: Cambridge University Press, 2000)
PELTONEN, MARKKU, *The Duel in Early Modern England: Civility, Politeness, and Honour* (Cambridge: Cambridge University Press, 2003)
PORTER, ROY, '"The whole secret of health": Mind, Body and Medicine in *Tristram Shandy*', in *Nature Transfigured: Science and Literature, 1700–1900*, ed. by J. Christie and S. Shuttleworth (Manchester: Manchester University Press, 1989), 61–84
POWELL, MARTYN J., 'Ireland: Radicalism, Rebellion and Union', in *A Companion to Eighteenth-Century Britain*, ed. by H. T. Dickinson (Oxford: Blackwell, 2002), 414–28
PRICE, CECIL, 'Thomas Harris and the Covent Garden Theatre', in *The Eighteenth-Century English Stage*, ed. by K. Richards and P. Thomson (London: Methuen, 1972), 105–22
PRICE, LEAH, *The Anthology and the Rise of the Novel* (Cambridge: Cambridge University Press, 2000)
RAGUSSIS, MICHAEL, 'Jews and Other "Outlandish Englishmen": Ethnic Performance and the Invention of British Identity under the Georges', *Critical Inquiry*, 26 (2000), 773–97
RAVEN, JAMES, *Judging New Wealth: Popular Publishing and Responses to Commerce in England, 1750–1800* (Oxford: Clarendon Press, 1992)
———, HELEN SMALL, and NAOMI TADMOR, 'The Practice and Representation of Reading in England', in *The Practice and Representation of Reading in England*, ed. by J. Raven, H. Small, and N. Tadmor (Cambridge: Cambridge University Press, 1996), 1–21
REGAN, SHAUN PATRICK, 'Laurence Sterne, Wit, and Politeness: Comedy and Cultural Politics in Eighteenth-Century England' (doctoral thesis, University of Wales, Aberystwyth, 1999)
RICE, SCOTT B., 'Smollett's *Travels* and the Genre of Grand Tour Literature', *Costerus*, 1 (1972), 207–20
RICHARDSON, RUTH, *Death, Dissection and the Destitute* (London: Routledge and Kegan Paul, 1987)
ROBSON, MARK, 'The Ethics of Anonymity', *MLR*, 103 (2008), 350–63
ROSE, MARK, *Authors and Owners: The Invention of Copyright* (Cambridge, MA: Harvard University Press, 1993)
ROSS, IAN CAMPBELL, *Laurence Sterne: A Life* (Oxford: Oxford University Press, 2001)
RUBENHOLD, HALLIE, *The Covent Garden Ladies: Pimp General Jack & the Extraordinary Story of Harris's List* (Stroud: Tempus, 2006)
RUSSELL, GILLIAN, *The Theatres of War: Performance, Politics, and Society, 1793–1815* (Oxford: Clarendon Press, 1995)
RUTHVEN, K. K., *Faking Literature* (Cambridge: Cambridge University Press, 2001)
SAPPOL, MICHAEL, *A Traffic of Dead Bodies: Anatomy and Embodied Social Identity in Nineteenth-Century America* (Princeton, NJ: Princeton University Press, 2002)
SCHEIL, KATHERINE WEST, *The Taste of the Town: Shakespearian Comedy and the Early Eighteenth-Century Theater* (Lewisburg: Bucknell University Press, 2003)
SCHLENTHER, BOYD STANLEY, *Queen of the Methodists: The Countess of Huntingdon and the Eighteenth-Century Crisis of Faith and Society* (Durham: Durham University Press, 1997)

SCHOCH, RICHARD W., *Not Shakespeare: Bardolatry and Burlesque in the Nineteenth Century* (Cambridge: Cambridge University Press, 2002)

SECHELSKI, D. S., 'Garrick's Body and the Labor of Art in Eighteenth-Century Theater', *Eighteenth-Century Studies*, 29 (1996), 369–89

SEIDEL, MICHAEL, *Satiric Inheritance, Rabelais to Sterne* (Princeton, NJ: Princeton University Press, 1979)

SHERBO, ARTHUR, 'The Dissection of Laurence Sterne', *N&Q*, 232 (1987), 348

SHOEMAKER, ROBERT B., *The London Mob: Violence and Disorder in Eighteenth-Century England* (London: Hambledon and London, 2004)

—— 'Reforming Male Manners: Public Insult and the Decline of Violence in London, 1660–1740', in *English Masculinities, 1660–1800*, ed. by T. Hitchcock and M. Cohen (Harlow: Longman, 1999), 133–50

SINFIELD, MARK, 'Uncle Toby's Potency: Some Critical and Authorial Confusions in *Tristram Shandy*', *N&Q*, 223 (1978), 54–55

SMITH, K. E., 'Ordering Things in France: The Travels of Sterne, Tristram and Yorick', *Studies on Voltaire and the Eighteenth Century*, 292 (1991), 15–25

SMITH, WOODRUFF D., *Consumption and the Making of Respectability, 1600–1800* (London: Routledge, 2002)

SOLOMON, HARRY M., *The Rise of Robert Dodsley: Creating the Age of Print* (Carbondale: Southern Illinois University Press, 1996)

SPACKS, PATRICIA MEYER, *Privacy: Concealing the Eighteenth-Century Self* (London: University of Chicago Press, 2003)

SPENCER, LIESE, 'The Postmodernist Always Wings It Twice', *Sight&Sound*, 16.2 (February 2006), 14–17

STEPHANSON, RAYMOND, '"Epicœne Friendship": Understanding Male Friendship in the Early Eighteenth Century, with Some Speculations about Pope', *The Eighteenth Century: Theory and Interpretation*, 38 (1997), 151–70

STERN, J. P., *Lichtenberg: A Doctrine of Scattered Occasions* (Bloomington: Indiana University Press, 1959)

STERN, TIFFANY, *Rehearsal from Shakespeare to Sheridan* (Oxford: Clarendon Press, 2000)

STRAUB, KRISTINA, *Sexual Suspects: Eighteenth-Century Players and Sexual Ideology* (Princeton, NJ: Princeton University Press, 1992)

SUTTON, R. B., 'Further Evidence of David Garrick's Portrayal of Hamlet from the Diary of Georg Christoph Lichtenberg', *Theatre Notebook*, 50 (1996), 8–14

TADIÉ, ALEXIS, *Sterne's Whimsical Theatres of Language: Orality, Gesture, Literacy* (Aldershot: Ashgate, 2003)

TANKARD, PAUL, 'The "Great Cham" and the "English Aristophanes": Samuel Johnson, Samuel Foote, and Harmless Pleasure', *The Age of Johnson: A Scholarly Annual*, 15 (2004), 83–96

THOMPSON, KARL F., 'The Authorship of *Yorick's Sentimental Journey Continued*', *N&Q*, 195 (1950), 318–19

TRISTRAM, PHILIPPA, *Living Space in Fact and Fiction* (London: Routledge, 1989)

TURNER, KATHERINE, *British Travel Writers in Europe, 1750–1800* (Aldershot: Ashgate, 2001)

VAN SANT, ANN JESSIE, *Eighteenth-Century Sensibility and the Novel: The Senses in Social Context* (Cambridge: Cambridge University Press, 1993)

WATTS, CAROL, *The Cultural Work of Empire: The Seven Years' War and the Imagining of the Shandean State* (Edinburgh: Edinburgh University Press, 2007)

WELLS, STANLEY, ed., *Shakespeare in the Theatre: An Anthology of Criticism* (Oxford: Oxford University Press, 1997)

WERNER, FLORIAN, 'Kindred Spirits? John Cleland's *Fanny Hill* and Laurence Sterne's *A Sentimental Journey*', *Zeitschrift für Anglistik Und Amerikanistik*, 48 (2000), 17–30

WILLIAMS, RAYMOND, *The Country and the City* (London: Chatto & Windus, 1973)
——*Keywords: A Vocabulary of Culture and Society* (London: Fontana, 1983)
WOODS, LEIGH, *Garrick Claims the Stage: Acting as Social Emblem in Eighteenth-Century England* (London: Greenwood Press, 1984)

INDEX

*References to illustrations are in **bold***

actors:
   Bannister, Charles 53
   Brydon, Rob 128
   Catley, Ann 82, 103 n. 26
   Coogan, Steve 127–29, 130 n. 5
   Delane, Dennis 11
   Edwin, John 68
   Fawcett, John 67
   Hull, Thomas 69, 71
   Kennedy, Margaret 68, 70–71, 73, 75 n. 87
   Powell, William 30–31, 49 n. 11
   Shuter, Edward (Ned) 67
   Wilkinson, Tate 11
   Woodward, Henry 11
Addison, Joseph 72
anatomisation:
   as literary concept 4, 5, 6, 9, 14, 23, 57, 81–82, 86, 87–88
   of Sterne's body 2–3, 6, 24 nn. 6 & 7, 88
Aretino, Pietro 79
articulation:
   and Jeremy Bentham 6, 25 n. 54
   as literary concept 4–6, 23, 57, 58, 121
   in osteology 2, 4–6, 58
Auburn, Mark 39

Bandry, Anne 26 n. 86
Bannet, Eve Tavor 124 n. 48
Barchas, Janine 31, 124 n. 35
Barker, Hannah 101, 106 n. 134
Barrington, Sir Jonah 61
Becket, Thomas 4, 93, 105 n. 84
Benedetti, Jean 33, 34
Benedict, Barbara 115
Berg, Maxine 123 n. 5
Black, Jeremy 97, 106 nn. 121 & 122
Blackwell, Mark 4, 17, 19, 21
Bosch, René 4, 17, 21, 25 n. 40, 26 n. 65, 94, 103 n. 22
Boswell, James 10, 25 n. 46, 79, 93, 101, 118
Brewer, David A. 5, 7, 25 nn. 36 & 51
Briggs, Peter 15–16
Burke, Edmund, *A Philosophical Enquiry* 19, 118
Burnim, Kalman 33, 41–43
Burton, Francis Pierpoint (Baron Conyngham) 110, 112–13, 121
Butler, Marilyn 72–73

Caricature Shop 89
Carter, Philip 10, 38, 110, 114–15, 118, 124 n. 24, 125 nn. 73 & 80, 126 n. 98
Cash, Arthur H. 24 n. 6, 26 n. 65, 38, 104 n. 56, 105 n. 100, 118
Cavendish, Georgiana (Duchess of Devonshire) and the Devonshire House circle 111
Churchill, Charles, *The Rosciad* 29
Cibber, Theophilus 33
Clark, Peter 91, 115
Cleland, John 79, 81, 82, 93–94
   and *Memoirs of a Woman of Pleasure* 82, 92, 104 n. 49
Cohen, Michèle 120
Collignon, Charles 2, 6, 24 n. 6
Colman, George (the elder) 45
Combe, William:
   and anonymity 11, 16, 19, 21, 109, 110, 117, 119, 120, 122
   finances 107, 111, 123 nn. 5 & 8, 130
   and forgery 23, 108, 123 n. 14
   friendships (both actual and textual) 107–08, 109–10, 111–13, 118, 122–23
   obituaries 113–14, 124 nn. 56 & 57
   works 5, 10, 11, 14, 16–17, 19, 21, 23, 26 n. 78, 107–10, 111–15, 117–23, 124 nn. 38 & 42, 128, 130
      advertisement of 120–21
      popularity of 16, 113–14
      reception of 13, 114
Copeland, Nancy 43
Cruise, James 22–23
Cumberland, Richard 9–10, 13, 16
   and *The West Indian* 13–14, 15–16, 26 n. 66
Cunningham, Vanessa 43, 51 n. 60
Curtis, Lewis Perry 108, 120, 121, 125 n. 93

Dashwood, Sir Francis, and the Hell-Fire Club 92, 105 nn. 96 & 98
Davies, Thomas, *Memoirs of the Life of David Garrick* 30–31, 33
Defoe, Daniel 22
Dodsley, James and Robert 93, 105 nn. 83 & 103
Dundas, Henry 66–67

Ellis, Markman 32, 114–15
Erickson, Robert 70, 75 nn. 82 & 84
erotica:
   and anonymity 12, 83, 84, 92–93, 100–01, 104 n. 64

attitudes to 13, 79, 82, 83, 88–89, 90, 91–93, 100–02, 106 n. 136
and bacchanalian clubs 14, 23, 84–85, 89–92, 94, 97, 130
consumption of 13, 23, 90–92, 94–96, 97, 99
flagellation literature 77–79, 102 nn. 9 & 11, 103 n. 14
and Sterne's *Journey* 78–79
formats of 84, 93, 94, 95–96, 105 n. 115, 106 n. 118
and geographical exploration 78, 95–97, 102 n. 7, 106 n. 124
glove fetish 78–79, 102 n. 12
in newspapers 77, 98–101, 103 n. 20, 106 n. 129
and politeness 89, 97, 101, 118
Sternean erotica 3, 5, 6, 9, 10, 12, 13, 14, 21, 23, 77–78, 81–88, 89–98, 102 n. 6, 103 n. 23, 118
works:
   An Account of the Remains of the Worship of Priapus 94
   Bon Ton 78
   'COUNTER EPISTLES FROM BRIGHT-HELMSTONE' 21, 82, 98–102, 106 nn. 129 & 136, 118
   L'ecole des Filles 88
   Exhibition of Female Flagellants 77, 102 nn. 4 & 11
   Harris's List of Covent Garden Ladies 95–96, 106 nn. 117 & 118
   Lady Bumtickler's Revels 77
   Madame Birchini's Dance 77, 79, 102 n. 4
   Memoirs of a Woman of Pleasure 82, 92, 104 n. 49
   Merryland Displayed 78
   A New Description of Merryland 78
   The Sublime of Flagellation 77

Ferguson, Frances 82
Fielding, Sarah, *The Adventures of David Simple* 31
Fitzpatrick, Thaddeus 33
Flint, Christopher 22
Foote, Samuel:
   as manager of the Haymarket 11–12, 25 n. 50, 26 n. 60
   as mimic 6, 8, 9–10, 25 nn. 48 & 56

Gamelin, Jacques, *Nouveau recueil d'ostéologie et de myologie* 5–6
Garrick, David:
   acting career 7, 11, 29, 30–31, 33–34, 36, 37, 38, 43, 45–47, 48, 49, 50 n. 26
   and Lichtenberg's description of 40–41, 50 nn. 48 & 55
   and Smollett's description of 33–34, 36, 37, 38, 47, 51 n. 85
   management of Drury Lane theatre 6, 29, 45
   and stagecraft 39–43, 49
   portrait of 17, 18
   and Shakespeare 34–35, 40–43, 45–46, 51 nn. 60 & 76
   and Sterne (friendship with, and influence upon) 11, 23, 29–31, 32–33, 34–39, 43–49, 49 n. 4, 120
Gatrell, Vic 89, 103 n. 15

Gay, John, *The Beggar's Opera* 53, 68
gentlemanliness 5, 19, 21, 34, 101, 102, 109, 110–11, 114, 117, 118–20, 122, 123, 125 n. 61, 127
Gerard, W. B. 102 n. 6, 103 n. 16
Gilliland, Thomas 76 n. 98
Gillray, James, *A Sale of English-Beauties* 77, 102 n. 4
Goring, Paul 62
Goulemot, Jean Marie 88–89, 104 n. 55
Graham, James 117
Griffin, Robert 19
Griffiths, Ralph 48–49

hacks 4, 17, 19, 128
Hall-Stevenson, John:
   and anonymity 11, 16, 19, 21, 84, 91, 92–93, 100–01, 122
   critical responses to 13, 26 n. 65, 82, 93, 97, 99–102, 106 n. 136, 128
   and the Demoniacs 10, 84, 89, 91–92, 93–94, 105 n. 100, 110, 122, 130
   and newspaper erotica 12–13, 21, 98–102, 106 n. 129
   and Sterne's personae 10, 16, 90, 92, 127
   works 10, 11, 12, 13, 14, 21, 26 n. 65, 30, 81, 82, 84, 86, 89–93, 94, 95, 98–102, 103 n. 23, 105 n. 115, 106 nn. 129 & 136, 122, 128, 130
   and *Yorick's Sentimental Journey Continued* 11, 83, 84–85, 86, 104 n. 43
Hamilton, Harlan 107, 124 n. 38
Harries, Elizabeth Wanning 32, 75 n. 91
Harris, Thomas:
   casting of MacNally's *Tristram Shandy* 54–55, 67–68, 70–72, 129, 130
   management of Covent Garden theatre 53, 67, 68, 69, 72, 76 n. 98
   posthumous reputation 53, 73 n. 4
Hartley, Lodwick 104 n. 43
Harvey, Karen 75 n. 87, 77, 88, 89, 104 nn. 70 & 77, 124 n. 53
Hawley, Judith 70, 75 n. 84
Hill, Aaron, *Meropé* 41
Hitchcock, Tim 89
Hogarth, William 7, 115
Holland, William 77–79, 81, 88, 102
Hunter, John 4–5
Hunter, J. Paul 31

Johnson, Samuel 8–9, 10, 12, 22, 29, 32, 33, 119

Kendrick, Walter 88
Kernan, Alvin 22
Keymer, Thomas 22, 27 n. 101
Kiernan, V. G. 119
Knox, Vicesimus 12, 57

Lackington, James 22
Langford, Paul 61, 125 n. 84
Lanham, Richard 70

Largier, Niklaus 78
Leppert, Richard 125 n. 78
libel 12, 98, 100
Lichtenberg, Georg Christoph 3, 24 n. 12, 40–41, 43, 50 nn. 47, 48 & 55, 112, 124 n. 44
Lynch, Deidre 47, 51 n. 84
Lyser, Michael, *The Art of Dissecting the Human Body* 5

McCormick, Donald 92
MacDonald, John, *Travels in Various Parts of Europe* 6–7
Mackenzie, Henry, *The Man of Feeling* 77, 79, 87
Macklin, Charles:
    acting career 61–62
    and *Love à-la-Mode* 61–66
MacNally, Leonard:
    and Macklin 61–62
    political involvement 60–61
    works:
        The Claims of Ireland 61
        Fashionable Levities 66, 75 nn. 63 & 64
        The Retaliation 66, 75 nn. 63 & 64
        Robin Hood 66, 75 nn. 63 & 64
        Sentimental Excursions to Windsor 55–56, 61–62, 65
        Tristram Shandy: A Sentimental, Shandean Bagatelle 5, 6, 21, 23, 27 n. 94, 49, 53–76, 129, 130
            casting 6, 54–55, 67–68, 69, 70–72, 73, 75 n. 87
            literary influences 57–59, 63–65
            performances of 6, 23, 53–54, 56, 67, 70–71, 72, 73 n. 7, 128
                as a burlesque 8, 23, 71–72, 73
            political context 59, 60–61, 66, 72–73, 74 n. 36, 76 n. 100
                American War of Independence 59, 60, 66–67, 72–73
                King William's Wars 59
                Seven Years War 59
            politics of 21, 59–60, 65–66
            reception of 54, 58, 66, 71, 75 n. 63
            representation of Toby 21, 54–55, 59–60, 63–66, 67–73
            scripting 5, 21, 23, 27 n. 94, 54, 55–57, 58, 59–60, 63–66, 71–72, 73, 74 n. 18
Madoff, Mark S. 44
Malone, Edmond 2
Marshall, Joseph, *Travels through Holland* 97
Medalle, Lydia and *Letters of the Late Rev. Mr. Laurence Sterne* 16–17, 19-20, 50 n. 31, 120–21, 125 n. 92
Methodism:
    and Hastings, Selina (Countess of Huntingdon) 98, 100
    and sexual scandal 82, 98–102
    and Wesley, Charles and John 98
Milhous, Judith 53
mimicry:
    and associated concepts 8–9, 23, 25 nn. 39 & 40, 71–72, 73
    definitions of 8–9, 25 n. 43, 32, 33

and friendship 1, 11, 14, 17, 29, 30, 84–85, 91, 94, 97, 104 n. 43, 107, 110, 122–23
as illegitimate entertainment 11–12, 16, 26 n. 60
as literary concept 7–10, 11–12, 81–82
in literature:
    and anonymity 1, 16, 19, 21, 84, 92–93, 117, 119, 120, 122
    as autobiography/biography 10–11, 15–16, 17–19, 20, 21–22, 23, 60–65, 83, 84–85, 122–23, 127, 128
    and deception 9, 83–84, 104 n. 38
    as self-promotion 1, 19, 20, 23, 93, 107–11, 112–14, 115, 122–23, 123 n. 21, 128
    Sterne's engagement with 7–8, 23, 29–31, 32, 33, 34, 36–39, 43, 45–49, 49 n. 4, 120, 128
in the theatre 6, 8, 9–10, 11–12, 25 n. 50, 56
Monkman, Kenneth 6–7, 11
    and W. G. Day 24 nn. 1 & 2
Moody, Jane 12, 26 n. 60
Morash, Christopher 66
Mortimer, John Hamilton, *A Caricature Group* 44
Mullan, John 25 n. 36, 88, 121

Nagle, Christopher C. 43
New, Melvyn 128, 129
    and Peter de Voogd, *The Letters* 49 n. 11, 50 n. 28, 51 n. 78, 105 nn. 83 & 84, 108, 118, 120, 121, 123 nn. 1 & 13, 124 nn. 29 & 45, 125 nn. 74, 92 & 93, 130 n. 4
Newbould, M.-C. 27 n. 94
Nicholson, George 12, 57
Nicoll, Allardyce 39, 50 n. 53
Nollekens, Joseph, and the bust of Sterne 11
Nugent, Thomas, *The Grand Tour* 97, 106 n. 123

O'Brien, John 40, 52 n. 90
Oya, Reiko 32

Parsons, John 2
Patch, Thomas, and the caricature of Sterne 79, 103 n. 17
Peacock, George 81, 87, 92
Peakman, Julie 77; 89; 92; 102 nn. 1, 6, 7, 9, 11 & 12; 103 nn. 14 & 18; 104 nn. 48 & 49; 105 nn. 96 & 108
Peltonen, Markku 120
politeness:
    challenges to 6, 9–10, 23, 34, 38–39, 68–69, 73, 89, 91, 97, 99, 108, 112, 117–20, 122, 130
    and erotica 89, 97, 101–02, 118
    guides to 19, 38–39, 72, 114, 119
    principles 10, 38, 63, 89, 93, 101–02, 109, 110, 115, 118, 119, 120, 121, 122–23, 126 n. 98
    and Stanhope, Philip Dormer (Earl of Chesterfield) 19, 117, 119
Pope, Alexander, *Imitations of Horace* 8
Powell, Martyn J. 74 n. 36
Price, Leah 57, 74 nn. 17 & 21

Ragussis, Michael 62
Ravenet, Simon François, *Mr. Garrick and Miss Bellamy in the Characters of Romeo and Juliet* 42
Regan, Shaun 112
Reynolds, Sir Joshua 11, 125 n. 74
Rice, Scott 97
Richardson, Ruth 3; 24 nn. 9, 13, 15 & 16; 25 n. 31
Richardson, Samuel 22
Robson, Mark 84
Ross, Ian Campbell 24 nn. 6 & 7
Rowlandson, Thomas:
  Connoisseurs 94
  Cunnyseurs 94
  The Man of Feeling (1788) 79
  A Man of Feeling (1811) 79-80, 103 n. 17
Rubenhold, Hallie 95, 106 nn. 117 & 118
Russell, Gillian 72, 76 n. 99

Scheil, Katherine West 67
Schlenther, Boyd Stanley 100, 106 nn. 131 & 132
Scrope, Thomas 110
Seidel, Michael 73, 75 n. 83
Shakespeare, William:
  and Garrick's productions of:
    Hamlet 40-41, 45-46, 47, 50 nn. 48 & 55
    Romeo and Juliet 7, 34, 35, 41-43, 51 n. 60
  influence upon *the Bramine's Journal* 45-46
Sheridan, Thomas, *A Course of Lectures on Elocution* 38-39
Shoemaker, Robert 101, 120
Sinfield, Mark 70
Spacks, Patricia Meyer 43, 51 n. 64
Spencer, John (Viscount of Althorp) 110, 124 n. 29
Stage Licensing Act (1737) 12, 26 n. 60
Stephanson, Raymond 110
Stern, Tiffany 33, 50 n. 36
Sterne, Laurence:
  and the anthology:
    The Beauties of Sterne 5, 16, 57-59, 72, 74 n. 25, 87-88, 103 n. 16, 121, 122
    Extracts from the Tristram Shandy and the Sentimental Journey 57
    Gleanings from the Works of Laurence Sterne 57, 58, 74 n. 25, 126 n. 94
    The Narrative Companion 57
    The Prose Epitome 57
  and appropriations of:
    A Cock and Bull Story 127-30
    Continuation of Yorick's Sentimental Journey (1788) 27 n. 93
    Crazy Tales 10-11, 12, 13, 14, 26 n. 65, 81, 82, 84, 86, 89-93, 94, 95, 98, 100, 103 n. 23, 122, 128, 130
    Letters of the Late Rev. Mr. Laurence Sterne (1775) 16-17, 19, 20, 50 n. 31, 120-21, 125 n. 92
    Maria; or, The Generous Rustic 27 n. 93
    Maria; or, The Vicarage 27 n. 93
    Miss C--Y's Cabinet of Curiosities 12, 81, 82, 103 n. 26
    Original Letters 5, 10, 11, 14, 16, 19, 23, 107-10, 112-15, 117, 122-23, 123 nn. 1, 13, 14, 18, 20 & 21, 124 n. 32
    Sentimental Excursions to Windsor 55-56, 61-62, 65
    A Sentimental Journey: Intended as a Sequel to Mr. Sterne's (1793) 27 n. 93
    A Sentimental Tour, Collected from a Variety of Occurrences 14
    Sentiments on the Death of the Sentimental Yorick 16, 27 n. 103
    La Souriciere 9, 10, 81-83, 87-88, 89, 94-97, 104 n. 65, 128
    Sterne's Letters on Various Occasions 10, 16-17, 21, 26 n. 78, 108-09, 117-23
    Sterne's Maria: A Pathetic Story 27 n. 93
    Sterne's Witticisms 115, 116, 117, 118
    Tristram Shandy: A Sentimental, Shandean Bagatelle 5, 6, 21, 23, 27 n. 94, 49, 53-76, 129, 130
    Two Lyric Epistles 30, 92, 94, 105 n. 115
    Yorick's Sentimental Journey Continued 2, 5, 9, 11, 12, 81-82, 83-87, 88, 96, 103 nn. 21 & 23, 104 nn. 38 & 43, 106 n. 124, 122
  and Archbishop Richard Sterne 108
  and the Demoniacs 10-11, 84-85, 89, 91, 92, 93, 94, 110, 122
  identification of remains 2, 11, 25 n. 54
  literary reviews (eighteenth-century) 12, 13-15, 26 n. 64, 48-49, 79, 82, 83, 86, 87, 93-94
  literary style:
    the dash 4, 23, 31-32, 34, 37, 45-46, 46-47, 87, 120
    eroticism 1, 5, 9, 14, 21, 23, 58, 77-79, 81, 82, 83, 85-86, 87, 88, 93-94, 118
    patriotism 13, 21, 54, 55, 57, 59-60, 63-64, 73, 74 n. 19, 75 n. 82
    sentimentalism 1, 4, 5, 12, 13-15, 21, 43-44, 45, 47, 54, 55, 56, 57, 58-59, 72, 81, 83, 85, 88, 119, 120, 121
    theatricality 7, 29-31, 32-33, 34, 36-39, 43, 45-49, 51 n. 78, 56, 120
    typography 22-23, 31-32, 87, 94, 120
  posthumous representation:
    and anatomisation 2-3, 6, 24 nn. 6 & 7, 88
    financial embarrassment 2-3, 108, 112, 123 n. 11
    grave and headstone 1, 2-3, 17, 24 nn. 1 & 2
    sexual activity 83, 117-19
    violence 119-20
  relationships (both actual and textual):
    Combe, William 10, 11, 17, 107, 109-10, 111-13, 118, 122-23
    Dillon, John Talbot 44
    Draper, Eliza 19, 30, 36, 43-49
    Garrick, David 29, 30-31, 36, 38, 49, 62
    Hall-Stevenson, John 10-11, 17, 30, 36, 44, 84, 86, 91-92, 107, 108

James, Anne and William 44, 47–48
Lascelles, Peter 44
Spencer, Margaret Georgiana Poyntz (Viscountess of Althorp) 44
Vesey, Elizabeth 118, 125 n. 74
Warkworth, Lady Anne Stuart 37
works:
   Bramine's Journal 29–30, 34, 39, 43–49, 51 nn. 75, 78 & 79
   A Sentimental Journey 4, 9, 14, 22, 43, 45, 47, 57, 78–79, 81, 84, 85–86, 88, 96, 97, 102 n. 10, 103 n. 16, 113, 121
   Tristram Shandy 3, 6, 7, 8, 12, 13–14, 15, 17, 22–23, 26 n. 64, 27 n. 101, 31, 32, 37, 45, 48–49, 54–56, 57, 58, 59, 60, 62, 65, 70, 71, 73, 74 n. 18, 75 nn. 60, 82 & 83, 77–78, 81, 82, 84, 87, 88, 93, 95, 102 n. 6, 105 nn. 83, 103 & 115, 109, 117, 127–28, 129, 130 n. 2
Straub, Kristina 75 n. 76
Swift, Jonathan 14

Tadié, Alexis 56

Tegg, Thomas 79
Thompson, Karl F. 85

Voogd, Peter de 26 n. 88, 27 n. 101, 75 nn. 82 & 86

Watts, Carol 21, 27 n. 93, 76 n. 100, 103 n. 22
Wells, Stanley 40
Williams, David 11, 52 n. 87
Williams, Raymond 50 n. 52
Wilson, Benjamin 7, 17
   and the monument scene from *Romeo and Juliet* 41–43
Wilson, Richard:
   as Mrs. Peachum 68
   off-stage life 69–70
   reviews 55, 68, 69–70, 71, 129
   as Uncle Toby 6, 54–55, 67–73, 128
Woodfall, Henry Sampson 100

Young, Edward, *Conjectures on Original Composition* 8

Zoffany, Johan, and the portrait of David Garrick 17, **18**

www.ingramcontent.com/pod-product-compliance
Lightning Source LLC
Chambersburg PA
CBHW080639170426
43200CB00015B/2897